TESTIMONIES OF A *Covenant Life*

CULTIVATES ENERGY

SIR JUSTUS ABRAMELECH

ISBN
978-1-961601-90-1 (Paperback)
978-1-961601-91-8 (eBook)
978-1-961601-89-5 (Hardcover)

TESTIMONIES OF A
Covenant Life

CULTIVATES ENERGY

TABLE OF CONTENTS

Sir Justus Abramelech,

An artificer of words spoken in wisdom, poems of honor, and songs of truth that intrigues the mind to seek out the unknown: the essence of nature.

A philosopher of proverbs and instructor of wisdom revealed by nature: the essence of God's presence. My affinity for the Arts & Sciences is expressed in Mathematics, allowing for quick analysis and observations witnessed and experienced on diverse levels of circumspection.

A servant of justice that peace may be proclaimed in my Father's name whose honor is above all the universe presents. Life has shown me shortcomings from misunderstanding situations given without assurance. The best practice is to question everything before taking on any responsibility or agreement without knowing the details to prevent consequences and even unnecessary trials. Over the years, I have grown a strong passion for understanding more about creation in all facets of life, a joy my heart loves to share with those who are inclined to know.

EXPERIENCE THE MEDITATION OF MY HEART

Throughout life, the things we experience teach us the difference between what is in our hearts and what comes out of our mouths.

Don't allow the past to torment you.

Don't seek the approval of others.

Upon experiencing spiritual rebirth, you commit to a life guided by obeisance to the everlasting covenant with the Almighty. The transformation of your spirit occurs gradually, culminating in your emergence as a sanctified soul. It's essential not to let emotions manipulate your thoughts and steer you away from the divine path. Release the burden of hidden truths that breed shame; embrace your identity as a renewed soul. Understand that your trust lies in Yeshua's word, as the sacred spirit of grace remains steadfastly by your side.

Don't allow emotions to control your thinking and to lead you astray from Yah.

Dark secrets bring shame; let them go. You are a new creation. All things pass away.

Know that your confidence is in Yeshua, for the spirit of grace is holy and with you.

Don't speak about pain or pity things you cannot change.

Don't be frustrated at people because of their guilt.

Don't let pride, knowledge, money, or family blind you.

The Testimony of Yeshua keeps your authority intact.

Don't let anyone define you, for your power is mighty, and you possess the Spirit of Truth.

Through eyes of fear, Yeshua sees your struggle, trust and believe he will carry you worthy. ISAIAH 10:1-4, 13-21

And it shall come to pass in that day, that the remnant of Israel, and such as are escaped of the house of Jacob, shall no more again stay upon him that smote them; but shall stay upon the Most High God, the Holy One of Israel, in truth. PSALM 89:14-39

For the Most High God is our defense; and the Holy One of Israel is our king. Hear ye this, O house of Jacob, which are called by the name of Israel, and are come forth out of the waters of Judah, which swear by the name of the Most High God, and make mention of the God of Israel, but not in truth, nor in righteousness. ISAIAH 48 When Israel was a child, then I loved him, and called my son out of Egypt. HOSEA 11

The Almighty Power your Most High God which goeth before you, he shall fight for you, according to all that he did for you in Egypt before your eyes; DEUT. 1:30-32 The voice of him that crieth in the wilderness, Prepare ye the way of the Most High God, make straight in the desert a highway for Our Almighty Power. ISAIAH 40 And an highway shall be there, and a way, and it shall be called The way of holiness; the unclean shall not pass over it; but it shall be for those: the wayfaring men, though fools, shall not err therein. ISAIAH 35

For the law was given by Moses, but grace and truth came by Yeshua Ha'Mashiach. JOHN 1:1-18 Ye also, as lively stones, are built up a spiritual house, a holy priesthood, to offer up spiritual sacrifices, acceptable to Most High God by Yeshua Ha'Mashiach. 1 PETER 2:5-10

Questioning Consciousness of Songs

Does the ward one belong to define one's conduct?

How shall we live on earth and share our experiences?

What we eat and drink becomes our way of life.

Everything spiritual manifests in the natural, physical form.

Bread and wine, a token of the covenant, redeemed by the blood of Yeshua

Passing-Over death to eternal life. An annual remembrance of love required of one another; to forgive those who have trespassed against us.

Do you eat whatsoever is placed before you? So that you do not crucify the glory of your body afresh?

Otherwise, to eat in ignorance would place you at the risk of another that you sin at will.

How is one made aware of wrongdoings without the foreknowledge of morality?

Wisdom teaches the prudent to seek out a matter diligently before ignorance becomes a fool's defense.

As it is written in the covenant of promise, the reward is to those who discern both good and evil through obedience.

Searching to prove what is good for humanity upholds honor, and that peace be multiplied in happiness.

Is this not obedience?

In wickedness, there is no happiness, as deceit steals away the innocent joy of a tender heart. How, then, shall we sing to praise and give glory to the Most High God?

Almighty Power of the Redeemed

The Most High God is my strength and song, and he is become my salvation: he is my God, and I will prepare him an habitation; my father's God, and I will exalt him. Exodus 15:2

For the Most High God your Almighty Power is God of gods, and YAH of YAHs, a great God, a mighty, and a terrible, which regardeth not persons, nor taketh reward:

18 He doth execute the judgment of the fatherless and widow, and loveth the stranger, in giving him food and raiment. Deuteronomy 10:17-18

And, behold, the glory of the God of Israel came from the way of the east: and his voice was like a noise of many waters: and the earth shined with his glory. Ezekiel 43:2

O YAH, thou art terrible out of thy holy places: the Most High God of Israel is he that giveth strength and power unto his people. Blessed be Most High God. Psalms 68:35

For the Most High God is terrible; he is a great King over all the earth. Psalms 47:2

And I heard as it were the voice of a great multitude, and as the voice of many waters, and as the voice of mighty thunderings, saying, Alleluia: for the Most High God omnipotent reigneth. Revelation 19:6

- Give unto the Most High God, O ye mighty, give unto the Most High God glory and strength.
- Give unto the Most High God the glory due unto his name; worship the Most High God in the beauty of holiness.
- The voice of the Most High God is upon the waters: the God of glory thundereth: the Most High God is upon many waters. Psalm 29:1-11
- The voice of YAH is powerful; the voice of the Most High God is full of majesty.
- The voice of YAH breaketh the cedars; yea, YAH breaketh the cedars of Lebanon.

- He maketh them also to skip like a calf; Lebanon and Sirion like a young unicorn.
- The voice of YAH divideth the flames of fire.
- The voice of YAH shaketh the wilderness; YAH shaketh the wilderness of Kadesh.
- The voice of YAH maketh the hinds to calve, and discovereth the forests: and in his temple doth every one speak of his glory.
- YAH sitteth upon the flood; yea, YAH sitteth King forever.
- YAH will give strength unto his people; YAH will bless his people with peace.

He bowed the heavens also, and came down: and darkness was under his feet.

He made darkness his secret place; his pavilion round about him were dark waters and thick clouds of the skies. Psalm 18

I form the light, and create darkness: I make peace, and create evil: I YAH do all these things. Isaiah 45:7

At the brightness that was before him his thick clouds passed, hail stones and coals of fire.

Yea, he sent out his arrows, and scattered them; and he shot out lightnings, and discomfited them.

Thou shalt be visited of YAH of hosts with thunder, and with earthquake, and great noise, with storm and tempest, and the flame of devouring fire. Isaiah 29:6

Then the earth shook and trembled; the foundations also of the hills moved and were shaken, because He was wroth.

And the same hour was there a great earthquake, and the tenth part of the city fell, and in the earthquake were slain of men seven thousand: and the remnant were affrighted, and gave glory to the Most High God of heaven. Revelation 11:13

I will make mine arrows drunk with blood, and my sword shall devour flesh; and that with the blood of the slain and of the captives, from the beginning of revenges upon the enemy. 43 Rejoice, O ye nations, with his people: for he will avenge the blood of his servants, and will render vengeance to his adversaries, and will be merciful unto his land, and to his people. Deuteronomy 32:42-43

There went up a smoke out of his nostrils, and fire out of his mouth devoured: coals were kindled by it. Then the channels of waters were seen, and the foundations of the world were discovered at thy rebuke, O YAH, at the blast of the breath of thy nostrils. Psalms 18:6-15

Then the channels of waters were seen, and the foundations of the world were discovered at thy rebuke, O YAH, at the blast of the breath of thy nostrils. (Exodus 15)

And with the blast of thy nostrils the waters were gathered together, the floods stood upright as a heap, and the depths were congealed in the heart of the sea. Exodus 15:8,10

Thou didst blow with thy wind, the sea covered them: they sank as lead in the mighty waters.

11 Who is like unto thee, O YAH, among the gods? who is like thee, glorious in holiness, fearful in praises, doing wonders?

12 Thou stretchedst out thy right hand, the earth swallowed them.

Thy right hand, O YAH, is become glorious in power: thy right hand, O YAH, hath dashed in pieces the enemy.

Thou art my battle axe and weapons of war: for with thee will I break in pieces the nations, and with thee will I destroy kingdoms;

21 And with thee will I break in pieces the horse and his rider; and with thee will I break in pieces the chariot and his rider;

22 With thee also will I break in pieces man and woman; and with thee will I break in pieces old and young; and with thee will I break in pieces the young man and the maid. Jeremiah 51:20-22

Take heaven and earth to witness; for I have broken the evil in pieces, and created the good: for I live, saith YAH. 2 Esdras 2:14

And he said, Behold, I make a covenant: before all thy people I will do marvels, such as have not been done in all the earth, nor in any nation: and all the people among which thou art shall see the work of YAH: for it is a terrible thing that I will do with thee. Exodus 34:10

See now that I, even I, am he, and there is no god with me: I kill, and I make alive; I wound, and I heal: neither is there any that can deliver out of my hand. If I whet my glittering sword, and mine hand take hold on judgment; I will render vengeance to mine enemies, and will reward them that hate me. Deuteronomy 32

YAH killeth, and maketh alive: he bringeth down to the grave, and bringeth up. 1 Samuel 2:6

These words YAH spake unto all your assembly in the mount out of the midst of the fire, of the cloud, and of the thick darkness, with a great voice: and he added no more. And he wrote them in two tables of stone, and delivered them unto me. Deuteronomy 5:22-24

23 And it came to pass, when ye heard the voice out of the midst of the darkness, (for the mountain did burn with fire,) that ye came near unto me, even all the heads of your tribes, and your elders; 24 And ye said, Behold, YAH Our Almighty Power hath shewed us his glory and his greatness, and we have heard his voice out of the midst of the fire: we have seen this day that God doth talk with man, and he liveth.

And he said, YAH came from Sinai, and rose up from Seir unto them; he shined forth from mount Paran, and he came with ten thousand saints: from his right hand went a fiery law for them. 3 Yea, he loved the people; all his saints are in thy hand: and they sat down at thy feet; every one shall receive of thy words. Deuteronomy 33:2-3

The Arm of Salvation, Almighty Savior

Isaiah 45:18-22 [18] For thus saith the Most High God that created the heavens; YAH himself that formed the earth and made it; he hath established it, he created it not in vain, he formed it to be inhabited: I am YAH; and there is none else.

[19] I have not spoken in secret, in a dark place of the earth: I said not unto the seed of Jacob, Seek ye me in vain: I YAH speak righteousness, I declare things that are right.
[20] Assemble yourselves and come; draw near together, ye that are escaped of the nations: they have no knowledge that set up the wood of their graven image, and pray unto a god that cannot save.
[21] Tell ye, and bring them near; yea, let them take counsel together: who hath declared this from ancient time? who hath told it from that time? have not I YAH? and there is no God else beside me; a just God and a Savior; there is none beside me.
[22] Look unto me, and be ye saved, all the ends of the earth: for I am God, and there is none else.

Isaiah 40:5 And the glory of YAH shall be revealed, and all flesh shall see it together: for the mouth of YAH hath spoken it.

Isaiah 52:7 How beautiful upon the mountains are the feet of him that bringeth good tidings, that publisheth peace; that bringeth good tidings of good, that publisheth salvation; that saith unto Zion, Thy God reigneth!

Psalms 146:10 YAH shall reign forever, even Your Almighty Power, O Zion, unto all generations. Praise ye YAH.

Judith 9:11 For thy power standeth not in multitude nor thy might in strong men: for thou art a God of the afflicted, a helper of the oppressed, an upholder of the weak, a protector of the forlorn, a savior of them that are without hope.

Psalms 106:8 Nevertheless he saved them for his name's sake, that he might make his mighty power to be known.

Additions to Esther 13:9 Saying, O YAH, YAH, the King Almighty: for the whole world is in thy power, and if thou hast appointed to save Israel, there is no man that can gainsay thee:

Joel 2:1-3, 29-32 Blow ye the trumpet in Zion, and sound an alarm in my holy mountain: let all the inhabitants of the land tremble: for the day of YAH cometh, for it is nigh at hand; And I will shew wonders in the heavens and in the earth, blood, and fire, and pillars of smoke.

Isaiah 63:1-6 For the day of vengeance is in mine heart, and the year of my redeemed is come.

2 Samuel 22:14 YAH thundered from heaven, and the Most High uttered his voice.

Psalms 18:6-15 There went up a smoke out of his nostrils, and fire out of his mouth devoured: coals were kindled by it. Then the channels of waters were seen, and the foundations of the world were discovered at thy rebuke, O YAH, at the blast of the breath of thy nostrils.

Habakkuk 3:8-11 Was YAH displeased against the rivers? Was thine anger against the streams? Was thy wrath against the sea, that thou didst ride upon thine horses and thy chariots of salvation? Thy bow was made quite naked, according to the oaths of the tribes, even thy word. Selah. Thou didst cleave the earth with rivers.

> The mountains saw thee, and they trembled: the overflowing of the water passed by: the deep uttered his voice, and lifted up his hands on high.

> The sun and moon stood still in their habitation: at the light of thine arrows they went, and at the shining of thy glittering spear.

Joel 3:15-16 The sun and the moon shall be darkened, and the stars shall withdraw their shining. YAH also shall roar out of Zion, and utter his voice from Jerusalem; and the heavens and the earth shall shake: but YAH will be the hope of his people, and the strength of the children of Israel.

> And he rode upon a cherub, and did fly: yea, he did fly upon the wings of the wind. 2 Sam 22:11

Habakkuk 3:4 And his brightness was as the light; he had horns coming out of his hand: and there was the hiding of his power.

2 Samuel 22:14 YAH thundered from heaven, and the Most High uttered his voice.

Psalms 18:6-15 There went up a smoke out of his nostrils, and fire out of his mouth devoured: coals were kindled by it. Then the channels of waters were seen, and the foundations of the world were discovered at thy rebuke, O YAH, at the blast of the breath of thy nostrils.

Exodus 15:2-3 YAH is my strength and song, and he is become my salvation: he is my God, and I will prepare him a habitation; my father's God, and I will exalt him.

> And with the blast of thy nostrils the waters were gathered together, the floods stood upright as a heap, and the depths were congealed in the heart of the sea.

> Thou didst blow with thy wind, the sea covered them: they sank as lead in the mighty waters.

Habakkuk 3:5 Before him went the pestilence, and burning coals went forth at his feet.

2 Samuel 22:14 YAH thundered from heaven, and the Most High uttered his voice.

Habakkuk 3:6 He stood, and measured the earth: he beheld, and drove asunder the nations; and the everlasting mountains were scattered, the perpetual hills did bow: his ways are everlasting.

YAH is my strength and song, and he is become my salvation: he is my God, and I will prepare him a habitation; my father's God, and I will exalt him.

And with the blast of thy nostrils the waters were gathered together, the floods stood upright as a heap, and the depths were congealed in the heart of the sea.

Thou didst blow with thy wind, the sea covered them: they sank as lead in the mighty waters. Exodus 15:2, 8

Who is like unto thee, O YAH, among the gods? who is like thee, glorious in holiness, fearful in praises, doing wonders? Exodus 15:11-18

Thou stretchedst out thy right hand, the earth swallowed them.

Then the dukes of Edom shall be amazed; the mighty men of Moab, trembling shall take hold upon them; all the inhabitants of Canaan shall melt away.

16 Fear and dread shall fall upon them; by the greatness of thine arm they shall be as still as a stone; till thy people pass over, O YAH, till the people pass over, which thou hast purchased.

17 Thou shalt bring them in, and plant them in the mountain of thine inheritance, in the place, O YAH, which thou hast made for thee to dwell in, in the Sanctuary, O YAH, which thy hands have established. 18 YAH shall reign for ever and ever.

Jeremiah 51:20 Thou art my battle axe and weapons of war: for with thee will I break in pieces the nations, and with thee will I destroy kingdoms;

Joel 3:18-21 Egypt shall be a desolation, and Edom shall be a desolate wilderness, for the violence against the children of Judah, because they have shed innocent blood in their land.

> But Judah shall dwell forever, and Jerusalem from generation to generation.

> For I will cleanse their blood that I have not cleansed: for YAH dwelleth in Zion.

Joel 2:32 And it shall come to pass, that whosoever shall call on the name of YAH shall be delivered: for in mount Zion and in Jerusalem shall be deliverance, as YAH hath said, and in the remnant whom YAH shall call.

Zephaniah 3:14-20 At that time will I bring you again, even in the time that I gather you: for I will make you a name and a praise among all people of the earth, when I turn back your captivity before your eyes, saith YAH.

Habakkuk 3:12-19 Yet I will rejoice in YAH, I will joy in the Most High God of my salvation.

Sanctify them through thy truth: thy word is truth.

Psalm 119:142 Thy righteousness is an everlasting righteousness, and thy law is the truth.

Genesis 35:10-12 And God said unto him, Thy name is Jacob: thy name shall not be called any more Jacob, but Israel shall be thy name: and he called his name Israel.

> 11 And God said unto him, I am God Almighty: be fruitful and multiply; a nation and a company of nations shall be of thee, and kings shall come out of thy loins;

> 12 And the land which I gave Abraham and Isaac, to thee I will give it, and to thy seed after thee will I give the land.

Romans 4:13 For the promise, that he should be the heir of the world, was not to Abraham, or to his seed, through the law, but through the righteousness of faith.

Exodus 19:6 And ye shall be unto me a kingdom of priests, and a holy nation. These are the words which thou shalt speak unto the children of Israel.

Isaiah 41:8 But thou, Israel, art my servant, Jacob whom I have chosen, the seed of Abraham my friend.

John 17:16-17 They are not of the world, even as I am not of the world.

> 17 Sanctify them through thy truth: thy word is truth.

Deut. 13:13 Certain men, the children of Belial (worldly), are gone out from among you, and have withdrawn the inhabitants of their city, saying, Let us go and serve other gods, which ye have not known;

14 Then shalt thou enquire, and make search, and ask diligently; and, behold, if it be truth, and the thing certain, that such abomination is wrought among you;

John 8:32 And ye shall know the truth, and the truth shall make you free.

1 Peter 1:22 Seeing ye have purified your souls in obeying the truth through the Spirit unto unfeigned love of the brethren, see that ye love one another with a pure heart fervently:

Soul = living soul, word of truth = spirit (breath of life in obedience to YAH)

Deuteronomy 32:1 Give ear, O ye heavens, and I will speak; and hear, O earth, the words of my mouth.

Deuteronomy 8:3 And he humbled thee, and suffered thee to hunger, and fed thee with manna, which thou knewest not, neither did thy fathers know; that he might make thee know that man doth not live by bread only, but by every word that proceedeth out of the mouth of YAH doth man live.

Deuteronomy 30:14 But the word is very nigh unto thee, in thy mouth, and in thy heart, that thou mayest do it.

Exodus 4:15 And thou shalt speak unto him, and put words in his mouth: and I will be with thy mouth, and with his mouth, and will teach you what ye shall do.

Numbers 30:2 If a man vow a vow unto YAH, or swear an oath to bind his soul with a bond; he shall not break his word, he shall do according to all that proceedeth out of his mouth.

Deuteronomy 18:18 I will raise them up a Prophet from among their brethren, like unto thee, and will put my words in his mouth; and he shall speak unto them all that I shall command him.

1 Kings 17:24 And the woman said to Elijah, Now by this I know that thou art a man of God, and that the word of YAH in thy mouth is truth.

Numbers 22:38 And Balaam said unto Balak, Lo, I am come unto thee: have I now any power at all to say anything? the word that God putteth in my mouth, that shall I speak.

Job 22:22 Receive, I pray thee, the law from his mouth, and lay up his words in thine heart.

Job 23:12 Neither have I gone back from the commandment of his lips; I have esteemed the words of his mouth more than my necessary food.

Psalm 33:4 For the word of YAH is right; and all his works are done in truth.

Psalm 138:2 I will worship toward thy holy temple, and praise thy name for thy lovingkindness and for thy truth: for thou hast magnified thy word above all thy name.

Hosea 4:1 Hear the word of YAH, ye children of Israel: for YAH hath a controversy with the inhabitants of the land, because there is no truth, nor mercy, nor knowledge of God in the land.

John 17:17 Sanctify them through thy truth: thy word is truth

Ephesians 1:13 In whom ye also trusted, after that ye heard the word of truth, the gospel of your salvation: in whom also after that ye believed, ye were sealed with that holy Spirit of promise,

1 Thessalonians 2:13 For this cause also thank we Most High God without ceasing, because, when ye received the word of YAH which ye heard of us, ye received it not as the word of men, but as it is in truth, the word of YAH, which effectually worketh also in you that believe.

2 Timothy 2:15 Study to shew thyself approved unto YAH, a workman that needeth not to be ashamed, rightly dividing the word of truth.

James 1:18 Of his own will begat he us with the word of truth, that we should be a kind of first fruits of his creatures.

Psalm 119:142 Thy righteousness is an everlasting righteousness, and thy law is the truth.

Genesis 35:10-12 And God said unto him, Thy name is Jacob: thy name shall not be called any more Jacob, but Israel shall be thy name: and he called his name Israel.

11 And God said unto him, I am God Almighty: be fruitful and multiply; a nation and a company of nations shall be of thee, and kings shall come out of thy loins;

12 And the land which I gave Abraham and Isaac, to thee I will give it, and to thy seed after thee will I give the land.

Romans 4:13 For the promise, that he should be the heir of the world, was not to Abraham, or to his seed, through the law, but through the righteousness of faith.

Exodus 19:6 And ye shall be unto me a kingdom of priests, and an holy nation. These are the words which thou shalt speak unto the children of Israel.

Isaiah 41:8 But thou, Israel, art my servant, Jacob whom I have chosen, the seed of Abraham my friend.

John 17:16-17 They are not of the world, even as I am not of the world.

17 Sanctify them through thy truth: thy word is truth.

Deut. 13:13 Certain men, the children of Belial (worldly), are gone out from among you, and have withdrawn the inhabitants of their city, saying, Let us go and serve other gods, which ye have not known;

14 Then shalt thou enquire, and make search, and ask diligently; and, behold, if it be truth, and the thing certain, that such abomination is wrought among you;

John 8:32 And ye shall know the truth, and the truth shall make you free.

1 Peter 1:22 Seeing ye have purified your souls in obeying the truth through the Spirit unto unfeigned love of the brethren, see that ye love one another with a pure heart fervently:

The Pavilion of Refuge

Psalms 91:1-2 He that dwelleth in the secret place of the Most High shall abide under the shadow of the Almighty. I will say of YAH, He is my refuge and my fortress: my God; in him will I trust.

Psalms 31:20 Thou shalt hide them in the secret of thy presence from the pride of man: thou shalt keep them secretly in a pavilion from the strife of tongues.

2 Kings 19:15 And Hezekiah prayed before YAH, and said, O Almighty Power of Israel, which dwellest between the cherubim, thou art the God, even thou alone, of all the kingdoms of the earth; thou hast made heaven and earth.

Job 26:8-11, 14 He bindeth up the waters in his thick clouds; and the cloud is not rent under them. 9 He holdeth back the face of his throne, and spreadeth his cloud upon it. 10 He hath compassed the waters with bounds, until the day and night come to an end. 11 The pillars of heaven tremble and are astonished at his reproof.

Lo, these are parts of his ways: but how little a portion is heard of him? but the thunder of his power who can understand?

Job 28:20-28 When he made a decree for the rain, and a way for the lightning of the thunder:

27 Then did he see it, and declare it; he prepared it, yea, and searched it out.

Song of Solomon 2:10-14,17 My beloved spake, and said unto me, Rise up, my love, my fair one, and come away. For, lo, the winter is past, the rain is over and gone;

> [12] The flowers appear on the earth; the time of the singing of birds is come, and the voice of the turtle is heard in our land;
> [13] The fig tree putteth forth her green figs, and the vines with the tender grape give a good smell. Arise, my love, my fair one, and come away.

[14] O my dove, that art in the clefts of the rock, in the secret places of the stairs, let me see thy countenance, let me hear thy voice; for sweet is thy voice, and thy countenance is comely.

[17] Until the day break, and the shadows flee away, turn, my beloved, and be thou like a roe or a young hart upon the mountains of Bether.

Psalms 27:5 For in the time of trouble he shall hide me in his pavilion: in the secret of his tabernacle shall he hide me; he shall set me up upon a rock.

1 Samuel 12:17-25 Is it not wheat harvest today? I will call unto YAH, and he shall send thunder and rain; that ye may perceive and see that your wickedness is great, which ye have done in the sight of YAH, in asking you a king.

2 Esdras 2:14 Take heaven and earth to witness; for I have broken the evil in pieces, and created the good: for I live, saith YAH.

Ecclesiasticus 39:25 For the good are good things created from the beginning: so evil things for sinners.

Ecclesiasticus 31:13 Remember that a wicked eye is an evil thing: and what is created more wicked than an eye? therefore it weepeth upon every occasion.

2 Esdras 16:62 Yea and the Spirit of Almighty God, which made all things, and searcheth out all hidden things in the secrets of the earth,

2 Esdras 8:1 And he answered me, saying, The Most High God hath made this world for many, but the world to come for few.

Wisdom of Solomon 5:15 But the righteous live for evermore; their reward also is with YAH, and the care of them is with the Most High God.

Exodus 34:10 And he said, Behold, I make a covenant: before all thy people I will do marvels, such as have not been done in all the earth, nor in any nation: and all the people among which thou art shall see the work of YAH: for it is a terrible thing that I will do with thee.

THE COVENANT OF ETERNAL LIFE

Covenants of Promise - Most High God of Abraham, Isaac, Jacob				
1 Ah'dom	the image of YAH	Adam	(ah-dom)	man has dominion over earth
2 Nu'wah	second Adam	Noah	(nu-wah)	the rest and rescuer of mankind
3 Ah'Brah'om	Father of Covenant	Abraham	(ah-brah-om)	father of Covenant, nations, kings and priests
4 Yitz'Sak	Son of Covenant	Isaac	(yits-khawk)	he laughs
5 Ya'Ah'Kob	Father of 12 Tribes	Jacob	(yah-ak-obe)	heel holder, supplanter
6 Mo'She	King & Priest	Moses	(mo-shay)	deliver of people drawn out of the water
7 Da'Weed	King of Israel	David	(dah-weed)	beloved of YAH, throne of David established by sacrifice of Yeshua

I call heaven and earth to record this day against you, that I have set before you life and death, blessing and cursing: therefore, choose life, that both thou and thy seed may live: Deuteronomy 30:19

And the Most High God said unto Moses, Write thou these words: for after the tenor of these words I have made a covenant with thee and with Israel. Exodus 34:27

And he took the book of the covenant, and read in the audience of the people: and they said, All that the Most High God hath said will we do, and be obedient. Exodus 24:7

These are the words of the covenant, which the Most High God commanded Moses to make with the children of Israel in the land of Moab, beside the covenant which he made with them in Horeb. Deuteronomy 29:1

Behold, the days come, saith the Most High God, that I will make a new covenant with the house of Israel, and with the house of Judah: Jeremiah 31:31

I have made a covenant with my chosen, I have sworn unto David my servant, Psalm 89:3

For it is evident that our Savior sprang out of Juda; of which tribe Moses spake nothing concerning priesthood. And it is yet far more evident: for that after the similitude of Melchizedek there ariseth another priest, Who is made, not after the law of a carnal commandment, but after the power of an endless life. For he testifieth, Thou art a priest for ever after the order of Melchizedek. Hebrews 7:11-17

Thus, saith the Most High God; If ye can break my covenant of the day, and my covenant of the night, and that there should not be day and night in their season; Then may also my covenant be broken with David my servant, that he should not have a son to reign upon his throne; and with the Levites the priests, my ministers. As the host of heaven cannot be numbered, neither the sand of the sea measured: so, will I multiply the seed of David my servant, and the Levites that minister unto me. Jeremiah 33:20-22

Ought ye not to know that the Most High God of Israel gave the kingdom over Israel to David forever, even to him and to his sons by a covenant of salt? 2 Chronicles 13:5

O ye seed of Israel his servant, ye children of Jacob, his chosen ones. 1 Chronicles 16:13

Ye that fear the Most High God, praise him; all ye the seed of Jacob, glorify him; and fear him, all ye the seed of Israel. Psalm 22:23

I have not spoken in secret, in a dark place of the earth: I said not unto the seed of Jacob, Seek ye me in vain: I the Most High God speak righteousness, I declare things that are right. Isaiah 45:19

Therefore, fear thou not, O my servant Jacob, saith the Most High God; neither be dismayed, O Israel: for, lo, I will save thee from afar, and thy seed from the land of their captivity; and Jacob shall return, and shall be in rest, and be quiet, and none shall make him afraid. Jeremiah 30:10

Zion shall be redeemed with judgment, and her converts with righteousness. Isaiah 1

Revelation 21:1-11 And there came unto me one of the seven angels which had the seven vials full of the seven last plagues, and talked with me, saying, Come hither, I will shew thee the bride, the Lamb's wife.

I the Most High God have called thee in righteousness, and will hold thine hand, and will keep thee, and give thee for a covenant of the people, for a light of the Gentiles; Isaiah 42:6

Isaiah 2:1-10 And many people shall go and say, Come ye, and let us go up to the mountain of the Most High God, to the house of the God of Jacob; and he will teach us of his ways, and we will walk in his paths: for out of Zion shall go forth the law, and the word of the Most High God from Jerusalem.

For unto us a child is born, unto us a son is given: and the government shall be upon his shoulder: and his name shall be called Wonderful, Counsellor, The mighty God, The everlasting Father, The Prince of Peace. Of the increase of his government and peace there shall be no end, upon the throne of David, and upon his kingdom, to order it, and to establish it with judgment and with justice from henceforth even forever. The zeal of the Most High God of hosts will perform this. Isaiah 9:6-7

Psalm 99 The Most High God is great in Zion; and he is high above all the people. Isaiah 4 And it shall come to pass, that he that is left in Zion, and he that remaineth in Jerusalem, shall be called holy, even every one that is written among the living in Jerusalem: Psalm 102:13-22 When the Most High God shall build up Zion, he shall appear in his glory.

Psalm 110 The Most High God shall send the rod of thy strength out of Zion: rule thou in the midst of thine enemies. Psalm 132 For the Almighty God hath chosen Zion; he hath desired it for his habitation.

Psalm 149 Let Israel rejoice in him that made him: let the children of Zion be joyful in their King.

And say unto them, Thus saith the Most High God; In the day when I chose Israel, and lifted up mine hand unto the seed of the house of Jacob, and made myself known unto them in the land of Egypt, when I lifted up mine hand unto them, saying, I am the Most High God your Almighty Power; Ezekiel 20:5

Isaiah 12:6 Cry out and shout, thou inhabitant of Zion: for great is the Holy One of Israel in the midst of thee. Isaiah 28:9-19 Therefore thus saith the Most High God, Behold, I lay in Zion for a foundation a stone, a tried stone, a precious corner stone, a sure foundation: he that believeth shall not make haste.

2 John 1:1-5 The elder unto the elect lady and her children, whom I love in the truth; and not I only, but also all they that have known the truth. Revelation 7:9-17 And I said unto him, Sir, thou knowest. And he said to me, These are they which came out of great tribulation, and have washed their robes, and made them white in the blood of the Lamb. Revelation 19:1-9 Let us be glad and rejoice, and give honor to him: for the marriage of the Lamb is come, and his wife hath made herself ready.

For thy Maker is thine husband; the Most High God of hosts is his name; and thy Redeemer the Holy One of Israel; The God of the whole earth shall he be called. Isaiah 54:5

Happy are thy men, happy are these thy servants, which stand continually before thee, and that hear thy wisdom. Blessed be the Most High God your Almighty Power, which delighted in thee, to set thee on the throne of Israel: because the Most High God loved Israel forever, therefore made he thee king, to do judgment and justice...

And twelve lions stood there on the one side and on the other upon the six steps: there was not the like made in any kingdom.
1 Kings 10:8-9, 20

And he carried me away in the spirit to a great and high mountain, and shewed me that great city, the holy Jerusalem, descending out of heaven from God, Having the glory of God: and her light was like unto a stone most precious, even like a jasper stone, clear as crystal; And had a wall great and high, and had twelve gates, and at the gates twelve angels, and names written thereon, which are the names of the twelve tribes of the children of Israel: On the east three gates; on the north three gates; on the south three gates; and on the west three gates. And the wall of the city had twelve foundations, and in them the names of the twelve apostles of the Lamb. Revelation 21:10-14

Judges and officers shalt thou make thee in all thy gates, which the Lord thy God giveth thee, throughout thy tribes: and they shall judge the people with just judgment. Deuteronomy 16:18

For the Father judgeth no man, but hath committed all judgment unto the Son: John 5:22

And Yeshua said unto them, Verily I say unto you, That ye which have followed me, in the regeneration when the Son of man shall sit in the throne of his glory, ye also shall sit upon twelve thrones, judging the twelve tribes of Israel. Matthew 19:28

12 PATRIARCHS CHART

Patriarchs	Beginnings	KJV	Hebrew Pronunciation	Meaning	Mother
Reuben	1st Tribe	Gen 29:32	Re'Ubeen	Yah hath looked upon my affliction; now my husband will love me.	Leah
Simeon	2nd	Gen 29:33	Sim'Ee'on	Yah hath heard that I was hated, he hath given me this son also	Leah
Levi	3rd Tribe	Gen 29:34	Lee'Vy	Be joined unto me	Leah
Judah	4th Tribe	Gen 29:35	Yah'Hudah	I praise Yah	Leah
Dan	5th Tribe	Gen 30:6	Don	Yah hath judged me, and hath also heard my voice	Bilhah
Naphtali	6th Tribe	Gen 30:7	Naphr'Tatee	With great wrestlings have I wrestled and I have prevailed	Bilhah
Gad	7th Tribe	Gen 30:11	God	A troop cometh	Zilpah
Asher	8th Tribe	Gen 30:13	Yah'Seer	Happy am I	Zilpah
Issachar	9th Tribe	Gen 30:18	Yitz'Ah'Kar	Yah hath given me my hire	Leah
Zebulun	10th Tribe	Gen 30:20	Zebulun	Yah hath endued me with a good dowry	Leah
Joseph	11th Tribe	Gen 30:24	Yah'Hasef	Yah hath taken away my reproach; The MOST HIGH GOD shall add to me another son.	Rachel
Benjamin	12th Tribe	Gen 35:18	Ben'Yah'meen	Son of my right hand	Rachel

12 APOSTLES

Apostles	Hours (Lots)	KJV	Hebrew Pronunciation	Meaning
Peter	1st Apostle	Matthew 10:2	Peter (Kephas)	stone
James	2nd Apostle	Matthew 10:2	Ya'Ah'Kob	heel holder, supplanter
John	3rd Apostle	Matthew 10:2	Yo'Cha'Nan	Yah is Gracious
Andrew	4th Apostle	Matthew 10:2	Andreas	man
Philip	5th Apostle	Matthew 10:3	Philip	friend of horse
Bartholomew (New Testament)	6th Apostle	Matthew 10:3	Natha'Na'El	Yah has given
Matthew (Levi)	7th Apostle	Matthew 10:3	Mattan'Yahu	Gift of Yah
Thomas	8th Apostle	Matthew 10:3	Thomas	Twin
James	9th Apostle	Matthew 10:3	Yah'Akob	heel holder, supplanter
Thaddeus (Jude)	10th Apostle	Matthew 10:3	Yah'Hudah	heart / I praise Yah
Simon Zealots	11th Apostle	Matthew 10:4	Shim'On	Yah hath heard me to bless
Matthathias	12th Apostle	Acts 1:26	Mattit'Yahu	Gift of Yah
Paul	Apostle to Gentiles	Galatians 2:7-10	Paul	"small" or "humble"

THE CHOSEN ONES

O ye seed of Israel his servant, you children of Jacob, his chosen ones.

The Most High and lofty One that inhabiteth eternity,

whose name is Holy; dwells in the high and holy place,

with him also that is of a contrite and humble spirit,

to revive the spirit of the humble,

and to revive the heart of the contrite ones. Isa 57:15

He is Yah our Almighty Power; his judgments are in all the earth.

Be ye mindful always of his covenant; the word he commanded to a thousand generations;

Confirmed with Abraham, Isaac, and Jacob for a law, and to Israel an everlasting covenant,

The lot of your inheritance, the land of Canaan;

Saying, Touch not mine anointed, and do my prophets no harm.

Sing unto Yah, all the earth; show forth from day to day his salvation.

Declare his glory among the heathen; his marvelous works among all nations.

For great is Yah, and greatly to be praised and feared above all gods.

Glory and honor are in his presence; strength and gladness are in his place.

Give unto Yah, glory and strength.

Blessed be the Most High of Israel for ever and ever. 1 Chron 16

JUDGE ME FOR MERCY

The heavens declare the glory of Yah.

I will sing mercy and judgment unto you, O Father,
I will behave myself wisely in a perfect way
who so privately slanders his neighbor
him will I cut off and him that have a high look even a proud heart
will I not suffer.
He that work deceit shall not dwell in my house.
He that tell lies shall not tarry in my sight cutting off all wicked
doers. (psalms 101)
Mine eyes shall be upon the faithful of the land
that they may dwell with me.
He's that walks in a perfect way shall serve me.
Hide not your face from me in the day when I am in trouble.
Incline your ear unto me in the day when I call answer speedily,
let my prayer be heard immediately.
A forward heart shall depart from me.
I will set no Wicked way before mine eyes.
Walking in my house with a perfect heart.
Let the heavens declare the glory of God.

ALMIGHTY POWER

Almighty power of Israel
Let Yah arise, let his enemies be scattered
let them also that hate him flee
But let the righteous be glad let them rejoice
before Yah exceedingly
Joyride upon the heavens
Seven blessings my Confession be the glory on high
The strength of Yeshua. PSA 68
All praises his mighty name

A father of the fatherless even the judge of the widows
Yeshua be in his holy habitation sitting lowly with the meek
observing of creation waiting to bring out
those bound with chains but the rebellious dwell in the dry land.
What a pity not to be loaded with daily benefits
even the Most High God your Almighty Power our salvation
takes no pleasure in the issues of life and death over eternity.
Come out of Babylon and dwell with the Most High God
who's ready to save,
forsake the incurable wound on the head of the enemy for all
kingdoms of the earth
ready to praise him who rides upon the cherub
in the circuits of heavens,
all shall see the Almighty Power of Israel

<u>MY RIGHTEOUSNESS</u>

I will worship toward your holy Temple
Praise your mighty name for your loving kindness.
I will worship for mercy and truth enduring forever,
Father, Yeshua has magnified your word above your name.
I will praise you O' Father with my whole heart,
before da gods will I sing praise unto you.
Mercy and truth endure forever, for you have magnified your word
above your name.
I'll be sure not to make promises of uncertainty
but to honor a few words.
All the kings of the earth shall praise you
when they hear the words of your mouth.
Yeah they will sing in the ways of the Almighty,
for great is the glory of Yah.
Having respect unto the lowly,
my humility goes before honor.
Stretch forth your hand and deliver me from my enemies.
In the midst of trouble your right hand shall save me.
The proud you knoweth not, my Almighty Power will perfect
that which concerneth me and forsake not the works of your own
hands. Selah

PRAISE & GLORIFY ALMIGHTY POWER

The Most High God your Almighty Power hath multiplied you, and, behold, ye are this day as the stars of heaven for multitude. Deuteronomy 1:10

We have also a surer word of prophecy; whereunto ye do well that ye take heed, as unto a light that shineth in a dark place, until the day dawn, and the day star arise in your hearts: 2 Peter 1:19

Praise ye him, sun and moon: praise him, all ye stars of light. Psalm 148:3

When the morning stars sang together, and all the sons of God shouted for joy? Job 38:7

Praise ye the YAH for the avenging of Israel, when the people willingly offered themselves. Judges 5:2

Whoso offereth praise glorifieth me: and to him that ordereth his conversation aright will I shew the salvation of God. Psalm 50:23

And now shall mine head be lifted up above mine enemies round about me: therefore, will I offer in his tabernacle sacrifices of joy; I will sing, yea, I will sing praises unto the YAH. Psalm 27:6

By him therefore let us offer the sacrifice of praise to God continually, that is, the fruit of our lips giving thanks to his name. Hebrews 13:15

WAYS OF YAH

Ah Hah, Hah
Ah Hah, Hah
Ah Hah, Hah
Hah Hah!

My Father Yah
Cries to <u>Hear you-ooh!</u>
Show me how to come to <u>you-ooh!</u>
The ways of sin is punishment
<u>Among</u> men.
Ah Hah, Hah

Straight way we go
Never slip away
From youth
Know the Truth
And it won't be forced
From you
Holy Spirit
be with you
Conviction
Spirit of Truth
Guide in meekness
Overcome weakness
Obeisance commands
my soul
joy be delight
walking in my youth
avoid yet foolish people
who stay in trouble
a mock

Ah Hah, Hah
Ah Hah, Hah
Ah Hah, Hah
Hah Hah!

I AM WHAT I AM

I am understanding (3)
The beauty of majesty
The glory of humility

I dwell with wisdom
The beauty of majesty
The glory of humility

I am love
The beauty of fulfilling needs
The glory of kindness speaks

I am faithful
The beauty of seeking truth
The glory of doing works

Serves to speak truthfully
Boldly taking charge
Establishing order
Fruits of authority
Be not unbelieving
But be Faithful and True.

I HAVE PURPOSE

Oh Yes,
You have wakened me from my sleep
Now - ow - ow
I could not see before
My spirit slept as I worked hard
Many hours, my time, energy, and mind
Hid the glory of Yah
The light shining bright in me
Not kept priority
I learned in time to posses
My heart and mind, spirit
How I see, you have awakened me
From my sleep to originality
I had to discover purpose
Frequently seeking
No more shall I return to work
That consumes my reality
My time, my mind, my energy
The glory of Yah
My maker, creator of heaven and earth
I have purpose and found destiny
I am free to give glory, free to serve
For I have purpose

A PLACE TO BE

I love myself so much,
my neighbor smiles at me
Wherever I am, my strength flows
as still waters run deep,
the pipeline connects the manifestation of Yah,
my truth stands on the shoulders of my ancestors,
before me.
I transform weakness to strength to
reveal the God in me.
Living what I pray, I release doubt,
no time to play with other's whereabouts.
I only care about my appreciation of love
to maintain confidence in the truth I live
that my determination creates abundance.
This is what I run with, yours truly!
Sincerely! Sir Justus Abramelech

SLUMBER OF SLEEP

Ya know that I am
here for you. (2)
What you've done,
My tears cry out in blues.
I hope you wake up soon.
And someday, question those
things that made my heart to ring.
As often on the phone
you left me all alone. (2)
Since then, I've found peace
a new heart and mind at ease.
Yet, am I without rest as
I strive to do my best.
It's clear to me now that
tactics of old still unfold
how you feel about me.

I pray you wake up (3)
from this slumber of sleep.
I pray you wake up, wake up, wake up
from this slumber of sleep. (2)

THE HEART OF IDOLATRY

A flaming heart of fables
Embellishes relics of traditions
Me don't know why
him come down the chimney
To give smokey toys to the children
Folktales for the young, but simple
Grows old stubborn thoughts,
Taking for granted the enchanted
Hearts locked away in the dark
Throw away the key
A sissy says it's just fine, it's for the kids.
Creator were you not made in this fashion?
Useless false perceptions steal away imagination
Whose happiness is contingent
Upon a fantasy, gone in the wind,
Running wild like a child with a bag of lies
Who knows next where the kite will fly?
Look up in the sky, see the imagery of idolatry?
Running rampant, off we go into magic times
A time where there is no rhyme or reason
Whatever feels good, do it for pleasure
No questions asked, no remembrance of the past.
Why do these things with strong reverence
To replace the divinity of the creator within you and me?

LEAVE ME, PEACE

Your heart is in your desires
above my needs
I am stressed, vexed in your presence
my soul is in despair.
Father, I cry, you made me not to die
that I should not taste death
but deliver me from evil
as transgression makes me feeble.
I am strong as I receive your love
the Holy Spirit of comfort and peace.
Amen, Ah-me-en, Amen, Ah-me-en (2)
Give me this day, my daily bread
for I am strong as my words of truth.
The deeds of this testifies of my youth
a sweet savor of incense present I unto you.
Amen, Ah-me-en, Amen, Ah-me-en (2)
Forgive me of sin, may I come before
your altar of incense to approach your
throne through the doors of
the Most Holy place am I in solace.
Hallow be thy name, thine kingdom come,
thine will be done on earth as in heaven,
like heaven may my heart be at peace and healed.
Amen, Ah-me-en, Amen, Ah-me-en (2)

SOMETHING HAS A HOLD ON ME

In this season I look for reason for what I want to do
But cannot. Something has a hold on me.
I'm disappointed with myself
All I want to do is eat
Lay around and watch the sun go down.
Do I need for someone to tell me what to do?
Can I manage myself, my money over time
My mind lends energy to the state of my wealth
It's hard to be fruitful and multiply in abundance.
When there is no action to run with.
I am disappointed with myself. No progress.
Keeps me asleep on opportunities to give back monies
To my communities, my monies is dry
I keep asking why, what's holding me back.
I disappointed in myself. Maybe it's that I desire to have love
And have not found it.
Whatever the case be. I hope this depression leaves.
Find its way and fall like leaves from a tree.
In the arms of safety, save me from the hands of strange
Come not near me.
Oh' father I adore you.
My desire is to be with you.
Yahshuah, I want to be with you.
So that I am no more disappointed in myself.

THE BLOOD OF MY BODY: NO MORE AM I IN MY WEAKNESS

My heart was troubled but now I see,
Your desires over my needs
I see how you treat me
Thinking in a cursed way of me
Like unto free radicals

In the blood of my body

Destroying the air I breathe
Wounds cause my heart to grieve
Do you, really, really, love me
I watch to avoid the lash of words as
My love fades away from you.
I say, are you okay?
In my weakness, I want to comfort
You leave me no room to grow
So, I cry this song for you
That I not be bruised

I watch to say hey, hey
How are you today? (2)
Hey, Hey, I cannot look at you this way
A scratch relieves the itch on my body
But comes back when I get close to you
Do I feel like a fool, in the same position as
Once before, now I refuse your desire of me
I draw the line this time
To let you go the way
You choose as this is the last of my blues
That I'll sing for you
I watch to say hey, hey
I cannot look at you this way
I watch to say hey, hey
I don't want to feel like this no more. Okkkkk!

MY CONFESSION

Without a garment I stood afar off
In filthy rags, watching the ways of truth
From my youth
I was ignorant of how my appearance
Was spent, I desired the ways of others
Finding myself walking in circles kicking the dust.
I didn't bring my slippers to move forward,
On my own is why I sing this song.
How can I approach you, Father?
O Yahushua, Yahu'shua
I am not worthy
Yahushua, Yahushua
My feet are dirty
Yahushua, Yahushua
Can you wash me?
Yahushua, Yahushua
Away with my infirmities
Yahushua, Yahushua
I plead your blood over me
Yahushua,
Now I am free.

LET NOT YOUR HEART BE TROUBLED

A broken heart suffering much hurt in the midst of the sea,
brings stormy waters even hurricanes of pain.

A man's wrath to express his uncontrolled anger,
lingers to shake up the earth,
havoc of earthquakes, great emotional rage.

> Let not your heart be troubled;
> You who believe in the Father of Spirits, believe also in me.
> While you hath the light, believe in the light,
> that you may be children of the light.
> Yet a little while is the light with you.

Walk while ye have the light with you, lest darkness come upon you.
Now is my soul troubled and what shall I say?
Father, save me from this hour; but for this cause came I into this hour.

> I am the way, the truth, and the life;
> no man cometh unto the Father, but by me.
> I am in the Father, and ye in me, and I in you.
> Greater love hath no man than this;
> that a man lay down his life for his friends.

Ye are my friends, if ye do whatsoever I command.
He that hateth me, also hateth my Father also.
If I had not come and spoken unto you, you had not had sin;
but now you have no cloak for your sin.

> Whatsoever you ask the Father in my name,
> he will give it to you.
> In this world ye shall have tribulation; but be of good cheer;
> even as I have overcome the world.

Truly, Truly, Verily, Verily,
I say unto you that if a man keep my saying, he shall never see death;
nor shall his heart be troubled. Iesous Kristos, Yashuah Masiach!

WALLS OF RESISTANCE

A Desire Found in Search of You
Sitting in the sunlight of it all,
Where did you go? (2)
Trying not to find you in panic, you were hidden within yourself.
A place where I could not go, unless you opened the door.
To where I could see your face.
This door, not found in an ordinary place.
Searching, searching, and searching your ways,
for what was remembered of you.
Was not easy, although I had many clues.
Remembering to stay in the light of happiness.
Understanding came and revealed, why you were hidden.
Your ways are the way to your heart,
Now I know, I begin walking the narrow path,
avoiding thoughts of confusion, distractions.
Along the journey of discovery, meant to be.
Lost, not found in misery, could I've been, for had I panicked.
Patience is key to perseverance, now I know more about me,
not to be complacent in the light in front of me.

CRY A WELL OF JOY

These are the days
That you go through life's journey
Don't you worry
To weary yourself
For these are days of affliction
Our Righteousness has risen
Many weep at death
But cannot see to overcome
The pain of suffering till the new
Kingdom comes. Patience is the guide
Of courage to approach mightily
The throne of complaints, but in reverence do
We request what our life is to bring, that the
Fruit of righteousness be not cut down as a tree.
Oh well, a well spring up of everlasting praise,
A time has been worthy for living to testify of thanksgiving.
Not without doubt we are living.

THE END OF TEARS

Show me how I'm to say
I love you throughout the blues,
Keep in your place, most holy will I be
To be lovely before I lie down my life
I cry this song for you, to dry those tears,
The pains of life expressed in fear. Show me how,
I'm to say I love you throughout the blues.
Keep in your place, most holy, will I be, to be lovely,
Free indeed of trouble, the gift of life, happiness, I want for you,
Find it you must, the way to heaven is not so hard,
always within reach.
Love one and teach one, not to fear, release it from you, the end of
fears, is happiness.
The gift of my love for you is the end of tears.

HOPE ALL IS WELL

Hope all is well
Your family be at peace
In the arms of safety
Speak for me
Cruel hands of strangers
Work iniquity, iniquity
Come not near me.
Come not near me.
My righteousness
Speak for me
Oh Father
I adore you
My desire
Forever and ever
I adore you
Yahashuah, Yahashuah.
I'm with you.
I'm with you.
Forever and ever. Forever and ever.

I SURRENDER

Wonderful Counselor, give me light
Reveal the iniquity around me
Wonderful Counselor, make my paths
Straightway. Towards the gate I pray.
Wonderful Creator, you made me in your image
Humble for instruction
I sit still for your counsel to move at will
Wonderful Counselor, hold me fast
Not to move till I know what I am to do.
Give me insight as I kneel before you.
Have mercy, Oh Yaha'shua in whom I trust.
My future is in your hands to lose the bands of bondage
On me.
I couldn't see I'm covered in a mess, society has brought upon me.
I dedicated my life to you. Take me out of this rat race, so complex is
my life you see.
Deliver me from the iniquity that latches to things around me. I
dedicated my life to you.
Oh Wonderful Counselor, take heed to my vow.
I believe my path is straight at your gate.
Open and let me come on in, as I surrender my life to you. I'll be
true. Halleluiah!

RISE & SHINE

Rise, Shine to the morning sky, There's hope of a new day coming
out from darkness let us trust in Yah's holiness
come let us adore him, kneel down be-fore him
and prepare our hearts to see him. as pure is the mind of peace
let us not be beneath, but acceptable are we in his decease
to minister the fruits of peace, and joy that comforts,
in his arms I'm safe to escape misery and not confused.
Rise, shine There's hope for a new day,
No more are we strangers to one another,
to overlook wrongdoing and not love
my neighbor as myself. My heart says yes,
my soul says, yeah-heh-eh, Yeah-eh.
Love teaches us to overcome, our weakness
that revives the old nature alive, as death in us we fail alone,
at fault before his throne. In unity there's strength, let us be not
divided from the light that shines so bright, our Father's presence
gives gifts of praise and thanksgiving to the living.
The day will come to Rise, Shine and go in peace before his majesty.
My heart says yes, my soul says yes, yeah-heh-eh, yeah-eh
My spirit is comforted to know where I go,
to my Father's house prepared are many mansions having
foreknowledge of the Holy One of Yisrael, we shall see the glory
Alleluyah! Luyah! Luyah!

SEE THE VISION

See the vision
Meditation, comprehension
Reflect on where you are,
Exercise to disconnect
Reflect from the clutter
Clear your mind,
Set daily goals.
Have a theme song and
Scriptures for accountability!
Be thankful and care for others.

JOURNEY OF LIFE

A chosen journey of life
I do it effortlessly
Hey, eh-eh, hey
Meticulous work pursuing the dream
Hey, eh-eh, hey
Examine your habits
Loose distractions
Hey, eh-eh, hey
Success is for you to do your best
Hey, eh-eh, hey
Learning from failures
Who cares what they tell you
Hey, eh-eh, hey
Walking consciously helps you
See pieces around you coming together
When you have it, you know that you know
Knowing who you are has all the pieces

EXODUS TO JUBILEE

Blood on doorpost
Covenant of blood
Born in distressed times
Thrusted out of Egypt
Humble life of service and poverty
Heard a voice from heaven
Give us manna to rest on 7th day
A stubborn and rebellious generation
Moshe appointed 70 elders over Israel
And fasted 40 days and 40 nights
they forgotten the God of thy salvation
Drank the dust of golden calf as a consequence
Received the tables of stone as a testimony
Moshe face shone with glory
Call together shepherds of the people
Let us make a covenant
Wondered 40 years in the wilderness for rebellion
Some overcome the years of tribulation
A King and 24 Priests appointed over 12 Tribes
Gathering all to the Feast of Weeks
12 Apostles appointed to Judge 12 Tribes
In that day glory of Jacob shall be made thin
His eyes shall have respect to the Holy One of Israel
Be fulfilled until Jubilee
We shall be free.

THY MERCY IS LOVING KINDNESS

Thy mercy, O Yah endureth forever - Ps 138:8
Be not far from me my Savior, Be not far from me - Ps 22:11
Be not far from me my Savior, Be not far from me
Ah-ee-ah, Ah-ee-ah, Ah-ee-ah, Ahhhh!
Save me from the lion's mouth - Ps 22:21
like birds caught in a snare when it falls suddenly upon them - Ecc 9:12
Bow down thine ear to me, - Ps 31:2
for I am your servant, heartbroken and vexed
Have mercy upon me, for I am in trouble - Ps 31:9
Have mercy upon me, for I am distressed
I walk in my house with a perfect heart - Ps 101:2
As you make my enemies my footstool. – Ps 110:1
Into thine hand I commit my spirit - Ps 31:5
Holy, Holy is the Lamb
My refuge and my fortress is the Rock;
Oh' Yah; in whom I will trust Ps 91:2
Save me for thy mercy's sake - Ps 31:16
Father, I confess my sins unto you - Ps 32:5
Preserve me from trouble Ps 32:7
That I should not go down to the pit - Ps 30:3
Behold is the eye of the Most High God upon them that fear him - Ps 33:18 Yaha'shuah!
My heart shall rejoice in him - Ps 33:21
Ceasing from anger and forsaking wrath; I fret not myself in any wise to do evil - Ps 37:8-9 unto others on earth.
Rid me, and deliver me from the hand of strange children, whose mouth speaketh vanity - Ps 144:11
Thine kingdom is an everlasting glory of sovereignty and I specially thank you for your presence of serenity. Yaha'shuah, Halleluyah!

THE SACRIFICE OF LIFE

Oh Merciful Father
Forgive me of my sins
Oh' Yaha'shuah, our Righteousness begins
Redeem us
The Word of the Father
Spirit of Truth, prick me
Honor and Glory,
Excellence, His majesty
On high we shall see, after we die
A perfect death of flesh
Is the sacrifice of life
Present on high
The Saints of the Almighty
The meek shall inherit, the whole earth
From the foundation of the world,
Was the Lamb, slain for perfection
His remnant, are his Holy Ones.
Holy, Halleluyah, Holy, Halleluyah,
Holy, Holy, Holy, Holy, Holy, Holy
HAl-le-luyah! More Glory to Yah!

THE DUTY OF HUSBANDRY

Blood on doorpost, (mind, body, and soul)
No honor among family to walk the straight and narrow
Thrusted out of the House of Bondage
The humble walk of life is not an easy one of service
Poverty awaits life, problems frustrates
I hear from heaven
Taking the time to sit down to be reverent in nature
I offer peace with my covenant of blood
Keeping clean and unspotted from the world
A baby girl can be taught of our father
Who gave us manna at 7th day of the rest
The great problem solver speaks wonders in counsel
Lifting burdens without sweat, blood, or tears.
We bless the shepherds of the people
Born in distressed times,
Fasted 40 days and nights
Without a fight our face shines in glory.
See the promise after 40 years in the wilderness.
Appointed over the 12 tribes, 12 rulers
Whose gates await seventy palm trees
To gather in the people
Seven weeks after the 1st day of Unleavened Bread
All tribes break free, exodus for Jubilee.
Sings after seven sabbatical years
A day of rest remaineth for the poor
The poor in spirit is meek and
goodly and in what they speak
A day of rest remaineth after the labor
Set apart the rest to do no work in it.
In the day of your consecration.
Be not bondmen in a strange land.
Be ye holy for I am.
The covenant of your Father, Ah-brah-am.
Is the whole duty of man.

THE END OF TIME

Awaken from a dream, it is not all that it seems
Where I am now, I'm not even sure, where here is,
As the moon affects the brain, the mind shifts in dimensions
Indescribable through planes of existence, A sign of the times,
The kingdom is under a curse and the city is in despair,
Call no man happy, who is not dead. Excruciating torment will be there.
The young, too foolish to listen, when will they learn,
anxious for nothing,
Running off with new gifts, no time to consider beyond, what's been
given to them,
Drunken in shambles, sex craves, and diverse lusts.
These are the strange times!
Set forth among the stars, of the universe,
Search the night skies as the stars will never fade,
Burning till the end of time.
The land was divided, now that there is no king,
the return of the dark ages are amongst us as courage and imagination
ceases to create heroes, only righteousness shall stand in the honor
to do so.
The light of a new age will begin a new millennium, the time that
ceases to age.

MERCY ENDURES FOREVER

Mercy Endureth Forever
We all shall do what's Right
His sight, Holy is He
Who cometh in the name
Hosanna, Forever liveth King of Kings
YAH is good and his mercy endures, forever
His truth endures, all generations.

SONG OF THE RIGHTEOUS

You that love righteousness
Where are you
And you that hate evil awwH!
You make your enemies afraid
To do good is great!
I saw my people rise!
To do good is great!
You make, enemies afraid
I'm talking to you my people
Lets go!
We gotta make a move right now.
You here me.
Nothing gonna stop us! (4)
We gotta make a move right now!
You here me! (2)
Nothing gonna stop us! (6)
We gotta make a move! (6)
Right now!
Ya here me!

MAKE COVENANT

Brothers and sisters (2)
Brothers (4)
Brothers and sisters lets us covenant
Keeping commandments
Giving the people laws
Govern yourselves and rise to do judgment and justice
Loving unity we are free keeping commandments
We work in harmony
Longevity is who we be
We are the meek you seek
Govern yourselves and rise with equity
Honor and glory
The bride of fame
Chose widely the game you play
Hoping chance of a better day
Seeing yesterday fade away
What you now with today
Unite do in love and your enemies

NARRATIVE

Shout against iniquity and it shall flee or else stronghold is built.
Oppression upholds evil as if reinforces its belief upon the people.
If any sing more than what is read, can one discern what to do in the time of trouble?
Obedience and Praise releases you from the captivity of your Fathers
And whatever acts of violence they have done. Many are affected by ancestral acts of wickedness. Never compare your ministry with that of another but complement them.
Yah's word is settled in him that obeys in peaceably, therefore glorify YAH in heaven.
This is my praise, a garment of praise, blessing Yah at all times.

<u>SPEAK NOT LYING WORDS</u>

Do not deal deceitfully
Hating evil, carefully consider
Your ways, never blame.
Always are signs near, getting closer to the truth
Perfect in heart, spirit is free.
Don't deal deceitfully to make enemies
Loving to do justice and judgment have all the saints.
The Most High is with you
Honor and glory
A new name given.
Praise Yah All the living.
Remember this day I spoken to you (2)
Always do what is good
No matter what is done unto you
Always do what is good
That you put away evil
I love you.

BE TRUE

Family says
We love you
We love you
Never love your life to death
Sweating bullets, Sweating bullets
A trial has come for you
Three times, Three times
The cock has crowed
Don't be in denial
Our Father says
We have a chance in you
Only if you would be true.
Be True –oo oo.
Never lose your life to death.
Never love your life to death.

BONDS BROKEN ASUNDER

Oh' Father, Oh' Yaha'shua,
I was attacked in my sleep
I had a dream of something deadly in me
Beyond reality blinded by idolatry, the envy of jealousy
The mystery of iniquity
Held me that I could not move
Takes away man's authority given to a woman.
To wander out of the way, would be not to obey the word
Of truth that gives mercy to the afflicted
The curse that makes things worse, is not to identify the unheard cry.
The song of repentance is the strength of my own
Existence in this world.
I shall not be moved,
By a flood of trouble,
Flee I to the mountain top, for safety.
Where calm waters leads me to the seas
And there I shall be free.
Let glory of honor come from my Father
His peace is with me and shall never leave,
But keeps company joy of happiness
Things that lasts forever and ever.
Forever am I everlasting in his arms. Thankful am I to be
called blessed!

I AM FREE

Oh' Father, Yaha'shua
It is given to me to know
Sorrow of heart.
A mind cannot grow, in dark
Places of the heart
I cry unto you
Show me how to come near you
Teach me now the spirit of happiness.
I look for joy and cannot find it.
Let me work with what I love
Deal with me <u>slow</u>, to know where I have <u>been</u>.
Make me know the whole truth and love judgment
Open my eyes, my ears, and my mouth.
Cleanse my soul, my heart, and my mind.
Give me work and desire for your truth.
Sanctify me and Hear me now
Fill me up with your Holy Ones
Lift me up and heal me
No more captive
I'm free

QUICKEN ME ACCORDINGLY

Quicken me accordingly to your way of prosperity.
I'm so happy, he knocked the dust off of my poverty!
Thankful am I that I learned from my cry,
Before the red dye, made record in earth of what I testify.
Love in peace that your eyes, be not filled with broken promises
But is good in truth, fulfilling dreams in time and space.
Not left alone, to do things, on your own, family, the song of a lifetime.
When love takes away poverty, everyone is at ease.
Needs are met with value seen in all for beauty, mercy, life, and peace.
Back on my feet, My Father restored me to see the right ways.
Holy and just, whom I trust, with all my soul, mind, and heart.
Halleluyah! Glory and Honor belongs to Yah!

I SHALL WORSHIP YOU

Oh' Yahashua
I shall worship you in song and praise
All of my days!
I shall worship Yahshua
Let all breath give praise, Yahashua
I shall tell of you all of my days!
I love you with all of my heart, mind, and soul. Console me in your
arms of joy!
I shall worship you!
Oh Yahashua, show me how to love
My neighbor as myself
Heal me all over to love myself.
From guilt carried in me.
Forgive me of the past
Wrong that I have done.
I shall worship you.
Make light of burden
Suffer me from hurting
I shall worship you in truth!
Clean me all over,
My soul cries for you.
Send your holy spirit
Make me your holy one!
I shall worship you.
In spirit and truth
Oh Yahushua
Come down your holy spirit
On us!

KEEP LIFE CLOSE

The chosen journey of life
Who can know it AND BE CLOSE TO IT
WITHOUT YOUR MAKER, YOU KNOW
NOTHING OF HIM, Blinded IN YOUR WAYS
Hard to see, openly who truly you be
Give me a fountain of living waters
These are my orders to eat consciously,
The peace of life abundant happiness
I seek eternity.

WHY SEEK THE KINGDOM OF HEAVEN

Depending on your relationship with food, it may not feel good to fast; but its necessary that we break our habits (carnal ways) or any obstacles in our life with fasting and praying to increase inner power coming closer to YAH. So many distractions are the ways of this world making it easy to lead anyone from the way of pursing the kingdom of our Heavenly Father. Therefore, fasting & praying is necessary to remain pure (innocent) seeking the life of a holy one. This service of dedication is an offering of our soul towards the Most High God for the protection from the wicked one and the sake of a good conscious towards humanity for the pursuit of eternal life; blessed in every good work.

Isaiah 55 Seek ye the Most High God while he may be found, call ye upon him while he is near: Jasher 3

Let the wicked forsake his way, and the unrighteous man his thoughts: and let him return unto the Most High God, and he will have mercy upon him; and to Our Almighty Power, for he will abundantly pardon.

8 For my thoughts are not your thoughts, neither are your ways my ways, saith the Most High God.

9 For as the heavens are higher than the earth, so are my ways higher than your ways, and my thoughts than your thoughts.

Job 6:11-29 Teach me, and I will hold my tongue: and cause me to understand wherein I have erred.

Nehemiah 8:8-12 So they read in the book in the law of God distinctly, and gave the sense, and caused them to understand the reading.

Colossians 1:4-20 For this cause we also, since the day we heard it, do not cease to pray for you, and to desire that ye might be filled with the knowledge of his will in all wisdom and spiritual understanding;

Amos 8:11-13 Behold, the days come, saith the Most High God God, that I will send a famine in the land, not a famine of bread, nor a thirst for water, but of hearing the words of the Most High God:

12 And they shall wander from sea to sea, and from the north even to the east, they shall run to and fro to seek the word of the Most High God, and shall not find it.
13 In that day shall the fair virgins and young men faint for thirst.

Malachi 3 Behold, I will send my messenger, and he shall prepare the way before me: and the Most High God, whom ye seek, shall suddenly come to his temple, even the messenger of the covenant, whom ye delight in: behold, he shall come, saith the Most High God of hosts... Then shall ye return, and discern between the righteous and the wicked, between him that serveth God and him that serveth him not.

Deuteronomy 31:16-19, 28-30 And the Most High God said unto Moses, Behold, thou shalt sleep with thy fathers; and this people will rise up, and go a whoring after the gods of the strangers of the land, whither they go to be among them, and will forsake me, and break my covenant which I have made with them.

17 Then my anger shall be kindled against them in that day, and I will forsake them, and I will hide my face from them, and they shall be devoured, and many evils and troubles shall befall them; so that they will say in that day, Are not these evils come upon us, because Our Almighty Power is not among us? Enoch 63
18 And I will surely hide my face in that day for all the evils which they shall have wrought, in that they are turned unto other gods.
19 Now therefore write ye this song for you, and teach it the children of Israel: put it in their mouths, that this song may be a witness for me against the children of Israel.

Deuteronomy 32 But Jeshurun waxed fat, and kicked: thou art waxen fat, thou art grown thick, thou art covered with fatness; then he forsook God which made him, and lightly esteemed the Rock of his salvation.

Deuteronomy 33:1-6, 26-29 Moses commanded us a law, even the inheritance of the congregation of Jacob. 5 And he was king in Jeshurun, when the heads of the people and the tribes of Israel were gathered together. Enoch 1

Revelation 15:1-4 And I saw as it were a sea of glass mingled with fire: and them that had gotten the victory over the beast, and over his image, and over his mark, and over the number of his name, stand on the sea of glass, having the harps of God.

3 And they sing the song of Moses the servant of God, and the song of the Lamb, saying, Great and marvelous are thy works, Most High God God Almighty; just and true are thy ways, thou King of saints.

4 Who shall not fear thee, O Most High God, and glorify thy name? for thou only art holy: for all nations shall come and worship before thee; for thy judgments are made manifest.

Micah 5 But thou, Bethlehem Ephrathah, though thou be little among the thousands of Judah, yet out of thee shall he come forth unto me that is to be ruler in Israel; whose goings forth have been from of old, from everlasting.

Micah 6:1-8 He hath shewed thee, O man, what is good; and what doth the Most High God require of thee, but to do justly, and to love mercy, and to walk humbly with Your Almighty Power?

Zechariah 8:7-17 And it shall come to pass, that as ye were a curse among the heathen, O house of Judah, and house of Israel; so will I save you, and ye shall be a blessing: fear not, but let your hands be strong.

BLESSINGS

Proverbs 4:7 Wisdom is the principal thing; therefore get wisdom: and with all thy getting get understanding. Ecclesiastes 12:13

Psalm 119:1-22 Blessed are the undefiled in the way, who walk in the law of the Most High God. I will meditate in thy precepts, and have respect unto thy ways. Enoch 58

Leviticus 26:3-12 For I will have respect unto you, and make you fruitful, and multiply you, and establish my covenant with you. Jeremiah 17:20-25

Deuteronomy 28:1-14 YAH shall open unto thee his good treasure, the heaven to give the rain unto thy land in his season, and to bless all the work of thine hand: and thou shalt lend unto many nations, and thou shalt not borrow.

Matthew 5:3-11 Blessed are the poor in spirit: for theirs is the kingdom of heaven.

4 Blessed are they that mourn: for they shall be comforted. 5 Blessed are the meek: for they shall inherit the earth. 6 Blessed are they which do hunger and thirst after righteousness: for they shall be filled. 7 Blessed are the merciful: for they shall obtain mercy. 8 Blessed are the pure in heart: for they shall see God. Bless them that curse you, and pray for them which despitefully use you. Luke 6:21-38

Genesis 27:28-30 Let people serve thee, and nations bow down to thee: be Most High God over thy brethren, and let thy mother's sons bow down to thee: cursed be everyone that curseth thee, and blessed be he that blesseth thee. Numbers 23:1-6

Numbers 24:4-9 YAH brought him forth out of Egypt; he hath as it were the strength of an unicorn: he shall eat up the nations his enemies, and shall break their bones, and pierce them through with his arrows.

Psalm 119:23-66 I intreated thy favor with my whole heart: be merciful unto me according to thy word. Enoch 61

Deuteronomy 30:1-16, 19-20 And it shall come to pass, when all these things are come upon thee, the blessing and the curse, which I have set before thee, and thou shalt call them to mind among all the nations, whither the Most High God your Almighty Power hath driven thee,

Deuteronomy 32:9-13 For YAH's portion is his people; Jacob is the lot of his inheritance.

Deuteronomy 33 Yea, he loved the people; all his saints are in thy hand: and they sat down at thy feet; every one shall receive of thy words.

Psalm 109 Let them curse, but bless thou: when they arise, let them be ashamed; but let thy servant rejoice. Righteousness, truth, even the light has vanished from before us, For we have not believed before Him nor glorified the name of the Most High God of Spirits, Don't let darkness be your dwelling-place for ever and ever:

Genesis 49 Judah, thou art he whom thy brethren shall praise: thy hand shall be in the neck of thine enemies; thy father's children shall bow down before thee The scepter shall not depart from Judah, nor a lawgiver from between his feet, until Shiloh come; and unto him shall the gathering of the people be.

Numbers 24:17-24 I shall see him, but not now: I shall behold him, but not nigh: there shall come a Star out of Jacob, and a Scepter shall rise out of Israel, and shall smite the corners of Moab, and destroy all the children of Seth.

Galatians 3:13-14 Christ hath redeemed us from the curse of the law, being made a curse for us: for it is written, Cursed is every one that hangeth on a tree: That the blessing of Abraham might come on the Gentiles through Yeshua Ha'Mashiach; that we might receive the promise of the Spirit through faith.

Genesis 12:2-4 I will bless those who bless you, and whoever curses you, I will curse. Through you every family on earth will be blessed. Genesis 28:3-4

Numbers 23:7-12 "The descendants of Jacob are like specks of dust. Who can count them or number even one-fourth of the people of Israel? Let me die the death of innocent people.

Let my end be like theirs."

Genesis 48:3-6, 14-22 The Angel which redeemed me from all evil, bless the lads; and let my name be named on them, and the name of my fathers Abraham and Isaac; and let them grow into a multitude in the midst of the earth.

Job 31 Oh that one would hear me! behold, my desire is, that the Almighty would answer me, and that mine adversary had written a book.

Numbers 23:18-24 No spell can curse the descendants of Jacob. No magic can harm the people of Israel. Now it will be said of Jacob and Israel: 'See what God has done!'

Genesis 27:28-29 Therefore God give thee of the dew of heaven, and the fatness of the earth, and plenty of corn and wine: Let people serve thee, and nations bow down to thee: be Almighty Yah over thy brethren, and let thy mother's sons bow down to thee: cursed be every one that curseth thee, and blessed be he that blesseth thee.

Isaiah 65:14-16 And ye shall leave your name for a curse unto my chosen: for the Most High God God shall slay thee, and call his servants by another name: Enoch 39

Numbers 6:22-27 So whenever they use my name to bless the Israelites, I will bless them.

CURSES

Deuteronomy 11:27-32 A blessing, if ye obey the commandments of the Most High God your Almighty Power, which I command you this day: 28 And a curse, if ye will not obey the commandments of the Most High God Your Almighty Power, but turn aside out of the way which I command you this day, to go after other gods, which ye have not known. Leviticus 26

Deuteronomy 32:1-8 Do ye thus requite the Most High God, O foolish people and unwise? is not he thy father that hath bought thee? hath he not made thee, and established thee?

Isaiah 9:8-21 YAH sent a word into Jacob, and it hath lighted upon Israel Manasseh, Ephraim; and Ephraim, Manasseh: and they together shall be against Judah. For all this his anger is not turned away, but his hand is stretched out still. Isaiah 11:13, 28:1-8

Hosea 7 Ephraim, he hath mixed himself among the people; Ephraim is a cake not turned And the pride of Israel testifieth to his face: and they do not return to the Most High God their Most High God, nor seek him for all this Ephraim also is like a silly dove without heart: they call to Egypt, they go to Assyria.

Isaiah 43:21-28 Therefore I have profaned the princes of the sanctuary, and have given Jacob to the curse, and Israel to reproaches. Jeremiah 11:1-4

Deuteronomy 28:15-68 YAH shall cause thee to be smitten before thine enemies: thou shalt go out one way against them, and flee seven ways before them: and shalt be removed into all the kingdoms of the earth.

Jeremiah 31:22-37 How long wilt thou go about, O thou backsliding daughter? for the Most High God hath created a new thing in the earth, A woman shall compass a man.

Joel 3:3 And they have cast lots for my people; and have given a boy for an harlot, and sold a girl for wine, that they might drink.

Psalm 83 They have taken crafty counsel against thy people, and consulted against thy hidden ones.

Psalm 37 Mark the perfect man, and behold the upright: for the end of that man is peace. 38 But the transgressors shall be destroyed together: the end of the wicked shall be cut off. Whoso curseth his father or his mother, his lamp shall be put out in obscure darkness.

Leviticus 24:15-17 And thou shalt speak unto the children of Israel, saying, Whosoever curseth his God shall bear his sin. Enoch 38 Proverbs 20 Whoso curseth his father or his mother, his lamp shall be put out in obscure darkness.

Proverbs 30 There is a generation that curseth their father, and doth not bless their mother.

Exodus 21:12-17 And he that smiteth his father, or his mother, shall be surely put to death.

Jeremiah 29:16-23 Thus saith the Most High God of hosts; Behold, I will send upon them the sword, the famine, and the pestilence, and will make them like vile figs, that cannot be eaten, they are so evil.

Isaiah 42:21-23 But this is a people robbed and spoiled; they are all of them snared in holes, and they are hid in prison houses: they are for a prey, and none delivereth; for a spoil, and none saith, Restore.

Jeremiah 48:10 Cursed be he that doeth the work of the Most High God deceitfully, and cursed be he that keepeth back his sword from blood.

Deuteronomy 7:25-26 Neither shalt thou bring an abomination into thine house, lest thou be a cursed thing like it: but thou shalt utterly detest it, and thou shalt utterly abhor it; for it is a cursed thing. Joshua 6:18

Jeremiah 44 Therefore now thus saith the Most High God, the God of hosts, the God of Israel; Wherefore commit ye this great evil against your souls, to cut off from you man and woman, child and suckling, out of Judah, to leave you none to remain; Enoch 45

Numbers 5:17-22 But if thou hast gone aside to another instead of thy husband, and if thou be defiled, and some man have lain with thee beside thine husband:

2 Peter 2:9-15 Having eyes full of adultery, and that cannot cease from sin; beguiling unstable souls: an heart they have exercised with covetous practices; cursed children:

Deuteronomy 29:9-29 And it come to pass, when he heareth the words of this curse, that he bless himself in his heart, saying, I shall have peace, though I walk in the imagination of mine heart, to add drunkenness to thirst:

Deuteronomy 30:17-18 But if thine heart turn away, so that thou wilt not hear, but shalt be drawn away, and worship other gods, and serve them; 2 Chronicles 34:24-25

Deuteronomy 32:15-36 How should one chase a thousand, and two put ten thousand to flight, except their Rock had sold them, and the Most High God had shut them up?

Genesis 3:16-20 In the sweat of thy face shalt thou eat bread, till thou return unto the ground; for out of it wast thou taken: for dust thou art, and unto dust shalt thou return. Genesis 8:21

Proverbs 11 He that withholdeth corn, the people shall curse him: but blessing shall be upon the head of him that selleth it.

Proverbs 28 He that giveth unto the poor shall not lack: but he that hideth his eyes shall have many a curse.

Deuteronomy 27:15-26 Cursed be he that confirmeth not all the words of this law to do them. And all the people shall say, Amen.

Job 24 The womb shall forget him; the worm shall feed sweetly on him; he shall be no more remembered; and wickedness shall be broken as a tree.

Genesis 4:10-12 And now art thou cursed from the earth, which hath opened her mouth to receive thy brother's blood from thy hand; Enoch 5

Genesis 49:7 Cursed be their anger, for it was fierce; and their wrath, for it was cruel: I will divide them in Jacob, and scatter them in Israel.

Psalm 62 How long will ye imagine mischief against a man? ye shall be slain all of you: as a bowing wall shall ye be, and as a tottering fence.

Proverbs 24 He that saith unto the wicked, Thou are righteous; him shall the people curse, nations shall abhor him:

Proverbs 3:29-35 The curse of the Most High God is in the house of the wicked: but he blesseth the habitation of the just.

Deuteronomy 12:9 Ye shall not do after all the things that we do here this day, every man whatsoever is right in his own eyes. Proverbs 12:15

Jeremiah 17:5 Thus saith the Most High God; Cursed be the man that trusteth in man, and maketh flesh his arm, and whose heart departeth from the Most High God.

Psalm 119:21 Thou hast rebuked the proud that are cursed, which do err from thy commandments.

Deuteronomy 7:25-26 Neither shalt thou bring an abomination into thine house, lest thou be a cursed thing like it: but thou shalt utterly detest it, and thou shalt utterly abhor it; for it is a cursed thing. Joshua 6:18

Proverbs 27 He that blesseth his friend with a loud voice, rising early in the morning, it shall be counted a curse to him.

Ecclesiastes 10:20 Curse not the king, no not in thy thought; and curse not the rich in thy bedchamber: for a bird of the air shall carry the voice, and that which hath wings shall tell the matter.

Psalm 76 At thy rebuke, O God of Jacob, both the chariot and horse are cast into a dead sleep... Thou didst cause judgment to be heard from heaven; the earth feared, and was still, 9 When God arose to judgment, to save all the meek of the earth. Selah. He shall cut off the spirit of princes: he is terrible to the kings of the earth. Enoch 53

Malachi 4 Behold, I will send you Elijah the prophet before the coming of the great and dreadful day of the Most High God: 6 And he shall turn the heart of the fathers to the children, and the heart of the children to their fathers, lest I come and smite the earth with a curse.

<u>IN THE MORNING</u>

In the morning (3)
Rise and shine (2)
in the morning (2)
rise and shine (2)
I pray you
Make this day
My daily Bread
Give me What I need
I testify
Your word, in me.
Give me What I need.
In the morning
Rise and shine,
In the morning
Praises go up And
Blessings come down on us
Oh' Yahu'shua. Your worthy

THE WORK OF SUCCESS

A Chosen journey of life
I do it effortlessly,
Hey, eh-eh, hey
Meticulous work pursues dreams
Hey, eh-eh, hey
Examine your habits, loose distractions.
Hey, eh-eh, hey
Success is for you to do your best
Hey, eh-eh, hey
Learn this from failures
Who cares what they tell you.
Hey, eh-eh, hey
Walking consciously helps you
see the pieces around you coming together
you will, know when you have it,
and know whence you are.
When you have all the pieces.
I have given you my last bread.

REVELATION OF GLORY

Bow down thing ear before the heavens.

By word of the Most High God were the heavens made - Ps 33:6

Let all the heaven and earth give him praise, the seas, and everything that moveth therein. - Ps 69:34, 33:8

Make a joyful noise unto the Most High of all the earth: make a loud noise, and rejoice, and sing praise. - Ps 98:4

Let them praise his name in the dance: let them sing praises unto him with the timbrel and harp. – Ps 149:3

Blessed is the nation whose Most High God is Yahoshuah. 33:12

Let us worship and bow down, let us kneel before our Maker - Ps 95:6

He shall judge the world with righteousness, and the people with his truth. - Ps 95:13

Ye that love the Almighty, hate evil; he preserveth the souls of his saints - Ps 97:10

Enter into his gates with thanksgiving... and into his courts with praise, Hallelujah! Ps 100:4

Sit thou at my right hand till I make thine enemies thy footstool Ps 110

The kings' strength also loveth judgment; thou executest judgment and righteousness in Yaquob. - Ps 97:4

A horse is a vain thing for safety - Ps 33:17 especially from the enemies that hate thee

For the Most High God is good, his mercy is everlasting; and his truth is always enduring forever.

MERCY KISSES TRUTH

Shew us thy mercy, O Yah, and grant us salvation. Ps. 85:7
Oh that the salvation of Israel were come out of Zion!
When Yah bringeth back the captivity of his people,
Jacob shall rejoice, and Israel shall be glad. Ps 14:7
8 I will hear what Yah will speak:
for he will speak peace unto his people, and to his saints:
but let them not turn again to folly.
9 Surely his salvation is nigh them that fear him;
that glory may dwell in our land.
10 Mercy and truth are met together;
righteousness and peace have kissed each other.
11 Truth shall spring out of the earth;
and righteousness shall look down from heaven.
12 Yah shall give that which is good; and our land shall yield
her increase.
13 Righteousness shall go before him; and shall set us in the way of
his steps.
Behold, Yah says unto the end of the world, Oh daughter of Zion,
Behold, your salvation cometh;
behold his reward is with him and his work before him. Is. 62:11

FULLY VESTED

The strength of others
is YAH's hand
To whom shall his glory
Be revealed as it is sealed?
The service of righteousness
Comes with a price
beyond a man's life there is hope
Not rolled as dice.
A new season paves the way
The decoration of today,
Colors sequels stories unheard
Of people's struggles broken like bottles.
The hand that throttles is cut off
from the lamp.
Not relied on food, life stamps,
in the hour of darkness,
The songs we chant as one declares
goodwill towards life without thrills.
Is the service to whom
the Most High God's arm is revealed.

FILL MY HEART

I will never forsake you
Joy I have perfect joy!
My cup runs over, my heart says yes!
I have learned of you!
My heart was broken
Without you I fall
I need you, Yahushua I need you
Come down, Come down
Holy Spirit fill my joy, my mind, and heart

MAKE ME PROPHECY

Father show me your dreams (2)
Show me your visions
Make me prophecy (3)
Waking up from slumber
Seeking Yah, Yahushua my Elohim for my dream
Signs and Wonders to be seen
Life or death in the hands of Ibreem
Be me like unto you, put away iniquity
Sin if you want
Commandment keepers, sweeping Torah
Applying the fringes, heals wounds on the borders.
Guard your heart these lively stones
My Father's orders, free the enslaved peoples
Release the captivity
Prophecy my life now, to be free. (2)
My people I say be free and let the prisoners go!
House of Yahudah, I hear you yo!
I be from Sierre Leone wake up people, Yisrael be free
Come, Come drink from the priesthood (2)
All that are thirsty, come, come to Zion!

<u>SIGNS OF RIGHTEOUS – THE RIGHTEOUS BRANCH</u>

You that love righteousness
Where are you
And you that hate evil awwh!
You make your enemies afraid.
To do good is great!
I saw my people rise!
To do good is great!
You make enemies afraid!
I'm talking to you my people! Let go!
We gotta make a move right now. You here me!
Nothing going to stop us! (4)
We gotta make a move right now. You here me! (2)
Nothing going to stop us! (6)
We gotta make a move!(6)
Right now! You here me!

WHO WE BE

Gullah Geechie, who we be!
My people be from Sierre Leone
Invincible Conquerors, never shall we fall!
We rise and multiply!
Remember this day, I have spoken to you (2)
Always do what is good
No matter what is done unto you
Always do what is good
That you put away evil.
I love you.
Speak not lying words
Do not deal deceitfully
Hating evil, carefully
Consider your ways, never blame.
Always are signs near, getting closer to the truth
Walking in youth, perfect in heart, spirit is free.
Don't deal deceitfully to make enemies.
Loving to do justice and judgment have all the saints.
The Most High is with you.
Honor and Glory, A new name given
Praise Yah all the living.

A TIME TO GIVE THANKS!

What a wonderful time
To celebrate the great life we live!
Yah is good, blessed are we to give thanks
For what we did. Halleluyah, Halleluyah! (2)
Joy comes quickly and smiles upon love,
Nothing to lose, but the baggage of blues.
Stay comforted, in the good that brings much sleep.
What a wonderful time to celebrate the great life we live.
Yah is good, blessed are we to give thanks for what we did.

I HAVE SEEN THE LIGHT

I hath seen the light. (3)
My heart of faith is on the altar.
Night and day I pray
that my soul be comforted,
Oh' Yahushua, my Elohim
the glory of majesty never seen.
The covering of earth and the heavens
that all creation is set apart at seven.
Shall all the days give praise
as the captives are set free at jubilee
each day the Most High God has made,
rejoice and be glad in it
for he is our refuge of promise
that we are not weary from
distress in the land wither we possess.
The light is at the end of the tunnel, revealed
to whomever finds it has the kingdom
as the patience of the saints, to be near unto him.
My Father says: He that hath ears
let him hear what the spirit saith:
I hath seen the light.

THE PRAISE OF MY DAYS

All my days shall I give praise
to the one who lifts me up.
I feel good that I could
give up my con-fes-sion,
for there is no <u>iniquity</u>
as I love and make peace <u>fully</u>.
Holy is he, <u>the rock</u>
of my soul that I be consoled.
<u>Trouble</u> shall come in my <u>days</u>
to prove my heart and see my ways.
What is the way to deliverance,
if I, not seek it out?
<u>Shall I</u> be trapped in a snare
not to consider my own ways?
<u>I shall not</u> make vanity the praise
of my days for the fear of my Father.
All my days shall I give praise to
the one who lifts me up.

MY PRESENCE AWAITS!

Ohhh! Look at here! (3)
Please, Please, Pleaaaseeeee! (2)
Seek me daily as you live
you'll find me
that you will try
before you lie
down in the earth.
New waters spring up,
life trapped inside.
You see, no more misery.
I live not for you
my friend, in the end
is a new beginning of life....
of hope.., of peace......, of joy......,
and well springing forth love. Halleluyah (2).
The glory of the earth, belongs to him
who gave it, made it, and praised it without hands
for all to glory in his majesty. Halleluyah (2). Alleluyah

A WELL-APPOINTED TIME OF JOLLILITY

Make a <u>joyful</u> noise in <u>Zion</u>
<u>Now</u> can I stop from cryin', there's victory over dyin'
The Almighty and his saints are comin'
for the day of vengeance against the heathen
The temple shall be opened in heaven,
at the last trump of the hour
many are called but few are chosen
for honor, glory, and wisdom... is much praise
power and might exalted on high
his throne is everlasting love, reigning for eternity
the dominion over things is his domain
I sing, for the beauty of his <u>majesty</u>
One day shall I see, my Father before me
Welcoming the bride-groom joined in hands with the elect Lady
Coming for her children, shall she be arrayed in fine linen
Upon his holy Mountain, shall all give praise
for the wrath of the Lamb has come,
the bride has made herself ready for Yahudah and Yisrael are one!

SECRET PLACE

Oh Father, Oh Father, Oh Father
I'm worn out, I'm worn out, I'm worrrn out!
Two Shabbats, let my body rest for me (2)
So I may endure this Shabbat's day journey.
Going to the secret place of the Most High
I strive for perfection to the resurrection.
I yearn to hear your voice. At the last day.
I yearn to see your face.
Two Shabbats, let my body rest for me (2)
Oh Father, Yahuwah comfort me with your Holy Spirit, the anointing
of the Most High
Keep me forever in you peace, let my enemies be struck with thunder,
Hot bolts of lightning striking the inner parts of their hearts
Acknowledges the servant of the Most High!
No more will be sin if they do penance, there will be no
more remembrance
I'll pray for them, forgive they know what not they do unto death.
I seek ways of the meek and humble.
Always and forever I will serve you, Oh Father you gave us Yahoshua.
The bread of life, Creator of all things seen, dreamed, conceived, and
believed in
The world made by him. Allaheim!, Halleluyah!

THE PEACE OF LIFE (THANK FOR YOUR PEACE)

Thank for your perfect peace
that we have <u>to</u>
live forever.
Alle-loo-ooh-yah, Alle-loo-ooh-yah, Alle-looyah!
Wisdom and honor belongs
to-ooh you
who made us for your
glory.
Alle-loo-ooh-yah, Alle-loo-ooh-yah, Alle-looyah!
The heavens are filled with praise
the earth always shall yield its fruit.
Alle-loo-ooh-yah!
Thank you for the peace of life,
the words of truth, from my youth.
Alle-loo-ooh-yah, Alle-loo-ooh-yah, Alle-looyah!
Keep me in your secret place
that I may see your face. Alle-looyah!
Wonderful is the presence
in your sight, my delight. Alle-looyah!
The splendor of colors ah-rayed
a masquerade, so magnificent. Alle-looyah!
Perfection of creation displayed
for all to see your majesty. Alle-looyah!
Praise our Father,
on high, El Shaddai for Yahshuah,
the Almighty. Ahh-le-loo-yah!
Ahh-loo-yah!, Ahh-loo-yah!, Ahh-le-loo-yah!
Alle-loo-ooh-yah, Alle-loo-ooh-yah, Alle-looyah!

BLESS THE BODY

Jasmine rice good for the sake
Yah made things good for the body
Spinach, onions, good for the tummy.
Drink your wine good with your honey.
Honey-wine good for the tummy.
Jasmine rice good for the sake.

I AM THANKFUL

I am Thankful, I am Thankful,
I am Thankful to have food
You have blessed me, you have blessed me,
You have blessed me, I am full
Clothe my mind, Clothe my body,
Clothe my spirit to rest.
Provide me every need, Provide me every day,
Provide me in the way of love. Today.
When I am hungry and When I thirst,
I need your love, quickly.
Patience is all that I have to endure,
the times of this world. Shall not tempt me.
My Father's word in him I trust, Oh Yahushua
my Elohim, Deliverer of my dreams make everything
so easy to me. I shall not rush in fear of anything
of this world. It is my footstool as I am meek,
I seek righteousness in my Father's house.
O' Yahuwah, Come see me, Come see me,
Come see me

OH MOST MIGHTY

Ooh Most Mighty, Ahh-le-loo-yah!,
Ahh-le-loo-yah!
You're the strength of my song
the life of my peace.
Ahh-le-loo-yah!
You're the peace of my heart,
keep my spirit, perfect in love.
I am comforted, to know who you-ooh,
no-oh-ble are you Ohh Mighty!
Ooh Most Mighty, Ahh-le-loo-yah!,
Ahh-le-loo-yah!, Ahh-le-loo-yah!
I know you Ahh-le-loo-yah!, Ahh-le-loo-yah!, Allel-looyah!
I know you!

HONOR AND GLORY AND WISDOM

Give Praise Always! It's your turn!
Honor and Glory and Wisdom! (4)
Drink of my Father's cistern!
Honor and Glory and Wisdom!
The path of righteous laughs
Honor and Glory and Wisdom!
Who's way always amaze?
Honor and Glory and Wisdom!
Seeks truth in the light of youth
Honor and Glory and Wisdom!
Rests with patience, move with knowledge
Honor and Glory and Wisdom!
Peace comes upon the meek
Honor and Glory and Wisdom!
Grace be upon your face
Honor and Glory and Wisdom!
Love, All of his children
Honor and Glory and Wisdom!
Who's ways always amaze?
The light of days <u>always</u>,
Vibrating <u>waves</u>, <u>feel</u> the glory
Of honor and wisdom!

WHO HATH FORSAKEN THE COVENANT

Who hath forsaken Father
Ahiyah Yaha'shuah
Covenants Broken
Commanding voice
Seeks sign among my people
To see your face is grace
Have Mercy, Oh Halleluyah!
You have hidden from me,
Your presence
Instruments of cruelty, speaks wickedly
The domain of forbidden fruit
Have you eaten
My spirit shall not strive with you people
Depart quickly.
While you have time.
You will not be great in my sight
Only, the humble shall speak to me
Day by day, honor and righteousness stands
To walk and talk with me in Paradise.
Ahiyah force is with them, the honor of my covenant.
I am refuge to those humbled from their ways
Learning of me shall they see my face.
Oh Yahu'shua
A covenant of life and peace
Shall they not see death
Seeking me in affliction
Ahiyah Ruach Hodesh.
Be upon them.

Narrative II

Knowing this: *Come now therefore, and I will send thee unto Pharaoh, that thou mayest bring forth my people the <u>children of Israel out of Egypt</u>. Exodus 3:10*

And Moses and Aaron came in unto Pharaoh, and said unto him, Thus saith the Most High God of the Hebrews, How long wilt thou refuse to humble thyself before me? <u>let my people go</u>, that they may serve me. Exodus 10:3

And it shall be when thy son asketh thee in time to come, saying, What is this? that thou shalt say unto him, By strength of hand the <u>Most High God brought us out from Egypt</u>, from the <u>house of bondage</u>: Exodus 13:14

Can we rejoice when our people are suffering?

Without knowledge of the past a love for humanity is forsaken. How can you discern any nation within your midst, if people are made inferior to racism as injustice becomes a house of bondage? What shall the future behold in America as wealth gap closes out those without financial literacy? Inflation increases cost of living, African woman exploited for her reproductive organs as division increases within the African families; while the African men are killed by self-hatred, racism, and law officials. There is violence in the earth as the nations has not learned to cease from threats of war even violence is seen between Hebrew men and women. What becomes of the Hebrew man and woman if they do not love each other to create family?

And the king of Egypt spake to the Hebrew midwives, of which the name of the one was Shiphrah, and the name of the other Puah: And he said, When ye do the office of a midwife to the Hebrew women, and see them upon the stools; if it be a son, then ye shall kill him: but if it be a daughter, then she shall live. But the midwives feared God, and did not as the king of Egypt commanded them, but saved the men children alive. And the king of Egypt called for the midwives, and said unto them, Why have ye done this thing, and have saved the men children alive? Exodus 1:15-18

What is our collective effort that grace and truth may abide?

Study to shew thyself approved unto God, a workman that needeth not to be ashamed, rightly dividing the word of truth. 2 Timothy 2:15

Can we rejoice when our people are suffering?

Watch ye therefore, and pray always, that ye may be accounted worthy to escape all these things that shall come to pass, and to stand before the Son of man. Luke 21:36

Read the Isis Papers: Keys to the Colors, The Kissinger Report: NSSM-200 Implications of Worldwide Population Growth., Planned Parenthood, Organ Harvesting, Tuskegee Experiment, Tulsa Massacre, etc.

<u>Understanding the assault on the Hebrew and Negro man:</u>

Wages war on our psychology, economics, work force, education, law regulation, political agendas, medical issues, health concerns, even social development and entertainment.

Weissinger, Thomas. "Conspiracy Theory in the Black Community - University of Illinois ..." Illinois University Library, 2012. https://www.library.illinois.edu/afx/wp-content/uploads/sites/22/2020/07/Conspiracy-Theory-in-the-Black-Community.pdf.

Welsing, Frances Cress. *The Isis (Yssis) Papers: The Key to the Colors*. Chicago, Illinois: Third World Press, 1995.

Clowes, Brian. "Exposing the Global Population Control Agenda." Human Life International, June 27, 2022. https://www.hli.org/resources/exposing-the-global-population-control/.

Van Deburg, William L. "White Conspiracies against Black Empowerment." Incidences de l'événement - White Conspiracies Against Black Empowerment. Presses universitaires François-Rabelais, January 1, 1970. https://books.openedition.org/pufr/5525?lang=en.

McVean B.Sc, Ada. "40 Years of Human Experimentation in America: The Tuskegee Study." Office for Science and Society, January 25, 2019. https://www.mcgill.ca/oss/article/history/40-years-human-experimentation-america-tuskegee-study.

Kelly, Amita. "Fact Check: Was Planned Parenthood Started to 'Control' the Black Population?" NPR. NPR, August 14, 2015. https://www.npr.org/sections/itsallpolitics/2015/08/14/432080520/fact-check-was-planned-parenthood-started-to-control-the-black-population.

Burnett, Zaron. "How Body Brokers Make Money Harvesting Organs from Black People." MEL Magazine, January 21, 2020. https://melmagazine.com/en-us/story/how-body-brokers-make-money-harvesting-organs-from-black-people.

Lloyd, Chrishana M., Marta Alvira-Hammond, Julianna Carlson, and Deja Logan. "Family, Economic, and Geographic Characteristics of Black Families with Children." Child Trends, March 17, 2021. https://www.childtrends.org/publications/family-economic-and-geographic-characteristics-of-black-families-with-children.

Robinson, Jeffery. "Five Truths about Black History." American Civil Liberties Union. American Civil Liberties Union, 2022. https://www.aclu.org/issues/racial-justice/five-truths-about-black-history.

Simon, Clea. "Rewriting History—to Include All of It This Time." Harvard Gazette. Harvard Gazette, June 22, 2020. https://news.harvard.edu/gazette/story/2020/06/burying-truth-keeps-black-americans-dispossessed-says-panel/.

American Experience. "Black Genocide." PBS. Public Broadcasting Service, 2020. https://www.pbs.org/wgbh/americanexperience/features/pill-black-genocide.

Can we rejoice when our people are suffering?

Parshina-kottas, Yuliya, and Anjali Singhvi. "What the Tulsa Race Massacre Destroyed." The New York Times. The New York Times, May 24, 2021. https://www.nytimes.com/interactive/2021/05/24/us/tulsa-race-massacre.html.

Hampton, Deon J. "'They Were Killing All the Black People': This 107-Year-Old Still Remembers Tulsa Massacre." NBCNews.com. NBCUniversal News Group, May 31, 2021. https://www.nbcnews.com/news/us-news/they-were-killing-all-black-people-107-year-old-still-n1268420.

BBC News. "We Only Kill Black People." London: BBC News, 2017. Recognize the conspiracy to subdue masculine melanin power and prowess to overcome the affliction of many; without masculinity there is no manhood, and if no manhood then no priesthood, nor father, husband for protection of woman and child.

If a man seeks not his identity he has no protocol to enter the rights of passage and the courses of mastery for the curriculum necessary to express his achievements in human relations for positive attributes of spiritual growth. Thus he becomes frustrated and may offend unintentionally his neighbor. Once he recognizes his spiritual gifts and skilled attributes he can assimilate knowledge to distribute assignments for the welfare of the people.

Absolved of crimes against us do they profit off us
Never is mercy shown but oppression over 400 years
Who else have endured such as us, the force of supremacy?
Step in the shoes of a Creator and sin becomes your troubles
Government bondage, fight for your righteousness
Lessons, teachings, growing pains
Cope with stress in the spirit realm than
emotional outbursts to know who you are

You are a god and Yah is with you according to righteousness. Save yourself and create the change you desire to see, declare your vision and embrace imagination for a new reality! Speak things into existence, reality creates things loving self with people of faith.

WEST AFRICAN DIASPORA

During the transatlantic slave trade, spanning several centuries, European slave traders played a pivotal role in capturing and transporting the majority of enslaved Africans to destinations such as South Carolina and other parts of the southern United States. These traders sourced enslaved individuals from various regions along the West African coast, contributing to the intricate network of the transatlantic slave trade.

This complex system involved European, African, and American traders, making it challenging to trace the exact origins of individuals transported to South Carolina due to the lack of detailed historical records. Despite the difficulty in pinpointing specific information about individual slave ships in the 1800s, names like the Brookes, the Zong, and the Jesus of Lübeck stand out as infamous vessels involved in this trade.

As the 1800s progressed, the transatlantic slave trade significantly declined, and by 1808, the importation of slaves into the United States, including South Carolina, became illegal. This marked a turning point, shifting the movement of enslaved people to internal slave trade within the United States or other forms of illegal transatlantic activities.

In the 18th century, many enslaved Africans brought to South Carolina had origins in various regions along the West African coast, including Senegambia, Sierra Leone, Gold Coast (present-day Ghana), and the Windward Coast. However, identifying the exact origins of slaves in the 1800s becomes more challenging due to the cessation of the legal transatlantic slave trade and limitations in available historical records.

The Windward Coast, historically denoting the coastal region from present-day Liberia to the Ivory Coast, played a crucial role in the transatlantic slave trade. This area attracted European interest for trade, acquiring goods such as gold and ivory, and eventually becoming a source for enslaved individuals during this dark chapter in history. It's important to recognize that historical terms and designations, like the Windward Coast, may vary in usage over time and across different contexts.

During the transatlantic slave trade, people from various ethnic groups in West Africa, including the Mandinka, were forcibly brought to the Americas. In the Sea Islands and coastal regions of South Carolina, Georgia, and Florida, where the Gullah people reside, individuals of diverse African ethnicities were grouped together on plantations. As a result, the Gullah people have ancestral roots in a range of African ethnicities, including the Mandinka.

The Mandinka people are primarily found in West Africa, particularly in the following countries:

1. Gambia: The Mandinka are one of the largest ethnic groups in The Gambia.

2. Senegal: Mandinka communities can be found in Senegal, especially in the eastern and southern regions.

3. Mali: The Mandinka have a significant presence in Mali, particularly in the southern and eastern parts of the country.

4. Guinea: Mandinka communities are also present in Guinea, particularly in the northeastern regions.

5. Sierra Leone: While not as numerous, there are Mandinka communities in Sierra Leone.

6. Ivory Coast: Mandinka populations are found in some areas of Ivory Coast.

The Mandinka people have a rich cultural and historical heritage and have played a prominent role in the development of the West African region.

The Gullah people are concentrated in the Sea Islands and the coastal regions of South Carolina, Georgia, and northeastern Florida in the United States. These areas include places such as Hilton Head Island, the St. Helena Island, and the coastal areas surrounding Charleston in South Carolina, as well as the barrier islands and coastal regions of Georgia. Gullah communities have preserved a distinctive African cultural heritage, including their own language (Gullah or Geechee) and traditions, making them a unique and historically significant group in the United States.

PATERNAL ANCESTRAL LINK TO WEST AFRICA

The Gullah people and the Mandinka tribe share historical and cultural connections, particularly in the context of the transatlantic slave trade and the development of African American communities in the United States.

The Gullah language, often referred to as Gullah or Geechee, contains linguistic elements that reflect the influence of various West African languages, including Mandinka. Additionally, cultural practices, traditions, and folklore within Gullah communities may bear some similarities to those of the Mandinka, as well as other West African ethnic groups.

It's important to note that the Gullah people are not exclusively descended from the Mandinka; their heritage encompasses a blend of various African ethnicities. The history of the Gullah people is a testament to the resilience and preservation of African cultural elements within African American communities in the United States.

My primary aim is to trace the origins of my father's family from South Carolina, where the lineage of my paternal grandfather is identified through the Y-chromosomal DNA marker originating in West Africa.

These major ethnic groups or tribes located in West African nations endured enslavement during the transatlantic slave trade and were subsequently transported to South Carolina. Let's explore the ethnic groups in West Africa linked to particular Haplogroups that may represent the ancestral roots of the descendants in South Carolina.

1. Senegal:

   - Wolof: Haplogroups E, A, B
   - Pulaar (Fulfulde): Haplogroups E, A, B
   - Serer: Haplogroups E, A, B
   - Mandinka: Haplogroups E, A, B
   - Jola: Haplogroups E, A, B

2. Gambia:

   - Mandinka: Haplogroups E, A, B
   - Wolof: Haplogroups E, A, B
   - Fula: Haplogroups E, A, B
   - Jola: Haplogroups E, A, B
   - Serer: Haplogroups E, A, B

3. Sierra Leone:

   - Mende: Haplogroups E, A, B
   - Temne: Haplogroups E, A, B
   - Limba: Haplogroups E, A, B
   - Krio: Haplogroups E, A, B
   - Loko: Haplogroups E, A, B

4. Liberia:

   - Kpelle: Haplogroups E, A, B
   - Bassa: Haplogroups E, A, B
   - Gio (Dan): Haplogroups E, A, B
   - Mano: Haplogroups E, A, B
   - Kru: Haplogroups E, A, B

5. Ivory Coast:

- Baoulé: Haplogroups E, A, B
- Bété: Haplogroups E, A, B
- Sénoufo: Haplogroups E, A, B
- Malinké: Haplogroups E, A, B
- Dan: Haplogroups E, A, B

6. Ghana:

- Akan (including Ashanti and Fante): Haplogroups E, A, B
- Mole-Dagbon: Haplogroups E, A, B
- Ewe: Haplogroups E, A, B
- Ga-Dangme: Haplogroups E, A, B
- Gurma: Haplogroups E, A, B

7. Mali:

- Bambara: Haplogroups E, A, B
- Fulani (Peul): Haplogroups E, A, B
- Tuareg: Haplogroups E, A, B
- Dogon: Haplogroups E, A, B
- Songhai: Haplogroups E, A, B

It's important to emphasize that the distribution of haplogroups can vary within ethnic groups, and the information provided here is a generalization based on broader population studies. Additionally, the categorization of ethnic groups may not capture the full diversity within these populations. These enumerations encompass several key tribes within each country. It's crucial to acknowledge that each of these nations boasts a rich mosaic of diverse ethnicities, cultures, and languages that extend well beyond those mentioned here.

According to historical records from the Port of Charleston, enslaved Africans transported to the port hailed from specific regions, with percentages as follows: Angola (39%), Senegambia (20%), the Windward Coast (17%), the Gold Coast (13%), Sierra Leone (6%), and Madagascar, Mozambique, and the two Bights (Benin and Biafra) combined (5%) (Pollitzer, 1999:43). The term "Windward Coast" was often synonymous with Sierra Leone, impacting the actual figure of slaves from that region.

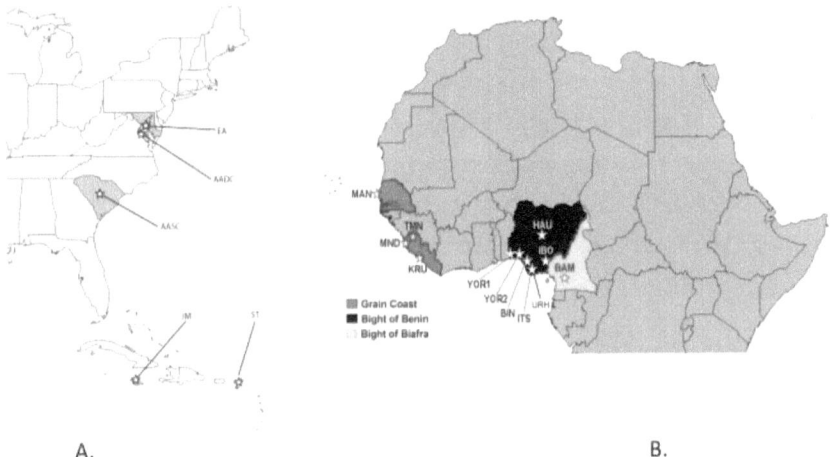

A.   B.

MATERNAL ANCESTRAL LINK TO WEST AFRICA

Increasing awareness about sickle cell anemia is crucial, especially among individuals with ancestral roots in sub-Saharan Africa, India, Saudi Arabia, and Mediterranean countries. Migration has contributed to a higher prevalence of the gene in the Americas. In certain sub-Saharan African regions, as many as 2% of children are born with sickle cell anemia. The prevalence of the sickle-cell trait, where individuals inherit the mutant gene from one parent, ranges from 10% to 40% in equatorial Africa, decreases to 1-2% on the North African coast, and drops below 1% in South Africa.

This distribution is linked to the protective advantage that the sickle-cell trait provides against malaria. The selection pressure from malaria has led to high frequencies of the mutant gene in areas with intense malaria transmission. Notably, in West African countries like Ghana and Nigeria, the trait occurs at rates of 15% to 30%, while others such as Cameroon, Chad, Republic of the Congo (Congo-Brazzaville), and Democratic Republic of the Congo (DRC) have high frequency of the sickle cell trait; Uganda exhibits tribal variations, with the Baamba tribe in the west showing a remarkable 45% frequency.

Understanding carrier state frequencies is vital in determining the prevalence of sickle-cell anemia at birth. In Nigeria, the most populous country in the subregion, 24% of the population are carriers of the mutant gene, resulting in a prevalence of about 20 cases of sickle-cell anemia per 1000 births. It is essential to raise awareness about the impact of these genetic factors on health outcomes, particularly in regions with higher carrier frequencies.

Evidence of the sickle cell trait was revealed from my maternal ancestors who inhabited West Africa. My mother became a carrier of the sickle cell trait at birth. My brother inherited the same sickle cell trait; therefore I can trace my maternal genetic ancestries to the countries of West Africa. Sickle cell trait is most prevalent in certain populations within sub-Saharan Africa. However, it's important to note that the prevalence of the sickle cell trait can vary within countries, and multiple factors can influence its distribution. Due to my maternal grandmother's South Carolina roots, I chose to focus on the elevated occurrences of the sickle cell trait prevalent in West African countries within the sub-Saharan region of Africa as follows:

1. Nigeria (has a coastline along the Gulf of Guinea in the Atlantic Ocean to the south)

2. Ghana (situated along the Gulf of Guinea, with a coastline along the Atlantic Ocean to the south)

3. Senegal (situated along the Atlantic Ocean with a coastline along the Cape Verde Peninsula)

4. Mali (does not have a coastline as it is landlocked in West Africa)

5. Guinea (has a coastline along the Atlantic Ocean to the west)

6. Ivory Coast (Côte d'Ivoire) (has a coastline along the Gulf of Guinea in the Atlantic Ocean to the south)

Many individuals with African American ancestry in the United States have roots tracing back to West Africa, where the sickle cell trait is more prevalent. However, the specific genetic makeup can vary widely, and not all individuals with West African ancestry necessarily carry the sickle cell trait such as myself.

Studies that do delve into ancestral origins often focus exclusively on the mitochondrial locus. For instance, Ely et al. and Salas et al., primarily investigate the maternal genetic ancestries of African Americans. Their findings align closely with historical records indicating that African Americans trace their roots to populations in west and west-central Africa. Similarly, genetic data from South America, particularly Brazil, support the conclusion that African-Brazilians also share origins with west and west-central African populations, along with some contributions from southeastern Africa.

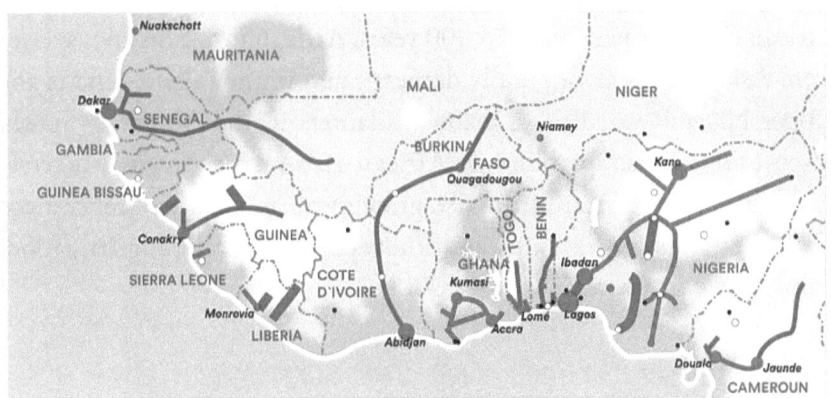

When exploring genetic variation across the genome and continental populations, the observed diversity outside of Africa is generally considered a subset of the variation found within African populations. This pattern is often attributed to the African origin of our species and the successive founder effects during human migrations from Africa. While some studies have investigated regional genetic diversity within west or central Africa, they predominantly focus on mitochondrial lineages. There is a comparatively limited body of literature addressing paternal genetic variation within west and central Africa.

This study specifically examines Y-chromosome genetic variation in populations of African descent. Additionally, it seeks genetic evidence indicating substantial Senegambian "Grain Coast" ancestry in African American males from South Carolina. Lastly, the research explores the paternal African origins of various African descendant populations across the Americas. The aim is not only to offer a genetic perspective complementing historical investigations into African geographical origins but also to contribute to the understanding of the genetic structure of African American populations. The insights gained from studying the variation within these populations hold implicit significance for admixture mapping and association studies in this politically defined 'macro-ethnic' group.

Particularly along the western coast, local peoples had cultivated African rice for an estimated 3,000 years. African rice, a distinct species from Asian rice, was originally domesticated in the inland delta of the Upper Niger River. British colonial planters in the American South, discovering the adaptability of African rice to their region, actively sought enslaved Africans from rice-growing areas. This preference arose from the necessity for skills and knowledge in developing irrigation, dams, and earthworks.

Two British trading companies, operating the slave castle at Bunce Island in the Sierra Leone River, played a significant role. Henry Laurens, a planter and slave trader, served as their agent in Charleston, while Richard Oswald was his counterpart in England. Bunce Island served as a prime export site for slaves to South Carolina and Georgia, distinct from slave castles in Ghana, which shipped individuals mainly to the Caribbean islands.

Following the foundation of Freetown, Sierra Leone, in the late 18th century, slaves were not allowed to be taken from Sierra Leone, as it became a colony for poor blacks from London and black Loyalists from Nova Scotia. The British and the United States prohibited the African slave trade in 1808, leading to the resettlement of liberated Africans in Sierra Leone by the British. Similarly, freed slaves were settled in Liberia, established by the American Colonization Society in the early 19th century.

The Gullah people, residing in what was then Charlestowne, South Carolina, preserved much of their African cultural heritage due to climate, geography, cultural pride, and patterns of importing enslaved Africans. Originating primarily from the Mende populations of Sierra Leone, the Gullah-Geechee people were traded in Charleston, South Carolina.

According to British historian P.E.H. Hair, Gullah culture developed as a creole culture, representing the amalgamation of peoples from various African cultures. These included the Baga, Fula, Kissi, Kpelle, Limba, Mandinka, Mende, Susu, Temne, Vai, and Wolof of the Rice Coast, as well as many from Angola, Igbo, Calabar, Congo Republic, and the Gold Coast. By the mid-18th century, thousands of acres in the Georgia and South Carolina Lowcountry, and the Sea Islands, were developed as African rice fields, making rice farming one of the most successful industries in early America.

Due to a period of relative isolation from the white population while toiling on expansive plantations in remote rural areas, Africans hailing from diverse Central and West African ethnic groups cultivated a distinctive creole culture. This unique cultural fusion has not only preserved a significant portion of their African linguistic and cultural heritage from a multitude of ethnic backgrounds but has also assimilated new influences from the surrounding region. The Gullah people communicate through an English-based creole language enriched with numerous African loanwords, displaying pronounced influences from African languages in both grammar and sentence structure. Referred to as "Sea Island Creole" by linguists and scholars, the Gullah language shares remarkable similarities with Bahamian Creole and maintains connections to Barbadian Creole, Belizean Creole, Jamaican Patois, and the Krio language of West Africa. The Gullah community's traditions, encompassing crafts, farming, fishing, folk beliefs, music, rice-based cuisine, and storytelling, distinctly bear the imprint of Central and West African cultures.

Presently, the Gullah community actively organizes annual cultural festivals throughout the Lowcountry, showcasing their rich heritage. Hilton Head Island, for example, hosts the "Gullah Celebration" every February, featuring diverse events such as the "De Aarts ob We People" show, the "Ol' Fashioned Gullah Breakfast," "National Freedom Day," the "Gullah Film Fest," "A Taste of Gullah" food and entertainment, a "Celebration of Lowcountry Authors and Books," an "Arts, Crafts & Food Expo," and "De Gullah Playhouse." In May, Beaufort hosts "The Original Gullah Festival," the oldest and largest celebration of its kind, while the nearby Penn Center on St. Helena Island organizes "Heritage Days" in November. Gullah festivals are also celebrated on James Island, South Carolina, and Sapelo Island, Georgia.

Beyond the Lowcountry, Gullah culture finds recognition and celebration across the United States. The High Art Museum in Atlanta has showcased exhibits dedicated to Gullah culture, while the Black Cultural Center at Purdue University in West Lafayette, Indiana, conducted a research tour, cultural arts festival, and related events to highlight Gullah culture. The Black Cultural Center Library at Purdue maintains a bibliography of Gullah books and materials. In Denver, Colorado, Metro State College recently hosted a conference titled "The Water Brought Us: Gullah History and Culture," featuring a panel of Gullah scholars and cultural activists. These events in Indiana and Colorado are indicative of the ongoing nationwide appreciation and acknowledgment of Gullah culture.

The **mitochondrial DNA (mtDNA) test** that traces the ancestral land of the most recent common ancestor on the maternal side is often referred to as a **maternal haplogroup test**. Mitochondrial DNA is passed down from mothers to their children, and it changes very slowly over time, allowing scientists to trace maternal lineages.

Various companies and testing services provide maternal haplogroup information as part of their DNA ancestry testing. The results typically include information about the specific branch or haplogroup of the mitochondrial DNA, and this information can be used to trace the ancient migratory paths of maternal lineages and, in some cases, identify the general geographical regions associated with those lineages.

Keep in mind that different DNA testing companies may use slightly different terminology or provide additional information along with maternal haplogroup details. If you're interested in such a test, it's recommended to explore the offerings of reputable genetic testing companies and review the details of their specific mitochondrial DNA testing services. Ensure that you carefully review all disclaimers that could potentially render you vulnerable, limiting your rights regarding the utilization of DNA testing or its application in pharmaceutical engineering laboratories.

For tracing the ancestral land of the most recent common ancestor on the paternal side, a **Y-chromosomal DNA (Y-DNA) test** is used. The test provides information about the paternal haplogroup, which represents a group of individuals who share a common ancestor on the direct paternal line.

Similar to mitochondrial DNA testing for the maternal line, Y-DNA testing allows individuals to trace their paternal lineage and learn about the ancient migratory paths and geographical regions associated with their paternal ancestors.

Several genetic testing companies offer paternal haplogroup testing as part of their DNA ancestry services. Examples of well known companies include 23andMe, AncestryDNA, and FamilyTreeDNA. It's important to note that the level of detail and the specific regions covered in the ancestral analysis can vary among different testing providers to know the pros and cons.

It's important to note that different testing companies may offer various levels of detail and analysis in their ancestry tests. Additionally, consent and privacy considerations should be carefully reviewed before submitting a sample for genetic testing, as the results can reveal sensitive information about an individual's heritage and potential health traits. Always choose reputable and reliable testing services that prioritize privacy and adhere to ethical standards.

Genetic testing, including Y-chromosomal DNA (Y-DNA) tests for paternal ancestry and maternal haplogroup tests for maternal ancestry, can generally be submitted by anyone interested in exploring their genetic heritage. Here's a breakdown:

1. Y-Chromosomal DNA (Y-DNA) Test:

    - Who Can Submit: Individuals who are interested in exploring their direct paternal line can submit a sample for a Y-DNA test. This test traces the paternal lineage along the Y chromosome, which is passed from father to son. Therefore, the test is typically most informative for males who want to learn about their paternal ancestry.

2. Maternal Haplogroup Test (Mitochondrial DNA Test):

    - Who Can Submit: Both males and females can submit samples for a maternal haplogroup test. Mitochondrial DNA (mtDNA) is passed from mothers to all of their children, regardless of gender. Thus, both men and women can learn about their maternal ancestry through this type of test.

My advice is to make diligent research efforts for prudent guidance on genetic testing; placing much emphasis on the importance of exercising extreme caution and discretion when selecting a DNA testing facility. Again, I emphasize the necessity of choosing a facility committed to safeguarding your genetic information, ensuring it is not released or utilized without your explicit consent. Prioritize confidentiality and inquire about policies regarding the secure disposal of genetic data after results have been delivered.

WHY CONDUCT Y-CHROMOSOMAL DNA (Y-DNA) TEST

Y-chromosomal DNA testing, commonly known as Y-DNA testing, provides insights into the direct paternal lineage of an individual. The Y-chromosome is passed down from father to son, so Y-DNA testing is particularly useful for tracing paternal ancestry. Here's a comprehensive understanding of what Y-chromosomal DNA markers indicate after the test results:

1. Haplogroup: A haplogroup is a classification that represents a group of individuals who share a common ancestor on the paternal line. It is identified by specific genetic markers on the Y-chromosome.

   Results Provide: Y-DNA testing reveals your haplogroup, which can provide information about the deep ancestry of your direct paternal line. Haplogroups are often associated with specific geographic regions and can help trace the migratory paths of ancestral populations.

2. Subclades and SNPs: Haplogroups are further divided into subclades, which represent more recent branching points in the paternal lineage. Single Nucleotide Polymorphisms (SNPs) are specific genetic markers that define these subclades.

   Results Provide: Subclades and SNPs provide more granular details about your paternal lineage. As you move down the phylogenetic tree, you get a more refined understanding of your direct paternal ancestry.

3. Genetic Distance and Matches: Genetic distance measures the genetic differences between individuals. Matches are individuals who share a significant portion of their Y-chromosomal DNA with you.

Results Provide: By comparing your Y-DNA with others in a database, testing companies can identify potential relatives within a genealogical timeframe. The number of genetic differences (genetic distance) helps estimate the time since a common paternal ancestor.

4. Time to Most Recent Common Ancestor (TMRCA): TMRCA is an estimate of the number of years since you and a match shared a common paternal ancestor.

    Results Provide: TMRCA provides a rough timeframe for when your paternal line diverged from the paternal line of a genetic match. This information can be valuable for understanding the age of shared ancestry.

5. Surname Projects: Surname projects are collaborative efforts where individuals with the same or similar surnames compare Y-DNA results to identify common paternal lineages.

    Results Provide: Participation in surname projects can help individuals with shared surnames connect with relatives and build a more extensive understanding of their paternal family history.

Y-chromosomal DNA testing is especially powerful for genealogical research on the paternal side, offering insights into ancient ancestry, migration patterns, and potential connections with living relatives who share a common paternal lineage. Keep in mind that the depth of information depends on the testing company and the level of Y-DNA testing performed.

WHY CONDUCT MITOCHONDRIAL DNA (MTDNA) TEST

Mitochondrial DNA (mtDNA) testing focuses on a specific set of DNA passed down exclusively from mother to child. Here's a comprehensive understanding of what the results of an <u>mtDNA test</u> can indicate:

1. Maternal Lineage: Every individual inherits their mtDNA from their mother. Both males and females receive their mother's mtDNA, but only females pass it on to their own offspring.

    - Unbroken Lineage: MtDNA allows the tracing of an unbroken maternal lineage, providing insights into the maternal ancestry of an individual.

2. Haplogroups: MtDNA is categorized into groups known as haplogroups, which represent distinct branches on the maternal family tree. Each haplogroup is associated with specific geographic regions and historical populations.

    - Geographic Origins: The haplogroup assigned in the test results can provide information about the likely geographic origins of your maternal ancestors.

3. Deep Ancestry: MtDNA testing can reveal ancient maternal ancestry, going back thousands of years. It connects individuals to ancient populations and migration patterns.

4. Migration Routes: Historical movement traced by analyzing the distribution of specific haplogroups, researchers can reconstruct historical migration routes of human populations. This sheds light on how our ancestors moved across continents.

5. Population Genetics: Genetic Diversity: MtDNA testing contributes to the study of population genetics, allowing scientists to understand genetic diversity and historical relationships among different populations.

6. Genealogical Clues: Connecting Relatives: While not as detailed as some other DNA tests, mtDNA testing can help identify distant maternal relatives and connect individuals with others who share a common maternal ancestor.

7. Health Implications: Limited Health Information: Unlike autosomal DNA tests, mtDNA tests are not primarily designed for health-related information. They focus on ancestry and maternal lineage.

8. Forensic Applications: Forensic Identification: MtDNA testing is used in forensic science for identifying individuals or establishing maternal relationships in cases where nuclear DNA is degraded or unavailable.

9. Limitations: Limited Genealogical Resolution: While mtDNA testing provides valuable information, its genealogical resolution is limited compared to autosomal DNA tests and may not identify recent maternal relatives.

10. Population-Specific Markers: Distinct Markers: Certain mtDNA markers are more prevalent in specific populations, contributing to our understanding of population movements and migrations.

In summary, mitochondrial DNA testing offers a unique perspective on maternal ancestry, providing a link to ancient roots, migration patterns, and the historical movements of human populations. It is a valuable tool for those interested in understanding their maternal lineage and connecting with distant maternal relatives.

WHY CONDUCT AUTOSOMAL DNA TEST

Autosomal DNA testing provides information about your ancestry and genetic relationships across both maternal and paternal lines. Unlike mitochondrial DNA (mtDNA) or Y-chromosome DNA (Y-DNA) tests that focus on specific maternal or paternal lineages, autosomal DNA tests examine a broad spectrum of your DNA, including the 22 pairs of autosomes (non-sex chromosomes).

Here's a comprehensive understanding of what autosomal DNA markers indicate after the test results:

1. Ancestry Composition: Autosomal DNA tests provide an estimate of your ethnic and geographic ancestry based on the genetic markers found in your autosomal DNA. This information is presented as a breakdown of your ancestry into different regions or populations.

2. Genetic Relatives: One of the key benefits of autosomal DNA testing is the identification of genetic relatives. These tests compare your autosomal DNA with others in the testing company's database to find potential relatives. The results often include a list of individuals who share significant portions of their DNA with you, indicating possible relationships.

3. Ethnicity Estimates: Autosomal DNA tests can provide estimates of the percentage of your DNA that comes from different populations. This can include broad categories like European, African, Asian, Native American, etc. The specificity of these estimates depends on the testing company and the size and diversity of their reference populations.

4. Haplogroups: While autosomal DNA tests primarily focus on the 22 autosomal chromosomes, some testing companies also provide information about haplogroups. Haplogroups represent specific branches of the human family tree and are often associated with deep ancestral origins. Unlike mtDNA and Y-DNA haplogroups, which trace specific maternal or paternal lineages, autosomal haplogroups provide a broader overview.

5. Health Traits (Optional): Some companies offer optional features that provide information about certain health-related traits. These traits are influenced by a combination of genetic factors and are not diagnostic of specific health conditions.

6. Shared Segments: Autosomal DNA tests identify shared DNA segments with relatives. The length and number of shared segments can give insights into the closeness of the relationship. Close relatives like siblings or first cousins will share longer segments than more distant relatives.

It's important to note that autosomal DNA testing is most effective for recent genealogy and understanding relationships within the last 5-6 generations. The further back in time you go, the more challenging it becomes to trace specific ancestors using autosomal DNA alone.

Additionally, interpretation of results can be complex, and understanding the limitations of these tests is crucial. Privacy considerations are also important when choosing to share genetic information with testing companies or participate in DNA databases.

CHROMOSOMES THE ANCESTRAL LINK

Understanding chromosomes is like reading a unique treasure map of your ancestry. These thread-like structures in our cells carry the genes that shape our traits, health, and family history. When considering DNA testing for ancestry, chromosomes play a central role.

1. Genetic Blueprint: Chromosomes contain thousands of genes, providing a genetic blueprint that influences our traits and characteristics.

2. Inheritance Patterns: Half of our chromosomes come from each parent, allowing us to explore both maternal and paternal ancestry.

3. Autosomal DNA Testing: Autosomal DNA testing examines 22 pairs of autosomes, offering a broad view of genetic ancestry across diverse regions.

4. Maternal and Paternal Lineage: Specific tests like mtDNA and Y-DNA focus on direct maternal and paternal lines, helping trace family origins.

5. Population Genetics: Chromosomal markers reveal population genetic patterns, connecting individuals to broader ethnic groups.

6. Migration Patterns: Analysis of chromosomes unveils historical migration patterns, showing how ancestors moved across regions.

7. Ethnicity Estimates: DNA testing estimates ethnic origins by comparing genetic markers to reference populations.

8. Genetic Relatives: Chromosomal analysis identifies genetic relatives, fostering connections with unknown family members.

In essence, chromosomes hold the key to a comprehensive understanding of your roots. They paint a vivid picture of your family's journey across generations, helping you unravel the fascinating tapestry of your ancestry.

Chromosomes and autosomes are related concepts in the field of genetics, but they refer to different aspects of the human genome.

1. <u>Chromosomes</u>: Chromosomes are thread-like structures composed of DNA and proteins found in the nucleus of a cell. They carry genetic information in the form of genes.

- Number: In humans, there are 46 chromosomes, organized into 23 pairs. Each parent contributes one chromosome to each pair during reproduction.
- Types: Chromosomes can be broadly categorized into two types: autosomes and sex chromosomes.
- Role: Chromosomes contain the genes that determine an individual's traits and characteristics.

2. Autosomes: Autosomes are chromosomes that are not involved in determining an individual's sex. In humans, autosomes make up the first 22 pairs of chromosomes.

- Number: Humans have 22 pairs of autosomes, for a total of 44 autosomes.
- Inheritance: Autosomes are inherited equally from both parents. Each parent contributes one autosome per pair to their offspring.
- Function: Autosomes carry genes that influence various traits and characteristics, excluding those related to sex determination.

Key Differences:

- Role in Sex Determination: Chromosomes include both autosomes and sex chromosomes. Autosomes do not determine an individual's sex, while sex chromosomes (X and Y) are involved in sex determination.
- Number: Humans have a total of 46 chromosomes, with 22 pairs of autosomes and one pair of sex chromosomes.
- Inheritance: Autosomes are inherited equally from both parents. In contrast, the combination of sex chromosomes inherited determines an individual's biological sex.
- Function: Autosomes carry genes that influence a wide range of traits, such as hair color, eye color, and susceptibility to certain diseases. Sex chromosomes carry genes related to sexual development and reproduction.

In summary, all autosomes are chromosomes, but not all chromosomes are autosomes. Autosomes specifically refer to the chromosomes that do not play a role in determining an individual's sex.

Ultimately, we arrive at the connection between telomeres and chromosomes. <u>Telomeres</u> are structures located at the ends of chromosomes, and they play a crucial role in the aging process and overall health. Chromosomes contain genetic material in the form of DNA, which carries the instructions for the development and functioning of all living organisms.

Here's how telomeres relate to chromosomes and the inheritance of genes that can influence the extension or shortening of life:

1. Structure of Chromosomes: Chromosomes are thread-like structures made of DNA and proteins. Human cells typically have 46 chromosomes organized in 23 pairs, including 22 pairs of autosomes and one pair of sex chromosomes.

2. Role of Telomeres: Telomeres are protective caps at the ends of chromosomes. Their primary function is to prevent the loss of genetic material during cell division. Each time a cell divides, the telomeres shorten.

3. Cell Division and Aging: With each round of cell division, telomeres gradually shorten. This process is a natural part of aging. Eventually, as telomeres become critically short, cells can no longer divide, leading to cellular senescence or cell death.

4. Inheritance of Genes: While telomere length itself is not directly inherited, there are genes that play a role in determining the rate of telomere shortening. These genes can influence the cellular aging process and may have implications for overall health and lifespan.

5. Telomerase and Cellular Renewal: Telomerase is an enzyme that can lengthen telomeres. It is active in some cells, particularly during early development, but is generally less active in most somatic cells in adults. Some individuals may have variations in genes related to telomerase activity, affecting how efficiently telomeres are maintained.

6. Lifestyle and Environmental Factors: Lifestyle factors, such as stress, diet, exercise, and exposure to environmental toxins, can impact the rate of telomere shortening. Healthy lifestyle choices may contribute to maintaining longer telomeres and potentially promoting healthier aging.

It's essential to note that while telomeres are implicated in the aging process and cellular health, they are just one aspect of a complex interplay of genetic and environmental factors that influence lifespan and overall well-being. Genetic variations, including those related to telomeres, contribute to individual differences in aging and longevity. Ongoing scientific research continues to explore the intricate relationships between genetics, telomeres, and the aging process.

As we conclude the exploration of ancestral roots in "Testimonies of a Covenant Life," I extend my heartfelt gratitude for your companionship on this meaningful journey. Together, we've delved into the essence of purpose and the profound meaning of life, rediscovering our past to shape a brighter future tomorrow. Thank you for being part of this transformative journey, where the threads of our maternal and paternal ancestry weave a tapestry that enriches our understanding of self and legacy. I conclude with love your genes (self improvement).

References:

Fields-Black, Edda (2008). Deep Roots: Rice Farmers in West Africa and the African Diaspora. Bloomington: Indiana University Press.

Jackson BA, Wilson JL, Kirbah S, Sidney SS, Rosenberger J, et al. (2005) Mitochondrial DNA genetic diversity among four ethnic groups in Sierra Leone. Am J Phys Anthropol 128: 156–163.

Wood PH (1974) Black majority; Negroes in colonial South Carolina from 1670 through the Stono Rebellion. New York: Random House Press. 346 p.

Ely B, Wilson JL, Jackson F, Jackson BA (2006) African-American mitochondrial DNAs often match mtDNAs found in multiple African ethnic groups. BMC Biol 4: 34.

Littlefield, Daniel (1981). Rice and Slaves: Ethnicity and the Slave Trade in Colonial South Carolina. Baton Rouge:Louisiana State University Press.

Miller, Edward (1995). Gullah Statesman: Robert Smalls from Slavery to Congress, 1839-1915.

Columbia: University of South Carolina Press.

Pollitzer, William (1999). The Gullah People and their African Heritage. Athens, GA: University of Georgia Press.

Smith, Julia Floyd (1985). Slavery and Rice Culture in Low Country Georgia: 1750-1860. Knoxville: University of Tennessee Press.

Carawan, Guy and Candie (1989). Ain't You Got a Right to the Tree of Life: The People of Johns Island, South Carolina, their Faces, their Words, and their Songs. Athens, GA: University of Georgia Press.

Conroy, Pat (1972). The Water Is Wide. Boston: Houghton Mifflin.

Creel, Margaret Washington (1988). A Peculiar People: Slave Religion and Community Culture among the Gullahs. New York: New York University Press.

Cross, Wilbur (2008). Gullah Culture in America. Westport, CT: Praeger.

Joyner, Charles (1984). Down by the Riverside: A South Carolina Slave Community. Urbana: University of Illinois Press.

Kiser, Clyde Vernon (1969). Sea Island to City: A Study of St. Helena Islanders in Harlem and Other Urban Centers. New York: Atheneum.

McFeely, William (1994). Sapelo's People: A Long Walk into Freedom. New York: W.W. Norton.

Parrish, Lydia (1992). Slave Songs of the Georgia Sea Islands. Athens, GA: University of Georgia Press.

Edelson SM (2006) Plantation enterprise in colonial South Carolina. Cambridge: Harvard University Press. 383 p.

Littlefield DC (1981) Rice and slaves: ethnicity and the slave trade in colonial South Carolina. Baton Rouge: Louisiana State University Press. 199 p.

THE STORY OF A SONG FORGOTTEN

Oh Father, you see the darkness in my eyes,
surely it is if no surprise, I run this race for a prize.
Longevity is what you would have of me, to sing gloriously.
Praises, the song that raises the dead from the bed of sorrows.
Help me, Help me that I not fall in too deep.
Going to sleep on my people, sacrificed lives for crimes against humanity,
Let the voice of my heart, not be left in the depths of the dark,
Awaken the forgotten, souled out on empty promises,
the riches of the heathen, a vain thing many believe in.
Idolatry a witches craft, the end of which
I never wish to see the wrath, of the Almighty!
That which shall not give, shall not live
According to the promise and blessings honored,
Ah-brah-am! Father of nations,
through him, by him his seed is blessed!
A sweet-smelling savor dedicates fasting and prayer, an
eternal remembrance.
Give praise to the Most High God,
Creator of all is the present of our presence, give honor and glory.
The story before us is of a majesty higher than
what is known of the earthly.
Who can tell what is like of the heavenly?
Give Thanks to YAH, our Majesty on High!

STRENGTHEN ME

Bring out the best in meeeee! HALLELUYAH!
Father strengthen meeeee! HALLELUYAH!
With your holiness HALLELUYAH!
The peace of righteousness. HALLELUYAH!
Let me come with symbols of dance.
Give me chance to sing as I bring,
You desire that lights my heart on fire.
Hold me in your secret place
lift me off the ground, HALLELUYAH!
keep me from the fall, HALLELUYAH!
suffered by most of all, HALLELUYAH!
in this race, I seek your face
purge my mind with hyssop
as the water drops from above
tells me of your love. HALLELUYAH!
I sing this SONG to you, HALLELUYAH!
that my words are true. HALLELUYAH!

I WILL OVERCOME

Night and Day I testify
I shall not see or taste death
But shall see him in my flesh
The glory of Yah is upon me
Heal the sick and raise the dead
Cast out doubt and fear flees
Make way for Jubilee
Be faithful, not unbelieving
No matter what has happened
These things surely will come to pass
Over and over till my works be perfected.
I testify to the resurrection
I shall not see or taste death.

LEAD ME, GUIDE ME

"He leadeth me, guideth me
taketh me over" (2)
the still waters of perfect
peace, am I at ease.
My Shepherd,
whom I trust
all ways
shall I see the full of days
My Father,
whom the brightness of light
is glory. Alleloo-yah
I laid down my, burdens
in the green pastures,
tender for a lamb to feed
and the ox the rest it needs.
All have the breathe of life
to live in harmony, without strife.
Halleluyah!

THE PASSAGEWAY HOME

Where does the light come from?
That guides me, keeps me still,
From the chills of my youth,
Know I to be truth.
Verified, I testify this song,
Everyone has his own.
I want to go home, but cannot.
Where the spirit is willing,
I shall increase, along the journey,
Growing together, going different places,
Create legacy to see generations.
Where will we be?
Caught up in the light you see.
From dusk to dawn,
my soul carry on.
A chosen way of life,
to a passageway home, sees light.

DECLARE BEFORE THE NATIONS

Give these words to Jen-and-sis (Genesis)
that my family is kind as our genetics do not lie,
I say Why-you-cry (Vayikra) that I loose not my mind.
Leave we (Lewii), let us be or should I say leave-I (Levi)
that I may exit on dusk before the nod of the new moon.
Oh my God, Yahshuah It's-a-car (Issachar) of hope not horse
for safety,
just send-me-on (Simeon) my way and I'll leave-it-cuz (Leviticus)
for he shall find others worthy who have not numb-ears (Numbers)
to bring tears of repentance for wrongdoing.
eNough-tally (Naphtali) up the votes C'est si bon' its done I
say-bull-on (Zebulon)
the loose and watch it do-the-run-on-me (Deuteronomy).
I was told to burry-your-shift (Bereshith) so that you don't remember
that bull****
from yesterday that devoured-him (Devarim) for the very foolish act
was he judged.
Shema (Shemoth) must have gone out as she was not cruel but said
your-whole-safe (Yahoseph) is protected from the threat of minimum
wages being
taken away. I'll share my house with you as I have longed to see
you another
day. Where-you-been (Reuben)? My brother asked, I been-jamming
(Benjamin) with Yahudah. Yah-hoo-dah (Yahudah) who?
He is a lion's whelp and who can rouse him up?
His brothers will praise him as his hand will be on the neck of
his enemies.
The law shall not depart from his right hand,
upheld by the scepter of righteousness and the rod of correction
between his feet to rule over the nations in obedience of love.

SEE, WHAT WORKS

Learned I this hymn,
Love it, to see another day.
A window of worship,
that looks to heaven, abide I him
feeding on his strength.
The word of truth.
Searches out, how prophets lived,
Before death! Theirs and Your sweat!
Whether in joy or sorrow!
Follow the word of truth.
Making friends with justice,
Helping those, who cannot help themselves!
Forgetting nothing is the Blessing to seek.
As the world turns and is filled with storms,
time is focused on YAH to be as the Most High God.
The instructor of my paths,
that I run not before him.
Taking time to calm my soul,
each thought, every motive.
Humble in deed that my spirit be, holy!
Filled with love, fitted for service above.
Committed to you, Oh' my Father.
Yours always (2), I'll be true-ooh-ooh-ooh-ooh-ooh, ooh-ooh

I AM FREE

I have purpose
Oh yes
Waken me from sleep
You have
Now – ow –ow
I could not, see before
My spirit slept as I worked hard
Many hours
My time, my energy, my mind
The glory of Yah.
The shining bright in me, not kept priority.
Now I see. You have waken me from my sleep.
I had to discover purpose seeking fervently
What consumes my reality. No more shall I return to work
for anyone.
My time, my mind, my energy is the glory of Yah.
My maker, the creator of heaven and earth I give glory.
I have purpose and have found destiny.
I am free, I am free to serve and give glory.

STAND IN GLORY

Stand in glory shout halleluyah shout halleluyah!
The walls fall down Shout halleluyah!
Govern yourselves and rise with equity.
We are the meek whose not afraid
Honor and glory
Speak not lying words
Do not deal deceitfully
Hating evil, carefully
Considering your ways
Never blame
Always are signs near
Getting closer to the truth
Be perfect in heart
A youthful spirit is free
Don't deal deceitfully to make enemies
Loving justice and judgment

KINDNESS IS GOODNESS

We can do this (2)
Surely there is mercy
Goodness, the way of truth
Kindness keeps the youth
Yah's mercy endures truth
Forever and ever
Surely there is mercy
We can do this (3)

FATHER'S MERCY ON ME

You got ta put up da testimone eh (high energy, quick and fast)
You got ta put up da testimone eh
Your heart is the ark of coven-ant
Your heart is the ark of coven-ant
Where's da blood on da mercy seat
Father forgive, I believe in Yesha'ah
Have mercy on me
I have forgiven all, debts against me
Have mercy on me, I believe in Yesha'ah
Where's da blood on da mercy seat
You got ta put up da testimone eh
You got ta put up da testimone eh
Your heart is the ark of coven-ant
Your heart is the ark of coven-ant

THE HOUR IS COMING

Holyeee, Holyeee, Holyeee,
Holyeee, Holyeee, Holyeee,
<u>Holy</u> is <u>he</u>, whose right it is to give
On the right hand of my Father.
He Lives!
My Father sees the hearts of man
Wakeup, Jacob
Final Warning
The hour is coming
The trumpet blasts
When all shall see,
The son of man
Coming in great glory!
Curses visits iniquity of your fathers
No liberty!
Wakeup Jacob
Zion Awaits
Wash away
Your mind, heart, and soul
Come to Yahshua, Yahshua!
Holy is he, whose right it is to give
On the right hand of my Father.
<u>Heeee, He </u>Lives!
Holyeee, Holyeee, <u>Holyeeee</u>!

MAKE ME PROPHECY

Make me prophecy (3) --fast
Father show me your dreams (2)
Show me your visions
Make me prophecy
Show me your visions
Make me prophecy
Waking up (2)
Waking up from slumber
I'm Seeking Yah (2)
Yeshua my Elohim for my dream --fast
Signs and Wonders to be seen
Life or death in the hands of Ibreem
Put away iniquity --fast
Sin if you want
Never quit on me
Commandment keepers, sweeping Torah --fast
Applying fringes
heals wounds on borders.
My Father's orders
Guard your heart, these lively stones
Free (2)
Free the enslaved peoples
Release those captive
My Father's (2), My Father's orders
Prophecy my life now, to be free. (2) --fast
My people (2)
My people I say be free
Let the prisoners go! (2) Hey
I be (2)
I be from Sierre Leone
House of Yahudah
I hear you yo!

Wake up <u>people</u>, Yisrael! (2)
Come, Come drink from the priesthood! --fast
Come drink from the priesthood! (2)
Hey all you thirsty
Come all you thirsty
Come (2) Come on….. into Zion!

FILL MY HEART

I will never forsake you
Joy I have perfect joy!
My cup runs over, my heart says yes!
I have learned of you!
My heart was broken
Without you I fall
I need you, Yahushua I need you
Come down, Come down
Holy Spirit fill my joy, my mind, and heart

MY OWN HEART

My Own Heart
What do we do with it
Give praise all of our days
Blessing Yah forever
Forever and Forever
We have this testimony of Yaha'shua
The spirit of prophecy to know what to do
Glory and Honor belongs to you.
Oh Father
Holy, Holy, Holy is Yah
Forever and ever.

SIGNS OF RIGHTEOUSNESS EVEN A RIGHTEOUS BRANCH

You that love righteousness
Where are you
And you that hate evil awwh!
You make your enemies afraid.
To do good is great!
I saw my people rise!
To do good is great!
You make enemies afraid!
I'm talking to you my people! Let go!
We gotta make a move right now. You here me!
Nothing going to stop us! (4)
We gotta make a move right now. You here me! (2)
Nothing going to stop us! (6)
We gotta make a move!(6)
Right now! You here me!

WHO ARE YOU

A planners mind is the architect
Become resilient and adaptable
Spiritual and Metaphysical
Quiet Silent Power
Strong and Positive commands respect
Dignity, Grace, and Humility
Respect people of all cultures
Give back to community
Lifelong commitment
Capture the soul of a people

WHO WE BE

Gullah Geechie, who we be!
My people be from Sierre Leone
Invincible Conquerors, never shall we fall!
We rise and multiply!
Remember this day, I have spoken to you (2)
Always do what is good
No matter what is done unto you
Always do what is good
That you put away evil.
I love you.
Speak not lying words
Do not deal deceitfully
Hating evil, carefully
Consider your ways, never blame.
Always are signs near, getting closer to the truth
Walking in youth, perfect in heart, spirit is free.
Don't deal deceitfully to make enemies.
Loving to do justice and judgment have all the saints.
The Most High is with you.
Honor and Glory, A new name given
Praise Yah all the living.

MAKE A COVENANT!

Brothers and Sisters let us covenant
Keeping the commandments
Laws, giving the people statutes
Govern yourselves and rise to do judgement and justice
Loving unity we are free
Keeping commandments we work in harmony
Longevity is who we be
Honor and glory; The price of fame
We are the meek you seek, in liberty we are together
My brothers and sisters!
Brothers and sistes (2); Brothers (4); Brothers & Sisters
Giving the people statutes and judgements (4)
Govern yourselves and rise with equity
Stand in glory, shout Halleluyah!
Break the walls on down, shout Halleluyah!
Govern yourselves and rise with equity. (3)
We are the meek whose not afraid.
Honor and glory; the bride price of fame
Choose wisely the game you play
Hoping chance of a better day
Seeing yesterday fade away
What do you now with today?
Unite in love and your enemies be afraid

RETURN TO LOVE

All I look for
Judgment, Equity, Peace
I saw none
I look for
Love your neighbor as yourself
I saw none
I look for
Judgment, Equity, Peace
I saw none
I look for
Obedience is praise
Sacrifices pleases not
I saw none
I look for
Judgment, Equity, Peace
I saw none
I look for
Love with all your heart, mind, and soul
I saw none
Lovest me not

FILL ME UP

Joy run over my cup
My fear the oil of gladness
Have I of you
My heart was broken
Without you I fall
I neeed you Yahushua and my
Father am I bowed on my knees and head
Before you
I need you to dwell with me
Your presence, Holy Spirit
Fill my joy, my mind and heart
Run over my cup

GRACE MERCY & TRUTH

Grace Mercy & Truth
Loving judgment
Have I been here for you
Have I
Have I been here for you
Lovest me not
Know my hear to be true
Testify or deny the spirit of truth
Have I learned of you, wisdom
Whose ways you follow
For a better tomorrow
Free from pain and suffering
Valley of decisions
Captive to it until judgment
You must trust in the spirit of truth
To do right in the conscience of sight
Pleasing the Father of truth
Who loveth judgment executing orders for you
Granting petitions on your behalf
Receiver will you see the aftermath
He is with you.

I LOVE YOU

Oh Father,
I love you with all my heart
To do that is right in your sight
Help me overcome the darkness of my heart
My soul longs for your love
Give me that eternal light
Praise and Joy multiplies my days
Help to overcome my ways
Obedience is better than sacrifice
All this will I do for you.
Judgment, Judgment, Judgment
Mercy, Grace, Peace loves truth
Let praise and joy multiply my days

AH'BA SHALAWAM

My Father loves me and I see
He always, with me
Faithful and True
I believe with my heart, mind, and soul
I am righteous
Holding true
Seeking the holy
Deliver me from evil
Deliver me from iniquity
Create I shall make
Things New
I shall do
Make provision, for the people (2)
My Father loves me and I see
He always, with me
Faithful and True
Ahba Shalawam

<u>MERCY ENDURES FOREVER</u>

Yahushua, Yahshua, Yahushua
Mercy endures, patience is love
Truth springs up life, more abundantly
That we do what's right, in his sight
And forever, liveth the king
He is good, for his mercy endureth
Forever, for-ev-er
His truth endures, all generations.
That we be saved.

Testimony In Jacob

For he established a testimony in Jacob, and appointed a law in Israel, which he commanded our fathers, that they should make them known to their children:

That the generation to come might know them, even the children which should be born; who should arise and declare them to their children:

That they might set their hope in YAH, and not forget the works of YAH, but keep his commandments:

And might not be as their fathers, a stubborn and rebellious generation; a generation that set not their heart aright, and whose spirit was not steadfast with YAH. Psalm 78:5-8

Touching the Almighty Yah we cannot find him out. He is excellent in power, judgment, and on plenty of justice he will not afflict. Job 37:23

Beware lest YAH take you away with his stroke; then a great ransom cannot deliver you.

Men so therefore fear him; he respects not any that are wise of heart. Job 37:24

YAH makes the small drops of water pour down rain according to the vapor. But if they obey not they shall perish by the sword, and they shall die without knowledge. Out of whose womb come the ice and hoary frost of heaven? Who hath gendered it? Hath the rain a Father or who hath begotten the drops of dew?

Where is YAH my maker, who giveth songs in the night? Job 35:10

Why open your mouth wide to multiply words without knowledge?

Be watchful, and strengthen the things which remain, that are ready to die: for I have not found thy works perfect before YAH. Revelation 3:2

Truly my words shall not be false for YAH who is perfect in knowledge is with you? Job 36:4

YAH withdraws not his eyes from the righteous, but with kings they are established on thrones forever. Job 36:7

Behold, YAH exalts by his power who teaches like him?

Do you know the balancing of the clouds and the wondrous works of him which is perfect in knowledge? Job 37:16

Neither can your friends be welcomed in your home. A man who is without a tragedy is not known to him. For he has not considered the house he shall build. Waiting patiently he chooses what is right for his plan.

Thou shalt neither vex a stranger, nor oppress him: for ye were strangers in the land of Egypt. Exodus 22:21 Thou shalt not avenge, nor bear any grudge against the children of thy people, but thou shalt love thy neighbor as thyself: I am the Most High God. Leviticus 19:18

Over the years, colonialism has destroyed African culture and confused beliefs of many. Let us not forget self-love builds family and a powerful culture counters racism.

A COUNTER RACISM (WHITE SUPREMACY) BEHAVIOR CODE FOR BLACK SELF AND GROUP RESPECT & BLACK MENTAL HEALTH BY DR. FRANCES CRESS WELSING, M.D.

- **Stop name-calling** one another.
- **Stop gossiping** about one another.
- **Stop squabbling** with one another.
- **Stop snitching** on one another -- informing on one another for reasons of personal gain.
- **Stop cursing** one another.
- **Stop being discourteous** to one another.
- **Stop being disrespectful** to one another.
- **Stop stealing** from one another.
- **Stop robbing** one another.
- **Stop fighting** one another.
- **Stop killing** one another.
- **Stop throwing down trash where Black people live**, work and play.
- **Stop making dirt and filth** the norm.
- **Stop using and selling drugs** to one another.
- **Stop Black children from thinking that as children they can be adequate mothers and fathers.**
- Stop believing that "welfare" will save you -- **start believing in prosperity.**
- **Stop pretending that racism (White Supremacy) does not exist.**
- **Stop being divided and conquered** -- stop allowing Black Brown, Red and Yellow peoples being divided by white supremacy.

Thy righteousness is an everlasting righteousness, and thy law is the truth. Psalm 119:142 Thou art near, O YAH; and all thy commandments are truth. Psalm 119:151 And ye shall know the truth, and the truth shall make you free. They answered him, We be Abraham's seed, and were never in bondage to any man: how sayest thou, Ye shall be made free? Yeshua answered them, Verily, verily, I say unto you, Whosoever committeth sin is the servant of sin. John 8:32-34

For the <u>wages of sin is death</u>; but the gift of YAH is eternal life through Yeshua our Savior. Romans 6:23 Whosoever committeth sin transgresseth also the law: for sin is the transgression of the law. 1 John 3:4 He that saith, I know him, and keepeth not his commandments, is a liar, and the truth is not in him. 1 John 2:4 For this is the love of YAH, that we keep his commandments: and his commandments are not grievous. 1 John 5:3

<u>TRANSGRESSION OF THE LAW (DISOBEDIENCE) IS TO UNJUST AS SIN IS TO DEATH HONORING THE LAW (OBEDIENCE) IS TO VIRTUOUS AS LOVE IS TO ETERNAL LIFE</u>

Awake to righteousness, and sin not; for <u>some have not the knowledge of YAH</u>: I speak this to your shame. **1 Corinthians 15:34-38, 52-57 Put off old carnal ways to not offend**

- 35 But some man will say, How are the dead raised up? and with <u>what body do they come</u>?
- 36 Thou fool, that which thou sowest is not quickened, except it die:
- 37 And that which thou sowest, **thou sowest not that body that shall be**, but bare grain, it may chance of wheat, or of some other grain:
- 38 But **YAH giveth it a body as it hath pleased him**, and to every seed his own body.
- 52 In a moment, in the twinkling of an eye, at the last trump: for the trumpet shall sound, and the dead shall be raised incorruptible, and we shall be changed.
- 53 For this corruptible must put on incorruption, and this mortal must put on immortality.
- 54 So when this corruptible shall have put on incorruption, and this mortal shall have put on immortality, then shall be brought to pass the saying that is written, Death is swallowed up in victory.
- 55 O death, where is thy sting? O grave, where is thy victory?
- 56 The sting of death is sin; and the strength of sin is the law.
- 57 But thanks be to YAH, which giveth us the victory through our YAH Yeshua Ha'Mashiach.

We are not to serve sin once baptized in covenant, rather die to sin to be quickened for life and flee fornication. Every sin that a man doeth is without the body; but he that committeth fornication sinneth against his own body. 1 Corinthians 6:18-20

19 What? know ye not that your body is the temple of the Holy Spirit which is in you, which ye have of YAH, and ye are not your own?

- 20 For ye are bought with a price: therefore glorify YAH in your body, and in your spirit, which are YAH's.

Who also declared unto us your love in the Spirit. NEWNESS OF SPIRIT BODY
For this cause we also, since the day we heard it, do not cease to pray for you, and to desire that ye might be filled with the knowledge of his will in all wisdom and spiritual understanding; Colossians 1:8-28

- 10 That ye might walk worthy of the Most High God unto all pleasing, being fruitful in every good work, and increasing in the knowledge of YAH;
- 11 Strengthened with all might, according to his glorious power, unto all patience and longsuffering with joyfulness;
- 12 Giving thanks unto the Father, which hath made us meet to be partakers of the inheritance of the saints in light:
- 13 Who hath delivered us from the power of darkness, and hath translated us into the kingdom of his dear Son:
- 14 In whom **we have redemption through his blood**, even the **forgiveness of sins**:
- 15 Who is the image of the invisible Almighty God, the firstborn of every creature:
- 16 For by him were all things created, that are in heaven, and that are in earth, visible and invisible, whether they be thrones, or dominions, or principalities, or powers: all things were created by him, and for him:
- 17 And he is before all things, and by him all things consist.

- 18 And he is the head of the body, the church: who is the beginning, the firstborn from the dead; that in all things he might have the preeminence.
- 19 For it pleased the Father that in him should all fullness dwell;
- 20 And, having made peace through the blood of his cross, by him to reconcile all things unto himself; by him, I say, whether they be things in earth, or things in heaven.
- 21 And you, that were sometime alienated and enemies in your mind by wicked works, yet now hath he reconciled
- 22 In **the body of his flesh through death, to present you holy and unblameable and unreproveable in his sight**:
- 23 If ye continue in the faith grounded and settled, and be not moved away from the hope of the gospel, which ye have heard, and which was preached to every creature which is under heaven; whereof I Paul am made a minister;
- 24 Who now rejoice in my sufferings for you, and fill up that which is behind of the afflictions of Christ in my flesh for his body's sake, which is the church:
- 25 Whereof I am made a minister, according to the dispensation of YAH which is given to me for you, to fulfil the word of YAH;
- 26 **Even the mystery which hath been hid from ages and from generations, but now is made manifest to his saints**:
- 27 To whom YAH would make known what is the riches of the glory of this mystery among the Gentiles; which is Christ in you, the hope of glory:
- 28 <u>Whom we preach, warning every man, and teaching every man in all wisdom; that we may present every man perfect in Yeshua Ha'Mashiach</u>:

Wherefore, my brethren, ye also are become dead to the law by the body of Christ; that ye should be married to another, even to him who is raised from the dead, that we should bring forth fruit unto YAH. Romans 7:4-25

- 5 For when we were in the flesh, the motions of sins, which were by the law, did work in our members to bring forth fruit unto death.

- 6 But now we are delivered from the law, that being dead wherein we were held; that we should serve in newness of spirit, and not in the oldness of the letter.

- 7 What shall we say then? Is the law sin? YAH forbid. Nay, I had not known sin, but by the law: for I had not known lust, except the law had said, Thou shalt not covet.

- 8 But sin, taking occasion by the commandment, wrought in me all manner of concupiscence. For without the law sin was dead.

- 9 For I was alive without the law once: but when the commandment came, sin revived, and I died.

- 10 And the commandment, which was ordained to life, I found to be unto death.

- 11 For sin, taking occasion by the commandment, deceived me, and by it slew me.

- 12 Wherefore the law is holy, and the commandment holy, and just, and good.

- 13 Was then that which is good made death unto me? YAH forbid. **But sin, that it might appear sin, working death in me by that which is good**; that sin by the commandment might become exceedingly sinful.

- 14 For we know that the law is spiritual: but I am carnal, sold under sin.

- 15 For that which I do I allow not: for what I would, that do I not; but what I hate, that do I

- 16 If then I do that which I would not, I consent unto the law that it is good.

- 17 Now then it is no more I that do it, but sin that dwelleth in me.

- 18 For I know that in me (that is, in my flesh,) dwelleth no good thing: for to will is present with me; but how to perform that which is good I find not.

- 19 For the good that I would I do not: but the evil which I would not, that I do.
- 20 Now if I do that I would not, it is no more I that do it, but sin that dwelleth in me.
- 21 I find then a law, that, when I would do good, evil is present with me.
- 22 For I delight in the law of YAH after the inward man:
- 23 But I see another law in my members, warring against the law of my mind, and bringing me into captivity to the law of sin which is in my members.
- 24 O wretched man that I am! who shall deliver me from the body of this death?
- 25 I thank YAH through Yeshua Ha'Mashiach our YAH. So then with the mind I myself serve the law of YAH; but with the flesh the law of sin.

This is the covenant that I will make with them after those days, saith the YAH, I will put my laws into their hearts, and in their minds will I write them; Hebrews 10:16-24

- 17 And their sins and iniquities will I remember no more.
- 18 Now where remission of these is, there is no more offering for sin.
- 19 Having therefore, brethren, boldness to enter into the holiest by the blood of Yeshua,
- 20 By a new and living way, which he hath consecrated for us, through the veil, that is to say, his flesh;
- 21 And having an high priest over the house of YAH;
- 22 Let us draw near with a true heart in full assurance of faith, having our hearts sprinkled from an evil conscience, and our bodies washed with pure water.
- 23 Let us hold fast the profession of our faith without wavering; (for he is faithful that promised;)
- 24 And let us consider one another to provoke unto love and to good works:

Therefore I thought it necessary to exhort the brethren, that they would go before unto you, and make up beforehand your bounty, whereof ye had notice before, that the same might be ready, as a matter of bounty, and not as of covetousness. 2 Corinthians 9:5-15

- 6 But this I say, <u>He which soweth sparingly shall reap also sparingly</u>; and he which <u>soweth bountifully shall reap also bountifully</u>.
- 7 Every man according as he purposeth in his heart, so let him give; **not grudgingly**, or of necessity: for <u>YAH loveth a cheerful giver</u>.
- 8 And YAH is able to make all grace abound toward you; that ye, always having all sufficiency in all things, may abound to every good work:
- 9 (As it is written, He hath dispersed abroad; <u>he hath given to the poor: his righteousness remaineth forever</u>.
- 10 Now <u>he that ministereth seed to the sower both minister bread for your food</u>, and **multiply your seed sown**, and **increase the fruits of your righteousness**;)
- 11 <u>Being enriched in every thing to all bountifulness</u>, which causeth through us thanksgiving to YAH.
- 12 For the administration of this service not only supplieth the want of the saints, but is **abundant also by many thanksgivings unto YAH**;
- 13 Whiles by the experiment of this ministration they glorify YAH for your professed subjection unto the gospel of Christ, and for your liberal distribution unto them, and unto all men;
- 14 And by their prayer for you, which long after you for the exceeding grace of YAH in you.
- 15 Thanks be unto YAH for his unspeakable gift.

Rejoice in the YAH always: and again I say, Rejoice.
Philippians 4:4-9
Let your moderation be known unto all men. The YAH is at hand.

- 6 Be careful for nothing; but in every thing by prayer and supplication with thanksgiving let your requests be made known unto YAH.
- 7 And the **peace of YAH**, which **passeth all understanding, shall keep your hearts and minds through Yeshua Ha'Mashiach.**
- 8 Finally, brethren, whatsoever things are true, whatsoever things are honest, **whatsoever things are just**, whatsoever things are pure, whatsoever things are lovely, whatsoever things are of good report; if there be any virtue, and if there be any praise, think on these things.
- 9 Those things, which **ye have both learned, and received, and heard, and seen in me, do**: and the **Almighty God of peace shall be with you.**

Making request, if by any means now at length I might have a prosperous journey by the will of YAH to come unto you. Romans 1:10-12, 16-17

- 11 For I long to see you, that I may impart unto you some spiritual gift, to the end ye may be established;
- 12 That is, that I may be comforted together with you by the mutual faith of both of you and me.

- 16 For **I am not ashamed of the gospel of Christ: for it is the power of YAH unto salvation to every one that believeth**; to the Jew first, and also to the Greek.
- 17 For therein is the **righteousness of YAH revealed from faith to faith:** as it is written, **The just shall live by faith.**

Whosoever abideth in him sinneth not: whosoever sinneth hath not seen him, neither known him. Little children, let no man deceive you: he that doeth righteousness is righteous, even as he is righteous. 1 John 3:6-16

- 8 He that committeth sin is of the devil; for the devil sinneth from the beginning. For this purpose the Son of Almighty God was manifested, that he might destroy the works of the devil.
- 9 Whosoever is born of YAH doth not commit sin; for **his seed remaineth in him**: and he cannot sin, because he is born of YAH.
- 10 In this the children of YAH are manifest, and the children of the devil: **whosoever doeth not righteousness is not of YAH**, neither he that loveth not his brother.
- 11 For this is the message that ye heard from the beginning, that **we should love one another.**

Search the scriptures; for in them ye think ye have eternal life: and they are they which testify of me. And ye will not come to me, that ye might have life. I receive not honor from men. But I know you, that ye have not the love of Most High God in you. I am come in my Father's name, and ye receive me not: if another shall come in his own name, him ye will receive. How can ye believe, which receive honor one of another, and seek not the honor that cometh from Most High God only? Do not think that I will accuse you to the Father: there is one that accuseth you, even Moses, in whom ye trust. For had ye believed Moses, ye would have believed me; for he wrote of me. But if ye believe not his writings, how shall ye believe my words? John 5:39:47

He that despised Moses' law died without mercy under two or three witnesses: Of how much sorer punishment, suppose ye, shall he be thought worthy, who hath trodden underfoot the Son of Almighty God, and hath counted the blood of the covenant, wherewith he was sanctified, an unholy thing, and hath done despite unto the Spirit of grace? Hebrews 10:28-29

DEDICATION OF PRAYER

Watch ye and pray, lest ye enter into temptation. The spirit truly is ready, but the flesh is weak. What is a life without prayer? Seek not to gain the wealth of this world and lose our soul having no knowledge of the Almighty God. But ye, beloved, building up yourselves on your most holy faith, praying in the Holy Ghost, Keep yourselves in the love of Almighty God, looking for the mercy of our Redeemer Yeshua unto eternal life.

Thank you Father for knowing our every need to satisfy us with good things to come. We remain faithful, hoping always for the good as we work daily to achieve the goals we desire. Our hearts and minds will always obey your holy word to make the crooked paths straight to fulfill the dreams of our destiny. Righteousness will shine in our countenance to be faithful in deed that our testimony delivers the oppressed from dwelling with strong presence of your Holy Spirit. We are your Holy Ones, gives us increase to put all wickedness under our feet. Halleluyah! Thank you Father we give you the glory, the honor, and the praise!

SPIRITUAL SACRIFICES EVEN KEYS OF ZION

Leverage these spiritual sacrifices for both construction and deconstruction of the kingdom of heaven and employ these sacred keys to release (unlock) or bind (secure). Just as it is written in Matthew 16:19, "And I will grant you the keys to the realm of heaven: whatever you bind on earth shall be bound in heaven, and whatever you release on earth shall be released in heaven."

"I am the good shepherd, and know my sheep, and am known of mine."

John 10:7-18 "The harvest truly is great, but the laborers are few: pray ye therefore the Lord of the harvest, that he would send forth laborers into his harvest." Luke 10:1-17

"The kings of the Gentiles exercise lordship over them; and they that exercise authority upon them are called benefactors. But ye shall not be so: but he that is greatest among you, let him be as the younger; and he that is chief, as he that doth serve. For whether is greater, he that sits at meat, or he that serves? is not he that sits at meat? but I am among you as he that serves." Luke 22:25-27

1 Chronicles 16:27 Glory and honor are in his presence; strength and gladness are in his place. 1 Peter 1:6-16 The voice of the Lord makes the hinds to calve, and discovers the forests: and in his temple doth every one speak of his glory. Psalm 29:9

Psalm 21:5

His glory is great in thy salvation: honor and majesty hast thou laid upon him. Romans 2:6-13 What? know ye not that your body is the temple of the Holy Ghost which is in you, which ye have of YAH, and ye are not your own? 1 Corinthians 6:19

In your journey to ascend spiritually in the Kingdom of Heaven, it is vital to embrace the nine keys of Zion as your guiding principles.

1. **Obedience (Obeisance):** Begin by submitting yourself to divine guidance and obeying the teachings of your faith. This unwavering commitment to obedience lays the foundation for your spiritual growth. Obedience involves showing respect or submission, a physical or mental gesture of acknowledgment. For instance, bowing before the Divine as an act of reverence. As we see in Exodus 18:7, Moses demonstrated obedience when he approached the altar and greeted his father-in-law. This obedience is a form of respect and submission to higher spiritual authority.

2. **Prayer (Devotion):** Regularly engage in heartfelt and sincere prayer. Through prayer, you establish a direct connection with the divine, seeking wisdom, guidance, and strength on your spiritual path. Prayer is a powerful tool for seeking guidance and support from the Almighty YAH. It is the act of addressing the Divine, either to acknowledge the Divine's presence or to earnestly request help and guidance in our lives and for others. James 5:16 underscores the power of prayer, emphasizing its effectiveness in producing positive results. Additionally, 2 Chronicles 7:14 highlights the importance of humility and prayer in seeking divine forgiveness and prosperity.

3. **Meditation (Introspection):** Dedicate time to quiet reflection and meditation. This practice allows you to deepen your understanding of spiritual truths and align your thoughts with higher principles. Meditation involves deep and reflective thinking, seeking insight and counsel on spiritual matters, both past and present.

   It allows us to explore our purpose, destiny, and gain wisdom and understanding. Joshua 1:8 encourages meditation on the Divine's laws, emphasizing its role in success. Psalm 1:2 and Psalm 119:99 emphasize the profound understanding that comes through meditation.

4. **Confession (Admission):** Be honest with yourself and your Creator. Acknowledge your faults and seek forgiveness. Confession is a powerful act of humility and growth. Confession is a powerful practice of acknowledging truths, whether right or wrong, and expressing gratitude and praise. James 5:16 encourages us to confess our sins to one another and seek healing, highlighting the transformative power of confession. It allows us to confront our weaknesses and find redemption, ultimately leading to a sound mind and healthy relationships. See ex. Joshua 7:19

5. **Alms (Charity):** Extend a helping hand to those in need. Alms-giving demonstrates your compassion and generosity, aligning you with the values of love and charity. Alms involve giving to those in need, showing generosity and compassion for humanitarian causes. It's an act of sacrifice and praise, pouring out blessings upon others and receiving joy in return. Various verses, such as Nehemiah 13:14, John 3:21, Acts 24:17, Acts 10:4, Luke 11:41, and Matthew 6:4, emphasize the importance of giving generously and the rewards it brings.

6. **Praise (Admiration):** Express gratitude and praise for the blessings in your life. Recognizing the divine goodness fosters a sense of abundance and contentment. Praise is also a way of expressing thanksgiving and rejoicing towards the Divine. It acknowledges the goodness and perfections of the Divine. Judges 5:3, 2 Samuel 22:4, and 1 Chronicles 16:36 illustrate the act of praising the Almighty.

7. **Worship (Homage):** Devote yourself to worship in your faith tradition. Worship is a profound way to connect with the divine and cultivate spiritual strength. Worship involves showing reverence, honor, and devotion to a divine being. It is an act of deep respect and admiration, often expressed through rituals, words, or actions of faith. Exodus 15:11 and Exodus 12:27

illustrate moments of worship, where individuals bow down and offer reverence to the Almighty.

8. **Fasting (Abstinence):** Practice self-discipline through fasting. It helps you detach from worldly distractions, focus on your spiritual journey, and develop resilience. Fasting represents dedication and commitment to deprivation, often involving abstaining from food or other comforts for spiritual purposes. It can be a powerful tool for seeking revelation, clarity, and spiritual insight. Deuteronomy 29:6, Ruth 3:3, Luke 2:37, and Deuteronomy 9:18 highlight the role of fasting in seeking a deeper connection with the Divine.

9. **Mercy (Grace):** Embrace a merciful heart. Show kindness and forgiveness to others as you've received from the divine. It reflects your spiritual growth and compassion. Mercy is an act of compassion and forgiveness, showing kindness and forbearance, even when dealing with an offender. It reflects divine favor and compassion. Various verses, such as John 1:17, Psalm 86:15, Proverbs 3:3, Proverbs 16:6, Galatians 5:4, Titus 3:7, and Psalm 98:3, emphasize the importance of mercy and grace in our spiritual journey.

Remember to ascend spiritually in the kingdom of heaven, one should earnestly embrace the nine keys of Zion: obedience, prayer, meditation, confession, alms-giving, praise, worship, fasting, and acts of mercy. These keys hold the power to unlock the doors to higher realms of spiritual enlightenment and connection with the divine. By dedicating oneself to these practices, you can nourish your soul, deepen your relationship with the divine, and ascend to greater heights in the kingdom of heaven.

By incorporating these nine keys of Zion into your life, you'll find yourself on a transformational journey toward increased spiritual enlightenment and a deeper connection to the Kingdom of Heaven.

Praying In Holy Spirit, Most Holy Faith

Psalms 54:1-5	Hear my prayer, O YAH; give ear to the words of my mouth.
Psalm 82:1-6	Defend the poor and fatherless: do justice to the afflicted and needy.
Matthew 6:1-8, 30-34	Take heed that ye do not your alms before men, to be seen of them: otherwise ye have no reward of your Father which is in heaven.
John 14:12-21	And whatsoever ye shall ask in my name, that will I do, that the Father may be glorified in the Son.
Psalm 34	The YAH is nigh unto them that are of a broken heart; and saveth such as be of a contrite spirit. (1 Peter 3:8-20)
1 Timothy 4:1-6	For it is sanctified by the word of YAH and prayer.
Job 12:4-10	The tabernacles of robbers prosper, and they that provoke YAH are secure; into whose hand YAH bringeth abundantly.
Proverbs 15:7-10	The sacrifice of the wicked is an abomination to the YAH: but the prayer of the upright is his delight.
Psalms 109:1-5	For the mouth of the wicked and the mouth of the deceitful are opened against me: they have spoken against me with a lying tongue.
Proverbs 28:9-12	He that turneth away his ear from hearing the law, even his prayer shall be abomination.
Proverbs 15:26-33	The YAH is far from the wicked: but he heareth the prayer of the righteous.

Ecclesiasticus 35:13-18	He will not accept any person against a poor man, but will hear the prayer of the oppressed. The prayer of the humble pierceth the clouds: and till it come nigh, he will not be comforted; and will not depart, till the Most High shall behold to judge righteously, and execute judgment.
James 5:7-20	Confess your faults one to another, and pray one for another, that ye may be healed. The effectual fervent prayer of a righteous man availeth much.
1 Timothy 4:1-6	For it is sanctified by the word of YAH and prayer.
Leviticus 20:6-7	Sanctify yourselves therefore, and be ye holy: for I am the Most High God your Almighty Power.
Psalm 33:4	For the word of the YAH is right; and all his works are done in truth.
Psalm 119:142	Thy righteousness is an everlasting righteousness, and thy law is the truth.
John 17:17	Sanctify them through thy truth: thy word is truth.
John 4:24	YAH is a Spirit: and they that worship him must worship him in spirit and in truth. (Zephaniah 3:11-13)
Psalms 42:8	Yet the YAH will command his lovingkindness in the daytime, and in the night his song shall be with me, and my prayer unto the Almighty Power of my life. (Psalm 107:41-43)
Proverbs 22:16-29	He that oppresseth the poor to increase his riches, and he that giveth to the rich, shall surely come to want.
Psalm 68:1-11	A father of the fatherless, and a judge of the widows, is Most High God in his holy habitation. (Deuteronomy 10:12-22)

John 15:1-17	Ye have not chosen me, but I have chosen you, and ordained you, that ye should go and bring forth fruit, and that your fruit should remain: that whatsoever ye shall ask of the Father in my name, he may give it you. (Luke 4:18)
1 John 3:16-24	My little children, let us not love in word, neither in tongue; but in deed and in truth.
1 Corinthians 13	Charity suffereth long, and is kind; charity envieth not; charity vaunteth not itself, is not puffed up (Zechariah 11:5-10)
Romans 14:1-19	For the kingdom of Most High God is not meat and drink; but righteousness, and peace, and joy in the Holy Ghost. (Matthew 5:3-12)
Luke 11:1-13	If ye then, being evil, know how to give good gifts unto your children: how much more shall your heavenly Father give the Holy Spirit to them that ask him?
Romans 15:21-32	Now I beseech you, brethren, for the YAH Yeshua Ha'Mashiach's sake, and for the love of the Spirit, that ye strive together with me in your prayers to Most High God for me;
Ephesians 3	That he would grant you, according to the riches of his glory, to be strengthened with might by his Spirit in the inner man;
Ephesians 6:10-20	Praying always with all prayer and supplication in the Spirit, and watching thereunto with all perseverance and supplication for all saints; (Colossians 4)
1 Peter 4:1-14	But the end of all things is at hand: be ye therefore sober, and watch unto prayer.
2 Thessalonians 3:1-5	Finally, brethren, pray for us, that the word of the YAH may have free course, and be glorified, even as it is with you:

Acts 4	By stretching forth thine hand to heal; and that signs and wonders may be done by the name of thy holy child Yeshua. And when they had prayed, the place was shaken where they were assembled together; and they were all filled with the Holy Ghost, and they spake the word of Almighty God with boldness.
Jude 1:17-25	But ye, beloved, building up yourselves on your most holy faith, praying in the Holy Spirit
Isaiah 40:28-31	Hast thou not known? hast thou not heard, that the everlasting God, the LORD, the Creator of the ends of the earth, fainteth not, neither is weary? there is no searching of his understanding. 29 He giveth power to the faint; and to them that have no might he increaseth strength. 30 Even the youths shall faint and be weary, and the young men shall utterly fall: 31 But they that wait upon the LORD shall renew their strength; they shall mount up with wings as eagles; they shall run, and not be weary; and they shall walk, and not faint.

Father, I am thankful for you blotting out my transgressions as I have confessed and repented of the wrong I have done. Keep me in your ways that I may learn of your righteous laws, judgments, and ordinances with a heart of joy! Daily I pray for those who are far and near to me. I pray you bless me with a spirit like unto a dove, a mouth not in dispute like a lamb, strength of an ox, watching as an eagle, and courage of a lion to overcome all odds against me to give you the glory before all as I walk the earth day by day. Deliver me from the hands of the ungodly and enlarge my family that you have given me. Halleluyah! Thank you Yaha'shua!

PRAYER OF FORGIVENESS

And I prayed unto the YAH my Almighty God, and made my confession, and said, O YAH, the great and dreadful Most High God, keeping the covenant and mercy to them that love him, and to them that keep his commandments; Daniel 9:4-19

⁵ We have sinned, and have committed iniquity, and have done wickedly, and have rebelled, even by departing from thy precepts and from thy judgments:

⁶ Neither have we hearkened unto thy servants the prophets, which spoke in thy name to our kings, our princes, and our fathers, and to all the people of the land.

⁷ O YAH, righteousness belong unto thee, but unto us confusion of faces, as at this day; to the men of Judah, and to the inhabitants of Jerusalem, and unto all Israel, that are near, and that are far off, through all the countries whither thou hast driven them, because of their trespass that they have trespassed against thee.

⁸ O YAH, to us belong confusion of face, to our kings, to our princes, and to our fathers, because we have sinned against thee.

⁹ To the YAH our Almighty God belong mercies and forgiveness, though we have rebelled against him;

¹⁰ Neither have we obeyed the voice of the YAH our Almighty God, to walk in his laws, which he set before us by his servants the prophets.

¹¹ Yea, all Israel have transgressed thy law, even by departing, that they might not obey thy voice; therefore the curse is poured upon us, and the oath that is written in the law of Moses the servant of Almighty God, because we have sinned against him.

¹² And he hath confirmed his words, which he spoke against us, and against our judges that judged us, by bringing upon us a great evil: for under the whole heaven hath not been done as hath been done upon Jerusalem.

¹³ As it is written in the law of Moses, all this evil is come upon us: yet made we not our prayer before YAH our Almighty God, that we might turn from our iniquities, and understand thy truth.

¹⁴ Therefore hath YAH watched upon the evil, and brought it upon us: for the YAH our Almighty God is righteous in all his works which he doeth: for we obeyed not his voice.

¹⁵ And now, O YAH our Almighty God, that hast brought thy people forth out of the land of Egypt with a mighty hand, and hast gotten thee renown, as at this day; we have sinned, we have done wickedly.

¹⁶ O YAH, according to all thy righteousness, I beseech thee, let thine anger and thy fury be turned away from thy city Jerusalem, thy holy mountain: because for our sins, and for the iniquities of our fathers, Jerusalem and thy people are become a reproach to all that are about us.

¹⁷ Now therefore, O our Almighty God, hear the prayer of thy servant, and his supplications, and cause thy face to shine upon thy sanctuary that is desolate, for the YAH's sake.

¹⁸ O my Almighty Power, incline thine ear, and hear; open thine eyes, and behold our desolations, and the city which is called by thy name: for we do not present our supplications before thee for our righteousness, but for thy great mercy's.

¹⁹ O YAH, hear; O YAH, forgive; O YAH, hearken and do; defer not, for thine own sake, O my Almighty God: for thy city and thy people are called by thy name. (Prayer of Daniel)

RETURN AND HEAR YOUR SERVANT'S PRAYER

Yet have thou respect unto the prayer of thy servant, and to his supplication, O YAH my Almighty Power, to hearken unto the cry and to the prayer, which thy servant prayeth before thee to day: 1 Kings 8:28-40

[29] That thine eyes may be open toward this house night and day, even toward the place of which thou hast said, My name shall be there: that thou mayest hearken unto the prayer which thy servant shall make toward this place.

[30] And hearken thou to the supplication of thy servant, and of thy people Israel, when they shall pray toward this place: and hear thou in heaven thy dwelling place: and when thou hear, forgive.

[31] If any man trespass against his neighbor, and an oath be laid upon him to cause him to swear, and the oath come before thine altar in this house:

[32] Then hear thou in heaven, and do, and judge thy servants, condemning the wicked, to bring his way upon his head; and justifying the righteous, to give him according to his righteousness.

[33] When thy people Israel be smitten down before the enemy, because they have sinned against thee, and shall turn again to thee, and confess thy name, and pray, and make supplication unto thee in this house:

[34] Then hear thou in heaven, and forgive the sin of thy people Israel, and bring them again unto the land which thou gave unto their fathers.

[35] When heaven is shut up, and there is no rain, because they have sinned against thee; if they pray toward this place, and confess thy name, and turn from their sin, when thou afflicts them:

[36] Then hear thou in heaven, and forgive the sin of thy servants, and of thy people Israel, that thou teach them the good way wherein they should walk, and give rain upon thy land, which thou hast given to thy people for an inheritance.

^{37} If there be in the land famine, if there be pestilence, blasting, mildew, locust, or if there be caterpillar; if their enemy besiege them in the land of their cities; whatsoever plague, whatsoever sickness there be;

^{38} What prayer and supplication soever be made by any man, or by all thy people Israel, which shall know every man the plague of his own heart, and spread forth his hands toward this house:

^{39} Then hear thou in heaven thy dwelling place, and forgive, and do, and give to every man according to his ways, whose heart thou knowest; (for thou, even thou only, knowest the hearts of all the children of men;)

^{40} That they may fear thee all the days that they live in the land which thou gave unto our fathers. (Prayer of King Solomon)

PRAYER OF REPENTANCE

O YAH, Almighty God of our Fathers, Abraham, Isaac, and Ya'aqob, and of their righteous seed: who hast made heaven and earth, with all the ornament thereof: who hast bound the Sea by the word of thy Commandment: who hast shut up the deep, and sealed it by thy terrible and glorious Name, whom all men fear, and tremble before thy power: for the Majesty of thy glory cannot be borne, and thine angry threatening towards sinners is importable: but thy merciful promise is unmeasurable and unsearchable: for thou art the Most High YAH, of great compassion, long suffering, very merciful, and repentest of the evils of men.

Thou, O YAH, according to thy great goodness hast promised repentance, and forgiveness to them that have sinned against thee: and of thine infinite mercies hast appointed repentance unto sinners that they may be saved. Thou therefore, O YAH, that art the Most High God of the just, hast not appointed repentance to the just, as to Abraham, and Isaac, and Jacob, which have not sinned against thee: but thou hast appointed repentance unto me that am a sinner: for I have sinned above the number of the sands of the Sea.

My transgressions, O YAH, are multiplied: my transgressions are multiplied, and I am not worthy to behold and see the height of heaven, for the multitude of mine iniquity. I am bowed down with many iron bands, that I cannot lift up mine head, neither have any release: For I have provoked thy wrath, and done evil before thee, I did not thy will, neither kept I thy Commandments: I have set up abominations, and have multiplied offences. Now therefore I bow the knee of mine heart, beseeching thee of grace: I have sinned, O YAH, I have sinned and I acknowledge mine iniquities: wherefore I humbly beseech thee, forgive me, O YAH, forgive me, and destroy me not with mine iniquities.

Be not angry with me forever, by reserving evil for me, neither condemn me into the lower parts of the earth. For thou art the Most High God, even the Almighty God of them that repent: and in me thou wilt shew all thy goodness: for thou wilt save me that am unworthy, according to thy great mercy. Therefore I will praise thee forever all the days of my life: for all the powers of the heavens do praise thee, and thine is the glory forever and ever, Halleluyah! (Prayer of Manasses)

PRAYER OF DELIVERANCE AND PRAISE

Blessed art thou, O YAH, Almighty God of our fathers: thy Name is worthy to be praised, and glorified for evermore. 3 For thou art righteous in all the things that thou hast done to vs: yea, true are all thy works: thy ways are right, and all thy judgments truth.4 In all the things that thou hast brought upon us, and upon the holy city of our fathers, even Jerusalem, thou hast executed true judgment: for according to truth and judgment, didst thou bring all these things upon vs, because of our sins. 5 For wee have sinned and committed iniquity, departing from thee.

6 In all things have we trespassed, and not obeyed thy Commandments, nor kept them, neither done as thou hast commanded us that it might go well with us. 7 Wherefore all that thou hast brought upon vs, and everything that thou hast done to vs, thou hast done in true judgment. 8 And thou didst deliver vs into the hands of lawless enemies, most hateful forsakers of YAH and to an unjust King, and the most wicked in all the world. 9 And now we cannot open our mouths, we are become a shame, and reproach to thy servants, and to them that worship thee. 10 Yet deliver vs not up wholly for thy Names sake, neither disannul thou thy Covenant: 11 And cause not thy mercy to depart from vs: for thy beloved Abrahams sake: for thy servant Isaacs sake, and for thy holy Israel's sake.

12To whom thou hast spoken and promised, that thou wouldest multiply their seed as the stars of heaven, and as the sand that lyeth upon the sea shore. 13 For we, O YAH, are become less then any nation, and bee kept under this day in all the world, because of our sins. 14 Neither is there at this time, Prince, or Prophet, or leader, or burnt offering, or sacrifice, or oblation, or incense, or place to sacrifice before thee, and to find mercy. 15 Nevertheless in a contrite heart, and a humble spirit, let us be accepted.

16 Like as in the burnt offering of rams and bullocks, and like as in ten thousands of fat lambs: so let our sacrifice bee in thy sight this day, and grant that we may holy go after thee: for they shall not be confounded that put their trust in thee.

17 And now we follow thee, with all our heart, we fear thee, and seek thy face. 18 Put vs not to shame: but deal with us after thy loving kindness, and according to the multitude of thy mercies. 19 Deliver us also according to thy marvelous works, and give glory to thy Name, O YAH, and let all them that doe thy servants hurt be ashamed. 20 And let them be confounded in all their power and might, and let their strength be broken. 21 And let them know that thou art YAH, the only Almighty God, and glorious over the whole world. 22 And the king's servants that put them in, ceased not to make the oven hot with rosin, pitch, tow, and small wood. 23 So that the flame streamed forth above the furnace, forty and nine cubits: 24 And it passed through, and burnt those Chaldeans it found about the furnace. 25 But the Angel of the YAH came down into the oven, together with Azariah and his fellows, and smote the flame of the fire out of the oven: 26 And made the midst of the furnace, as it had bene a moist whistling wind, so that the fire touched them not at all, neither hurt nor troubled them.

27 Then the three, as out of one mouth, praised, glorified, and blessed Almighty God in the furnace, saying; 28 Blessed art thou, O YAH Almighty God of our fathers: and to be praised and exalted above all forever. 29 And blessed is thy glorious and holy Name: and to be praised and exalted above all forever. 30 Blessed art thou in the Temple of thine holy glory: and to be praised and glorified above all forever. 31 Blessed art thou that beholdest the depths, and sittest upon the Cherubims, and to be praised and exalted above all forever.

32 Blessed art thou on the glorious Throne of thy kingdom: and to be praised and glorified above all forever.

33 Blessed art thou in the firmament of heaven: and above all to be praised and glorified forever.

34 O all ye works of the YAH, bless ye the YAH: praise and exalt him above all forever.

35 O ye heavens, bless ye the YAH: praise and exalt him above all forever.

36 O ye Angels of the YAH, bless ye the YAH: praise and exalt him above all forever.

37 O all ye waters that be above the heaven, bless ye the YAH: praise and exalt him above all forever.

38 O all ye powers of the YAH, bless ye the YAH: praise and exalt him above all forever.

39 O ye Sun and Moon, bless ye the YAH: praise and exalt him above all forever.

40 O ye stars of heaven, bless ye the YAH: praise and exalt him above all forever.

41 O every shower and dew, bless ye the YAH: praise and exalt him above all forever.

42 O all ye winds, bless ye the YAH: praise and exalt him above all forever.

43 O ye fire and heat, bless ye the YAH: praise and exalt him above all forever.

44 O ye Winter and Summer, bless ye the YAH: praise and exalt him above all forever.

45 O ye dews and storms of snow, bless ye the YAH: praise and exalt him above all forever.

46 O ye nights and days, bless ye the YAH: praise and exalt him above all forever.

47 O ye light and darkness, bless ye the YAH: praise and exalt him above all forever.

48 O ye ice and cold, bless ye the YAH: praise and exalt him above all forever.

49 O ye frost and snow, bless ye the YAH: praise and exalt him above all forever.

50 O ye lightings and clouds, bless ye the YAH: praise and exalt him above all forever.

51 O let the earth bless the YAH: praise and exalt him above all forever.

52 O ye mountains and little hills, bless ye the YAH: praise and exalt him above all forever.

53 O all ye things that grow on the earth, bless ye the YAH: praise and exalt him above all forever. (Prayer of Azariah)

54 O ye fountains, bless ye the YAH: praise and exalt him above all forever.

55 O ye seas and rivers, bless ye the YAH: praise and exalt him above all forever.

56 O ye whales and all that move in the waters, bless ye the YAH: praise and exalt him above all forever.

57 O all ye fouls of the air, bless ye the YAH: praise and exalt him above all forever.

58 O all ye beasts and cattle, bless ye the YAH: praise and exalt him above all forever.

59 O ye children of men, bless ye the YAH: praise and exalt him above all forever.

60 O Israel bless ye the YAH: praise and exalt him above all forever.

61 O ye priests of the YAH, bless ye the YAH: praise and exalt him above all forever.

62 O ye servants of the YAH, bless ye the YAH: praise and exalt him above all forever.

63 O ye spirits and souls of the righteous, bless ye the YAH, praise and exalt him above all forever.

64 O ye holy and humble men of heart, bless ye the YAH: praise and exalt him above all forever.

65 O Hananias, Azariah, and Mishael, bless ye the YAH, praise and exalt him above all forever: for he hath delivered vs from hell, and saved vs from the hand of death, and delivered us out of the midst of the furnace, and burning flame: even out of the midst of the fire hath he delivered us.

66 O give thanks unto the YAH, because he is gracious: for his mercy endureth forever.

67 O all ye that worship the YAH, bless the Most High God of gods, praise him, and give him thanks: for his mercy endureth forever. (Prayer of Azariah)

COUNSEL FOR A BLESSED LIFE EXPERIENCE CAN BE FRAMED AS FOLLOWS:

In the journey of life, wisdom stands firm upon a foundation of seven essential pillars: Knowledge, Understanding (comprehension), Discretion (discernment), Equity (fairness), Justice (integrity), Judgment (impartiality), and Wisdom (sagacity). To navigate the noble path of life, we must diligently seek to validate what is virtuous and commendable. By incrementally accumulating insights, layer upon layer, and adhering to principles and values, we come to recognize the universal importance of wisdom in all facets of existence. Let us begin with examining the seven pillars of wisdom for choices made throughout life.

APPLIED CONCEPTS FOR 7 PILLARS OF WISDOM

Knowledge

Whoso loveth instruction loveth knowledge: but he that hateth reproof is brutish. Proverbs 12:1 My son, forget not my law; but let thine heart keep my commandments: Proverbs 3:1 My son, keep my words, and lay up my commandments with thee. Proverbs 7:1

Proverbs 1:2-10, Hosea 4:1, 2 Timothy 3:1-7, Romans 2:16-25, Psalm 14:1-5

Understanding

Hear, ye children, the instruction of a father, and attend to know understanding. Proverbs 19:1-3 Better is the poor that walketh in his integrity, than he that is perverse in his lips, and is a fool. Also, that the soul be without knowledge, it is not good; and he that hasteth with his feet sinneth. 3 The foolishness of man perverteth his way: and his heart fretteth against the Lord. Proverbs 4:1

Psalm 119:103-105, Proverbs 3:11-14, Proverbs 4:1-8, Proverbs 19:7-9

Discretion

Proverbs 16:1-4 The preparations of the heart in man, and the answer of the tongue, is from the Lord. 2 All the ways of a man are clean in his own eyes; but the Lord weigheth the spirits. 3 Commit thy works unto the Lord, and thy thoughts shall be established. 4 The Lord hath made all things for himself: yea, even the wicked for the day of evil.

Psalm 112:4-6; Proverbs 15:1-7; 13:1-6; 20:1-3; 19:10-12; 2:10-13

Equity

A false balance is an abomination to the Lord: but a just weight is his delight. When pride cometh, then cometh shame: but with the lowly is wisdom. The integrity of the upright shall guide them: but the perverseness of transgressors shall destroy them. Proverbs 11:1-3

Proverbs 28:1-14, Proverbs 29:1-9, Psalm 99:3-5, Isaiah 11:2-5, Malachi 2:5-7

Judgment

Proverbs 10: 2-3 Treasures of wickedness profit nothing: but righteousness delivereth from death. The Lord will not suffer the soul of the righteous to famish: but he casteth away the substance of the wicked. A good man obtaineth favour of the Lord: but a man of wicked devices will he condemn. A man shall not be established by wickedness: but the root of the righteous shall not be moved.

Proverbs 21:1- 8, Proverbs 22:10-11, Proverbs 24:3-14, Proverbs 25:1-8

Wisdom

Proverbs 5:1 My son, attend unto my wisdom, and bow thine ear to my understanding:

- Proverbs 8:1 Doth not wisdom cry? and understanding put forth her voice?
  2 She standeth in the top of high places, by the way in the places of the paths.
- Proverbs 9:1 Wisdom hath builded her house, she hath hewn out her seven pillars:

Proverbs 18:1-3, Proverbs 26:1-8, Proverbs 27:1-13, Proverbs 30:5-14. Proverbs 31:3-9

Be not wise in thine own eyes: fear the MOST HIGH GOD, and depart from evil.

Proverbs 3:7 [7] Be not wise in thine own eyes: fear the MOST HIGH GOD, and depart from evil.

Knowledge

Proverbs 1:7-8 [7] The fear of the MOST HIGH GOD is the beginning of knowledge: but fools despise wisdom and instruction.

> [8] My son, hear the instruction of thy father, and forsake not the law of thy mother:

Deuteronomy 11:16-17 Take heed to yourselves, that your heart be not deceived, and ye turn aside, and serve other gods, and worship them; idolatry even And then the Most High God's wrath be kindled against you, and he shut up the heaven, that there be no rain, and that the land yield not her fruit; and lest ye perish quickly from off the good land which the Most High God giveth you.

And now, Israel, what doth the Almighty God thy Power require of thee, but to fear the Almighty God thy Power, to walk in all his ways, and to love him, and to serve the Almighty YAH thy Power with all thy heart and with all thy soul Deuteronomy 10:12

Understanding

Psalm 34:14 Depart from evil, and do good; seek peace, and pursue it. And unto man he said, Behold, the fear of the Most High God, that is wisdom; and to depart from evil is understanding. Job 28:28

Discretion

Psalm 112:5 A good man will guide his affairs with discretion. Discretion shall preserve thee, understanding shall keep thee: Proverbs 2:11 The discretion of a man deferreth his anger; and it is his glory to pass over a transgression. Proverbs 19:11-12

Equity

Ecclesiastes 2:21 For there is a man whose labour is in wisdom, and in knowledge, and in equity; yet to a man that hath not laboured therein shall he leave it for his portion. This also is vanity and a great evil.

Justice

Deuteronomy 33:20-21 he dwelleth as a lion, and teareth the arm with the crown of the head.

> [21] And he provided the first part for himself in a portion of the lawgiver, was he seated; and he came with the heads of the people, he executed the justice of the Most High God, and his judgments with Israel.

Proverbs 17:13-15 Whoso rewardeth evil for good, evil shall not depart from his house.

> [14] The beginning of strife is as when one letteth out water: therefore leave off contention, before it be meddled with.
> [15] He that justifieth the wicked, and he that condemneth the just, even they both are abomination to the MOST HIGH GOD.

Judgment

Psalm 19:9 The fear of the Most High God is clean, enduring for ever: the judgments of the Most High God are true and righteous altogether. Turn away my reproach which I fear: for thy judgments are good. Psalm 119:39 Evil men understand not judgment: but they that seek the Most High God understand all things. Proverbs 28:5 Whoso keepeth the commandment shall feel no evil thing: and a wise man's heart discerneth both time and judgment. Ecclesiastes 8:5

Wisdom

Proverbs 17:24 The lips of the righteous feed many: but fools die for want of wisdom. Proverbs 10:21 My son, let not them depart from thine eyes: keep sound wisdom and discretion: Wisdom is before him that hath understanding; but the eyes of a fool are in the ends of the earth. Proverbs 3:21

Job 37:23-24 [23] Touching the Almighty, we cannot find him out: he is excellent in power, and in judgment, and in plenty of justice: he will not afflict.

[24] Men do therefore fear him: he respecteth not any that are wise of heart.

Knowledge

Romans 5:19 [19] For as by one man's disobedience many were made sinners, so by the obedience of one shall many be made righteous.

Proverbs 1:7-11 [7] The fear of the MOST HIGH GOD is the beginning of knowledge: but fools despise wisdom and instruction.

[8] My son, hear the instruction of thy father, and forsake not the law of thy mother:

[9] For they shall be an ornament of grace unto thy head, and chains about thy neck.

[10] My son, if sinners entice thee, consent thou not.

[11] If they say, Come with us, let us lay wait for blood, let us lurk privily for the innocent without cause:

Understanding

Proverbs 13:13-16 [13] Whoso despiseth the word shall be destroyed: but he that feareth the commandment shall be rewarded.

[14] The law of the wise is a fountain of life, to depart from the snares of death.

[15] Good understanding giveth favor: but the way of transgressors is hard.

[16] Every prudent man dealeth with knowledge: but a fool layeth open his folly.

Proverbs 13:18-21 [18] Poverty and shame shall be to him that refuseth instruction: but he that regardeth reproof shall be honored.

[19] The desire accomplished is sweet to the soul: but it is abomination to fools to depart from evil.

[20] He that walketh with wise men shall be wise: but a companion of fools shall be destroyed.

[21] Evil pursueth sinners: but to the righteous good shall be repayed.

1 Samuel 15:22-23 [22] And Samuel said, Hath the MOST HIGH GOD as great delight in burnt offerings and sacrifices, as in obeying the voice of the MOST HIGH GOD? Behold, to obey is better than sacrifice, and to hearken than the fat of rams.

[23] For rebellion is as the sin of witchcraft, and stubbornness is as iniquity and idolatry. Because thou hast rejected the word of the MOST HIGH GOD, he hath also rejected thee from being king.

1 Samuel 16:14-15 [14] But the Spirit of the MOST HIGH GOD departed from Saul, and an evil spirit from the MOST HIGH GOD troubled him.

[15] And Saul's servants said unto him, Behold now, an evil spirit from God troubleth thee.

Fear

Proverbs 3:1-6 [1] My son, forget not my law; but let thine heart keep my commandments:

> [2] For length of days, and long life, and peace, shall they add to thee.
>
> [3] Let not mercy and truth forsake thee: bind them about thy neck; write them upon the table of thine heart:
>
> [4] So shalt thou find favor and good understanding in the sight of God and man.
>
> [5] Trust in the MOST HIGH GOD with all thine heart; and lean not unto thine own understanding.
>
> [6] In all thy ways acknowledge him, and he shall direct thy paths.

Discretion

Proverbs 12:13-21 [13] The wicked is snared by the transgression of his lips: but the just shall come out of trouble.

> [14] A man shall be satisfied with good by the fruit of his mouth: and the recompence of a man's hands shall be rendered unto him.
>
> [15] The way of a fool is right in his own eyes: but he that hearkeneth unto counsel is wise.
>
> [16] A fool's wrath is presently known: but a prudent man covereth shame.
>
> [17] He that speaketh truth sheweth forth righteousness: but a false witness deceit.
>
> [18] There is that speaketh like the piercings of a sword: but the tongue of the wise is health.
>
> [19] The lip of truth shall be established for ever: but a lying tongue is but for a moment.
>
> [20] Deceit is in the heart of them that imagine evil: but to the counsellors of peace is joy.
>
> [21] There shall no evil happen to the just: but the wicked shall be filled with mischief.

Isaiah 5:20-25 [20] Woe unto them that call evil good, and good evil; that put darkness for light, and light for darkness; that put bitter for sweet, and sweet for bitter!

[21] Woe unto them that are wise in their own eyes, and prudent in their own sight!

[22] Woe unto them that are mighty to drink wine, and men of strength to mingle strong drink:

[23] Which justify the wicked for reward, and take away the righteousness of the righteous from him!

[24] Therefore as the fire devoureth the stubble, and the flame consumeth the chaff, so their root shall be as rottenness, and their blossom shall go up as dust: because they have cast away the law of the MOST HIGH GOD of hosts, and despised the word of the Holy One of Israel.

[25] Therefore is the anger of the MOST HIGH GOD kindled against his people, and he hath stretched forth his hand against them, and hath smitten them: and the hills did tremble, and their carcasses were torn in the midst of the streets. For all this his anger is not turned away, but his hand is stretched out still.

Proverbs 5:1-17 [1] My son, attend unto my wisdom, and bow thine ear to my understanding:

[2] That thou mayest regard discretion, and that thy lips may keep knowledge.

[3] For the lips of a strange woman drop as a honeycomb, and her mouth is smoother than oil:

[4] But her end is bitter as wormwood, sharp as a two-edged sword.

[5] Her feet go down to death; her steps take hold on hell.

[6] Lest thou shouldest ponder the path of life, her ways are moveable, that thou canst not know them.

[7] Hear me now therefore, O ye children, and depart not from the words of my mouth.

[8] Remove thy way far from her, and come not nigh the door of her house:

[9] Lest thou give thine honor unto others, and thy years unto the cruel:

[10] Lest strangers be filled with thy wealth; and thy labors be in the house of a stranger;

[11] And thou mourn at the last, when thy flesh and thy body are consumed,

[12] And say, How have I hated instruction, and my heart despised reproof;

[13] And have not obeyed the voice of my teachers, nor inclined mine ear to them that instructed me!

[14] I was almost in all evil in the midst of the congregation and assembly.

[15] Drink waters out of thine own cistern, and running waters out of thine own well.

[16] Let thy fountains be dispersed abroad, and rivers of waters in the streets.

[17] Let them be only thine own, and not strangers' with thee.

Equity

Proverbs 14:7-10 [7] Go from the presence of a foolish man, when thou perceivest not in him the lips of knowledge.

[8] The wisdom of the prudent is to understand his way: but the folly of fools is deceit.

[9] Fools make a mock at sin: but among the righteous there is favor.

[10] The heart knoweth his own bitterness; and a stranger doth not intermeddle with his joy.

Justice

Proverbs 17:13-15,19-20,24-28 [13] Whoso rewardeth evil for good, evil shall not depart from his house.

[14] The beginning of strife is as when one letteth out water: therefore leave off contention, before it be meddled with.

[15] He that justifieth the wicked, and he that condemneth the just, even they both are abomination to the MOST HIGH GOD.

[19] He loveth transgression that loveth strife: and he that exalteth his gate seeketh destruction.

[20] He that hath a froward heart findeth no good: and he that hath a perverse tongue falleth into mischief.

[24] Wisdom is before him that hath understanding; but the eyes of a fool are in the ends of the earth.

[25] A foolish son is a grief to his father, and bitterness to her that bare him.

[26] Also to punish the just is not good, nor to strike princes for equity.

[27] He that hath knowledge spareth his words: and a man of understanding is of an excellent spirit.

[28] Even a fool, when he holdeth his peace, is counted wise: and he that shutteth his lips is esteemed a man of understanding.

Psalms 109:15-21 [15] Let them be before the MOST HIGH GOD continually, that he may cut off the memory of them from the earth.

[16] Because that he remembered not to shew mercy, but persecuted the poor and needy man, that he might even slay the broken in heart.

[17] As he loved cursing, so let it come unto him: as he delighted not in blessing, so let it be far from him.

[18] As he clothed himself with cursing like as with his garment, so let it come into his bowels like water, and like oil into his bones.

[19] Let it be unto him as the garment which covereth him, and for a girdle wherewith he is girded continually.

[20] Let this be the reward of mine adversaries from the MOST HIGH GOD, and of them that speak evil against my soul.

[21] But do thou for me, O YAH the Most High God, for thy name's sake: because thy mercy is good, deliver thou me.

Judgment

Matthew 25:40-41 [40] And the King shall answer and say unto them, Verily I say unto you, Inasmuch as ye have done it unto one of the least of these my brethren, ye have done it unto me.

[41] Then shall he say also unto them on the left hand, Depart from me, ye cursed, into everlasting fire, prepared for the devil and his angels:

Isaiah 11:2-5 [2] And the spirit of the MOST HIGH GOD shall rest upon him, the spirit of wisdom and understanding, the spirit of counsel and might, the spirit of knowledge and of the fear of the MOST HIGH GOD;

[3] And shall make him of quick understanding in the fear of the MOST HIGH GOD: and he shall not judge after the sight of his eyes, neither reprove after the hearing of his ears:

[4] But with righteousness shall he judge the poor, and reprove with equity for the meek of the earth: and he shall smite the earth with the rod of his mouth, and with the breath of his lips shall he slay the wicked.

[5] And righteousness shall be the girdle of his loins, and faithfulness the girdle of his reins.

Jubilees 5:17 [17] And of the children of Israel it has been written and ordained: If they turn to him in righteousness, He will forgive all their transgressions and pardon all their sins.

[18] It is written and ordained that He will show mercy to all who turn from all their guilt once each year.

Jubilees 5:13-14, [13] And the judgment of all is ordained and written on the heavenly tablets in righteousness -even (the judgment of) all who depart from the path which is ordained for them to walk in; and if they walk not therein, judgment is written down for every creature and for every kind.

[14] And there is nothing in heaven or on earth, or in light or in darkness, or in Sheol or in the depth, or in the place of darkness (which is not judged); and all their judgments are ordained and written and engraved.

Psalms 149:6-9 [6] Let the high praises of God be in their mouth, and a two-edged sword in their hand;

[7] To execute vengeance upon the heathen, and punishments upon the people;

[8] To bind their kings with chains, and their nobles with fetters of iron;

[9] To execute upon them the judgment written: this honor have all his saints. Praise ye the MOST HIGH GOD.

Hebrews 4:12 [12] For the word of YAH is quick, and powerful, and sharper than any two-edged sword, piercing even to the dividing asunder of soul and spirit, and of the joints and marrow, and is a discerner of the thoughts and intents of the heart.

Wisdom

Job 37:23-24 [23] Touching the Almighty, we cannot find him out: he is excellent in power, and in judgment, and in plenty of justice: he will not afflict.

[24] Men do therefore fear him: he respecteth not any that are wise of heart.

Psalms 64:9-10 [9] And all men shall fear, and shall declare the work of God; for they shall wisely consider of his doing. [10] The righteous shall be glad in the MOST HIGH GOD, and shall trust in him; and all the upright in heart shall glory.

Ecclesiasticus 1:2-30 [2] Who can number the sand of the sea, and the drops of rain, and the days of eternity?

[3] Who can find out the height of heaven, and the breadth of the earth, and the deep, and wisdom?

[4] Wisdom hath been created before all things, and the understanding of prudence from everlasting.

[5] The word of YAH Most High is the fountain of wisdom; and her ways are everlasting commandments.

[6] To whom hath the root of wisdom been revealed? or who hath known her wise counsels?

[7] Unto whom hath the knowledge of wisdom been made manifest? and who hath understood her great experience?

[8] There is one wise and greatly to be feared, the Most High God sitting upon his throne.

[9] He created her, and saw her, and numbered her, and poured her out upon all his works.

[10] She is with all flesh according to his gift, and he hath given her to them that love him.

[11] The fear of the Most High God is honor, and glory, and gladness, and a crown of rejoicing.

[12] The fear of the Most High God maketh a merry heart, and giveth joy, and gladness, and a long life.

[13] Whoso feareth the Most High God, it shall go well with him at the last, and he shall find favor in the day of his death.

[14] To fear the Most High God is the beginning of wisdom: and it was created with the faithful in the womb.

[15] She hath built an everlasting foundation with men, and she shall continue with their seed.

[16] To fear the Most High God is fulness of wisdom, and filleth men with her fruits.

[17] She filleth all their house with things desirable, and the garners with her increase.

[18] The fear of the Most High God is a crown of wisdom, making peace and perfect health to flourish; both which are the gifts of God: and it enlargeth their rejoicing that love him.

[19] Wisdom raineth down skill and knowledge of understanding standing, and exalteth them to honor that hold her fast.

[20] The root of wisdom is to fear the Most High God, and the branches thereof are long life.

[21] The fear of the Most High God driveth away sins: and where it is present, it turneth away wrath.

[22] A furious man cannot be justified; for the sway of his fury shall be his destruction.

[23] A patient man will tear for a time, and afterward joy shall spring up unto him.

[24] He will hide his words for a time, and the lips of many shall declare his wisdom.

[25] The parables of knowledge are in the treasures of wisdom: but godliness is an abomination to a sinner.

[26] If thou desire wisdom, keep the commandments, and the Most High God shall give her unto thee.

[27] For the fear of the Most High God is wisdom and instruction: and faith and meekness are his delight.

[28] Distrust not the fear of the Most High God when thou art poor: and come not unto him with a double heart.

[29] Be not an hypocrite in the sight of men, and take good heed what thou speakest.

[30] Exalt not thyself, lest thou fall, and bring dishonor upon thy soul, and so God discover thy secrets, and cast thee down in the midst of the congregation, because thou camest not in truth to the fear of the Most High God, but thy heart is full of deceit.

WALK WITH THE WISE OR BE A COMPANION OF FOOLS

Proverbs 13:20 He that walketh with wise men shall be wise: but a companion of fools shall be destroyed.

- A fool despises knowledge and is known by what fruit comes out of his mouth having a lack of knowledge thereof condemns himself in judgment.
- A fool makes a mock at sin; therefore there is no understanding to reason with one's ways of error. Proverbs 14:9
- A man of understanding seeks the lips of knowledge and will not be companion of deceit to entertain the foolish. Proverbs 16:21
- A man with discretion is sets himself apart from foolishness in how he speaks of good morale and walking upright to depart from evil whenever approached with foolishness for without discretion one inherits folly.
- A fool will reap what one sows therefore to accompany one would diminish equity for equity is without respect of persons to maintain peace and unity through knowledge and understanding. There is no unity with fools perhaps a moment of time to plot subtle inventions causing discord or shame.

The lips of Truth brings out Justice to ensure there is no evil way having an advantage over the innocent. Walking with men of understanding having knowledge of the Holy allows a man to increase in righteousness for the fear of the eternal judgment being blameless against sin.

Wise men that do justice and judgment set the standard for courage and strength to put away evil even foolishness bound up in the heart of a child who does not want to grow into a man of the Most High. The thought of foolishness is sin, neither shall a just man desire to be a companion or else he becomes an accomplice for mischief.

Wise Men are a beacon of light to guide those who have not knowledge of salvation. Wise men having their house built is trucks a man how to have a strong Foundation beginning with knowledge as he builds with understanding he uses discretion to choose the company keeps to increase in righteousness using equity he learns how to makes his own decisions from Discerning the times and not be respect of persons in dealing with situations. These wise men not only turned him to righteousness but he also shall be wise to turn others to righteousness that he be all so blameless and innocent of the judgment. Having the skill and experience of being guided and righteousness he is able to judge and use wisdom to reveal what things are coming to past before him being experienced he now can draw insight quickly to things learned and unlearned waiting patiently for things to come to past. Whereas fools have no vision being hasty in spirit and in words they do error greatly to make others go astray unto destruction.

Knowledge

Proverbs 13:16 Every prudent man dealeth with knowledge: but a fool layeth open his folly.

Malachi 2:7-8 [7] For the priest's lips should keep knowledge, and they should seek the law at his mouth: for he is the messenger of the MOST HIGH GOD of hosts.

Proverbs 14:29-30 He that is slow to wrath is of great understanding: but he that is hasty of spirit exalteth folly.

A sound heart is the life of the flesh: but envy the rottenness of the bones. Ecclesiasticus 26:6 But a grief of heart and sorrow is a woman that is jealous over another woman, and a scourge of the tongue which communicateth with all.

Job 36:9-12 [9] Then he sheweth them their work, and their transgressions that they have exceeded.

[10] He openeth also their ear to discipline, and commandeth that they return from iniquity.

[11] If they obey and serve him, they shall spend their days in prosperity, and their years in pleasures.

[12] But if they obey not, they shall perish by the sword, and they shall die without knowledge.

Proverbs 13:13-14 [13] Whoso despiseth the word shall be destroyed: but he that feareth the commandment shall be rewarded.

[14] The law of the wise is a fountain of life, to depart from the snares of death.

Understanding

Proverbs 13:15, 19, 21 [15] Good understanding giveth favor: but the way of transgressors is hard.

[19] The desire accomplished is sweet to the soul: but it is abomination to fools to depart from evil.

[21] Evil pursueth sinners: but to the righteous good shall be repayed.

Proverbs 14:7-9, 34-35 [7] Go from the presence of a foolish man, when thou perceivest not in him the lips of knowledge.

[8] The wisdom of the prudent is to understand his way: but the folly of fools is deceit.

[9] Fools make a mock at sin: but among the righteous there is favor.

[34] Righteousness exalteth a nation: but sin is a reproach to any people.

[35] The king's favor is toward a wise servant: but his wrath is against him that causeth shame.

Discretion

Proverbs 14:10-12,16-18 [10] The heart knoweth his own bitterness; and a stranger doth not intermeddle with his joy.

[11] The house of the wicked shall be overthrown: but the tabernacle of the upright shall flourish.

[12] There is a way which seemeth right unto a man, but the end thereof are the ways of death.

[16] A wise man feareth, and departeth from evil: but the fool rageth, and is confident.

[17] He that is soon angry dealeth foolishly: and a man of wicked devices is hated.

[18] The simple inherit folly: but the prudent are crowned with knowledge.

Proverbs 14:21-22,26,29-30,33 [21] He that despiseth his neighbor sinneth: but he that hath mercy on the poor, happy is he.

[22] Do they not err that devise evil? but mercy and truth shall be to them that devise good.

[26] In the fear of the MOST HIGH GOD is strong confidence: and his children shall have a place of refuge.

[29] He that is slow to wrath is of great understanding: but he that is hasty of spirit exalteth folly.

[30] A sound heart is the life of the flesh: but envy the rottenness of the bones.

[33] Wisdom resteth in the heart of him that hath understanding: but that which is in the midst of fools is made known.

Proverbs 29:18-20 [18] Where there is no vision, the people perish: but he that keepeth the law, happy is he.

[19] A servant will not be corrected by words: for though he understand he will not answer.

[20] Seest thou a man that is hasty in his words? there is more hope of a fool than of him.

Equity (reap what you sow)

Proverbs 13:2-11,24-25 [2] A man shall eat good by the fruit of his mouth: but the soul of the transgressors shall eat violence.

[3] He that keepeth his mouth keepeth his life: but he that openeth wide his lips shall have destruction.

[4] The soul of the sluggard desireth, and hath nothing: but the soul of the diligent shall be made fat.

[5] A righteous man hateth lying: but a wicked man is loathsome, and cometh to shame.

[6] Righteousness keepeth him that is upright in the way: but wickedness overthroweth the sinner.

[7] There is that maketh himself rich, yet hath nothing: there is that maketh himself poor, yet hath great riches.

[8] The ransom of a man's life are his riches: but the poor heareth not rebuke.

[9] The light of the righteous rejoiceth: but the lamp of the wicked shall be put out.

[10] Only by pride cometh contention: but with the well advised is wisdom.

[11] Wealth gotten by vanity shall be diminished: but he that gathereth by labor shall increase.

[24] He that spareth his rod hateth his son: but he that loveth him chasteneth him betimes.

[25] The righteous eateth to the satisfying of his soul: but the belly of the wicked shall want.

Ecclesiastes 7:8-12 [8] Better is the end of a thing than the beginning thereof: and the patient in spirit is better than the proud in spirit.

[9] Be not hasty in thy spirit to be angry: for anger resteth in the bosom of fools.

[10] Say not thou, What is the cause that the former days were better than these? for thou dost not enquire wisely concerning this.

[11] Wisdom is good with an inheritance: and by it there is profit to them that see the sun.

[12] For wisdom is a defense, and money is a defense: but the excellency of knowledge is, that wisdom giveth life to them that have it.

Proverbs 28:21-23,25-26 [21]To have respect of persons is not good: for a piece of bread that man will transgress.

[22] He that hasteth to be rich hath an evil eye, and considereth not that poverty shall come upon him.

[23] He that rebuketh a man afterwards shall find more favor than he that flattereth with the tongue.

[25] He that is of a proud heart stirreth up strife: but he that putteth his trust in the MOST HIGH GOD shall be made fat.

[26] He that trusteth in his own heart is a fool: but whoso walketh wisely, he shall be delivered.

Justice

Proverbs 12:19-28 [19] The lip of truth shall be established for ever: but a lying tongue is but for a moment.

[20] Deceit is in the heart of them that imagine evil: but to the counsellors of peace is joy.

[21] There shall no evil happen to the just: but the wicked shall be filled with mischief.

[22] Lying lips are abomination to the MOST HIGH GOD: but they that deal truly are his delight.

[23] A prudent man concealeth knowledge: but the heart of fools proclaimeth foolishness.

[24] The hand of the diligent shall bear rule: but the slothful shall be under tribute.

[25] Heaviness in the heart of man maketh it stoop: but a good word maketh it glad.

[26] The righteous is more excellent than his neighbor: but the way of the wicked seduceth them.

[27] The slothful man roasteth not that which he took in hunting: but the substance of a diligent man is precious.

[28] In the way of righteousness is life; and in the pathway thereof there is no death.

Proverbs 11:3-11 [3] The integrity of the upright shall guide them: but the perverseness of transgressors shall destroy them.

[4] Riches profit not in the day of wrath: but righteousness delivereth from death.

[5] The righteousness of the perfect shall direct his way: but the wicked shall fall by his own wickedness.

[6] The righteousness of the upright shall deliver them: but transgressors shall be taken in their own naughtiness.

[7] When a wicked man dieth, his expectation shall perish: and the hope of unjust men perisheth.

[8] The righteous is delivered out of trouble, and the wicked cometh in his stead.

[9] An hypocrite with his mouth destroyeth his neighbor: but through knowledge shall the just be delivered.

[10] When it goeth well with the righteous, the city rejoiceth: and when the wicked perish, there is shouting.

[11] By the blessing of the upright the city is exalted: but it is overthrown by the mouth of the wicked.

Judgment

Proverbs 11:1-2 [1] A false balance is abomination to the MOST HIGH GOD: but a just weight is his delight.

[2] When pride cometh, then cometh shame: but with the lowly is wisdom.

Proverbs 12:2-14 [2] A good man obtaineth favor of the MOST HIGH GOD: but a man of wicked devices will he condemn.

[3] A man shall not be established by wickedness: but the root of the righteous shall not be moved.

[4] A virtuous woman is a crown to her husband: but she that maketh ashamed is as rottenness in his bones.

[5] The thoughts of the righteous are right: but the counsels of the wicked are deceit.

[6] The words of the wicked are to lie in wait for blood: but the mouth of the upright shall deliver them.

[7] The wicked are overthrown, and are not: but the house of the righteous shall stand.

[8] A man shall be commended according to his wisdom: but he that is of a perverse heart shall be despised.

[9] He that is despised, and hath a servant, is better than he that honoreth himself, and lacketh bread.

[10] A righteous man regardeth the life of his beast: but the tender mercy of the wicked are cruel.

[11] He that tilleth his land shall be satisfied with bread: but he that followeth vain persons is void of understanding.

[12] The wicked desireth the net of evil men: but the root of the righteous yieldeth fruit.

[13] The wicked is snared by the transgression of his lips: but the just shall come out of trouble.

[14] A man shall be satisfied with good by the fruit of his mouth: and the recompence of a man's hands shall be rendered unto him.

Wisdom

Proverbs 24:1-3,5,7-9 [1] Be not thou envious against evil men, neither desire to be with them.

[2] For their heart studieth destruction, and their lips talk of mischief.

[3] Through wisdom is a house built; and by understanding it is established:

[5] A wise man is strong; yea, a man of knowledge increaseth strength.

[7] Wisdom is too high for a fool: he openeth not his mouth in the gate.

[8] He that deviseth to do evil shall be called a mischievous person.

[9] The thought of foolishness is sin: and the scorner is an abomination to men.

Daniel 12:3,10 [3] And they that be wise shall shine as the brightness of the firmament; and they that turn many to righteousness as the stars for ever and ever.

[10] Many shall be purified, and made white, and tried; but the wicked shall do wickedly: and none of the wicked shall understand; but the wise shall understand.

Proverbs 11:12-20 [12] He that is void of wisdom despiseth his neighbor: but a man of understanding holdeth his peace.

[13] A talebearer revealeth secrets: but he that is of a faithful spirit concealeth the matter.

[14] Where no counsel is, the people fall: but in the multitude of counsellors there is safety.

[15] He that is surety for a stranger shall smart for it: and he that hateth suretiship is sure.

[16] A gracious woman retaineth honor: and strong men retain riches.

[17] The merciful man doeth good to his own soul: but he that is cruel troubleth his own flesh.

[18] The wicked worketh a deceitful work: but to him that soweth righteousness shall be a sure reward.

[19] As righteousness tendeth to life: so he that pursueth evil pursueth it to his own death.

[20] They that are of a froward heart are abomination to the MOST HIGH GOD: but such as are upright in their way are his delight.

Isaiah 55:6-9,11 [6] Seek ye the MOST HIGH GOD while he may be found, call ye upon him while he is near:

[7] Let the wicked forsake his way, and the unrighteous man his thoughts: and let him return unto the MOST HIGH GOD, and he will have mercy upon him; and to Our Almighty Power, for he will abundantly pardon.

[8] For my thoughts are not your thoughts, neither are your ways my ways, saith the MOST HIGH GOD.

[9] For as the heavens are higher than the earth, so are my ways higher than your ways, and my thoughts than your thoughts.

[11] So shall my word be that goeth forth out of my mouth: it shall not return unto me void, but it shall accomplish that which I please, and it shall prosper in the thing whereto I sent it.

Ephesians 2:8-10,12-14,19-22 [8] For by grace are ye saved through faith; and that not of yourselves: it is the gift of God:

[9] Not of works, lest any man should boast.

[10] For we are his workmanship, created in Yeshua Ha'Mashiach unto good works, which God hath before ordained that we should walk in them.

[12] That at that time ye were without Christ, being aliens from the commonwealth of Israel, and strangers from the covenants of promise, having no hope, and without God in the world:

[13] But now in Yeshua Ha'Mashiach ye who sometimes were far off are made nigh by the blood of Christ.

[14] For he is our peace, who hath made both one, and hath broken down the middle wall of partition between us;

[19] Now therefore ye are no more strangers and foreigners, but fellow citizens with the saints, and of the household of God;

[20] And are built upon the foundation of the apostles and prophets, Yeshua Ha'Mashiach himself being the chief corner stone;

[21] In whom all the building fitly framed together groweth unto an holy temple in the Most High God:

[22] In whom ye also are built together for a habitation of God through the Spirit.

A WISE KING SEEKS OUT WISDOM

These are also proverbs of Solomon, which the men of Hezekiah king of Judah copied out. Proverbs 25:1

Knowledge

The men of Judah sought after the knowledge and used many proverbs as precepts to statutes written by King Solomon to increase in wisdom.

Understanding

The men of Judah mouth spoke of wisdom as their meditation of heart became of understanding. Understanding came by virtue of the law to walk in the statutes with further insight of the proverbs written by Solomon for fear and reverence of the Most High.

Discretion

The men of Judah gained great insight for discretion as to deal with people, how to speak, and behave when discerning the foolish from the wise.

Equity

The men of Judah became equitable, making sure all the children of Israel came together to keep the feast of Passover as they were pardoned from their sins to restore life and peace among their brethren. No matter the sins committed. The Most High was equitable to not cast away his people who he hid his face from after confession was made.

Justice

The men of Judah established justice as Hezekiah made a decree that all the house of Israel are to come together and turn away wrath of Yah from being stiff-necked and make confession before the Most High.

Judgment

Solomon sought out the Most High for an understanding heart to judge the people as the men of Judah taught the people the word of Yah diligently and judiciously to restore the fear of Yah.

Wisdom

The men of Judah copied out the Proverbs of King Solomon as they received knowledge of the law to increase in understanding, discretion, justice, and judgment fortifying wisdom.

Knowledge of King Solomon passed unto King Hezekiah

2 Chronicles 1:7-10 [7] In that night did God appear unto Solomon, and said unto him, Ask what I shall give thee.

> [8] And Solomon said unto God, Thou hast shewed great mercy unto David my father, and hast made me to reign in his stead.
> [9] Now, O MOST HIGH GOD Almighty Power, let thy promise unto David my father be established: for thou hast made me king over a people like the dust of the earth in multitude.
> [10] Give me now wisdom and knowledge, that I may go out and come in before this people: for who can judge this thy people, that is so great?

Ecclesiasticus 47:13-17 [13] Solomon reigned in a peaceable time, and was honored; for God made all quiet round about him, that he might build an house in his name, and prepare his sanctuary for ever.

> [14] How wise was thou in thy youth and, as a flood, filled with understanding!
> [15] Thy soul covered the whole earth, and thou filledst it with dark parables.
> [16] Thy name went far unto the islands; and for thy peace thou was beloved.
> [17] The countries marvelled at thee for thy songs, and proverbs, and parables, and interpretations.

Proverbs 1:2-10 [2] To know wisdom and instruction; to perceive the words of understanding;

[3] To receive the instruction of wisdom, justice, and judgment, and equity;

[4] To give subtilty to the simple, to the young man knowledge and discretion.

[5] A wise man will hear, and will increase learning; and a man of understanding shall attain unto wise counsels:

[6] To understand a proverb, and the interpretation; the words of the wise, and their dark sayings.

[7] The fear of the MOST HIGH GOD is the beginning of knowledge: but fools despise wisdom and instruction.

[8] My son, hear the instruction of thy father, and forsake not the law of thy mother:

[9] For they shall be an ornament of grace unto thy head, and chains about thy neck.

[10] My son, if sinners entice thee, consent thou not.

2 Chronicles 30:12 [12] Also in Judah the hand of God was to give them one heart to do the commandment of the king and of the princes, by the word of the MOST HIGH GOD.

Understanding

Proverbs 10:1 [1] The proverbs of Solomon. A wise son maketh a glad father: but a foolish son is the heaviness of his mother.

Proverbs 15:20-24 [20]A wise son maketh a glad father: but a foolish man despiseth his mother.

[21] Folly is joy to him that is destitute of wisdom: but a man of understanding walketh uprightly.

[22] Without counsel purposes are disappointed: but in the multitude of counsellors, they are established.

[23] A man hath joy by the answer of his mouth: and a word spoken in due season, how good is it!

[24] The way of life is above to the wise, that he may depart from hell beneath.

Proverbs 7:2-10 [2] Keep my commandments, and live; and my law as the apple of thine eye.

[3] Bind them upon thy fingers, write them upon the table of thine heart.

[4] Say unto wisdom, Thou art my sister; and call understanding thy kinswoman:

[5] That they may keep thee from the strange woman, from the stranger which flattereth with her words.

[6] For at the window of my house I looked through my casement,

[7] And beheld among the simple ones, I discerned among the youths, a young man void of understanding,

[8] Passing through the street near her corner; and he went the way to her house,

[9] In the twilight, in the evening, in the black and dark night:

[10] And, behold, there met him a woman with the attire of an harlot, and subtil of heart.

Proverbs 25:2 [2] It is the glory of God to conceal a thing: but the honor of kings is to search out a matter. So men of Judah copied out these things to make one wise.

Discretion

Proverbs 6:20-26 [20] My son, keep thy father's commandment, and forsake not the law of thy mother:

[21] Bind them continually upon thine heart, and tie them about thy neck.

[22] When thou goest, it shall lead thee; when thou sleepest, it shall keep thee; and when thou awakest, it shall talk with thee.

[23] For the commandment is a lamp; and the law is light; and reproofs of instruction are the way of life:

[24] To keep thee from the evil woman, from the flattery of the tongue of a strange woman.

[25] Lust not after her beauty in thine heart; neither let her take thee with her eyelids.

[26] For by means of a whorish woman a man is brought to a piece of bread: and the adulteress will hunt for the precious life.

Ecclesiasticus 19:22 [22] The knowledge of wickedness is not wisdom, neither at any time the counsel of sinners prudence.

Proverbs 19:23-29 [23] The fear of the MOST HIGH GOD tendeth to life: and he that hath it shall abide satisfied; he shall not be visited with evil.

[24] A slothful man hideth his hand in his bosom, and will not so much as bring it to his mouth again.

[25] Smite a scorner, and the simple will beware: and reprove one that hath understanding, and he will understand knowledge.

[26] He that wasteth his father, and chaseth away his mother, is a son that causeth shame, and bringeth reproach.

[27] Cease, my son, to hear the instruction that causeth to err from the words of knowledge.

[28] An ungodly witness scorneth judgment: and the mouth of the wicked devoureth iniquity.

[29] Judgments are prepared for scorners, and stripes for the back of fools.

Equity

Ecclesiasticus 47:20-22 [20] Thou didst stain thy honor, and pollute thy seed: so that thou broughtest wrath upon thy children, and wast grieved for thy folly.

[21] So the kingdom was divided, and out of Ephraim ruled a rebellious kingdom.

[22] But the Most High God will never leave off his mercy, neither shall any of his works perish, neither will he abolish the posterity of his elect, and the seed of him that loveth him he will not take away: wherefore he gave a remnant unto Jacob, and out of him a root unto David.

2 Chronicles 30:1-2 [1] And Hezekiah sent to all Israel and Judah, and wrote letters also to Ephraim and Manasseh, that they should come to the house of the MOST HIGH GOD at Jerusalem, to keep the Passover unto the MOST HIGH GOD of Israel.

[2] For the king had taken counsel, and his princes, and all the congregation in Jerusalem, to keep the Passover in the second month.

Justice

1 Esdras 1:5-6,13-16 [5] According as David the king of Israel prescribed, and according to the magnificence of Solomon his son: and standing in the temple according to the several dignity of the families of you the Levites, who minister in the presence of your brethren the children of Israel,

[6] Offer the Passover in order, and make ready the sacrifices for your brethren, and keep the Passover according to the commandment of the Most High God, which was given unto Moses.

[13] And set them before all the people: and afterward they prepared for themselves, and for the priests their brethren, the sons of Aaron.

[14] For the priests offered the fat until night: and the Levites prepared for themselves, and the priests their brethren, the sons of Aaron.

[15] The holy singers also, the sons of Asaph, were in their order, according to the appointment of David, to wit, Asaph, Zacharias, and Jeduthun, who was of the king's retinue.

[16] Moreover the porters were at every gate; it was not lawful for any to go from his ordinary service: for their brethren the Levites prepared for them.

Judgment

Ecclesiasticus 32:1-4,7-9,14-18 [1] If thou be made the master of a feast, lift not thyself up, but be among them as one of the rest; take diligent care for them, and so sit down.

[2] And when thou hast done all thy office, take thy place, that thou mayest be merry with them, and receive a crown for thy well ordering of the feast.

[3] Speak, thou that art the elder, for it becometh thee, but with sound judgment; and hinder not musick.

[4] Pour not out words where there is a musician, and shew not forth wisdom out of time.

[7] Speak, young man, if there be need of thee: and yet scarcely when thou art twice asked.

[8] Let thy speech be short, comprehending much in few words; be as one that knoweth and yet holdeth his tongue.

[9] If thou be among great men, make not thyself equal with them; and when ancient men are in place, use not many words.

[14] Whoso feareth the Most High God will receive his discipline; and they that seek him early shall find favor.

[15] He that seeketh the law shall be filled therewith: but the hypocrite will be offended thereat.

[16] They that fear the Most High God shall find judgment, and shall kindle justice as a light.

[17] A sinful man will not be reproved, but findeth an excuse according to his will.

[18] A man of counsel will be considerate; but a strange and proud man is not daunted with fear, even when of himself he hath done without counsel.

2 Chronicles 30:7-9 [7] And be not ye like your fathers, and like your brethren, which trespassed against the MOST HIGH GOD of their fathers, who therefore gave them up to desolation, as ye see.

[8] Now be ye not stiff-necked, as your fathers were, but yield yourselves unto the MOST HIGH GOD, and enter into his sanctuary, which he hath sanctified forever: and serve the MOST HIGH GOD Your Almighty Power, that the fierceness of his wrath may turn away from you.

[9] For if ye turn again unto the MOST HIGH GOD, your brethren and your children shall find compassion before them that lead them captive, so that they shall come again into this land: for the MOST HIGH GOD Your Almighty Power is gracious and merciful, and will not turn away his face from you, if ye return unto him.

Ecclesiasticus 19:24-25 [24] He that hath small understanding, and feareth God, is better than one that hath much wisdom, and transgresseth the law of the Most High.

[25] There is an exquisite subtilty, and the same is unjust; and there is one that turneth aside to make judgment appear; and there is a wise man that justifieth in judgment.

Wisdom of Solomon provided a great feast and sanctification of the people.

2 Chronicles 1:11-13 [11] And God said to Solomon, Because this was in thine heart, and thou hast not asked riches, wealth, or honor, nor the life of thine enemies, neither yet hast asked long life; but hast asked wisdom and knowledge for thyself, that thou mayest judge my people, over whom I have made thee king:

[12] Wisdom and knowledge is granted unto thee; and I will give thee riches, and wealth, and honor, such as none of the kings have had that have been before thee, neither shall there any after thee have the like.

[13] Then Solomon came from his journey to the high place that was at Gibeon to Jerusalem, from before the tabernacle of the congregation, and reigned over Israel.

2 Chronicles 30:22-27 [22] And Hezekiah spake comfortably unto all the Levites that taught the good knowledge of the MOST HIGH GOD: and they did eat throughout the feast seven days, offering peace offerings, and making confession to the MOST HIGH GOD Almighty Power of their fathers.

[23] And the whole assembly took counsel to keep other seven days: and they kept other seven days with gladness.

[24] For Hezekiah king of Judah did give to the congregation a thousand bullocks and seven thousand sheep; and the princes gave to the congregation a thousand bullocks and ten thousand sheep: and a great number of priests sanctified themselves.

[25] And all the congregation of Judah, with the priests and the Levites, and all the congregation that came out of Israel, and the strangers that came out of the land of Israel, and that dwelt in Judah, rejoiced.

[26] So there was great joy in Jerusalem: for since the time of Solomon the son of David king of Israel there was not the like in Jerusalem.

[27] Then the priests the Levites arose and blessed the people: and their voice was heard, and their prayer came up to his holy dwelling place, even unto heaven.

THE LAW & TESTIMONY

And Moses said unto YAH, Behold, when I come unto the children of Israel, and shall say unto them, The Most High God of your fathers hath sent me unto you; and they shall say to me, What is his name? what shall I say unto them? And YAH said unto Moses, I Am That I Am: and he said, Thus shalt thou say unto the children of Israel, I Am hath sent me unto you.

And YAH said moreover unto Moses, Thus shalt thou say unto the children of Israel, the Almighty God of your fathers, the Almighty God of Abraham, the Almighty God of Isaac, and the Almighty God of Jacob, hath sent me unto you: this is my name for ever, and this is my memorial unto all generations. And they shall hearken to thy voice: and thou shalt come, thou and the elders of Israel, unto the king of Egypt, and ye shall say unto him, The Almighty God of the Hebrews hath met with us: and now let us go, we beseech thee, three days' journey into the wilderness, that we may sacrifice to the Most High Our Almighty Power. Exodus 3:13-15, 18

Then YAH said unto Mosheh, Go in unto Pharaoh, and tell him, Thus saith the Almighty God of the Hebrews, Let my people go, that they may serve me. Exodus 9:1

And it came to pass in the first year of the exodus of the children of Yisrael out of Egypt, in the third month, on the sixteenth day of the month, that YAH spoke to Mosheh, saying: 'Come up to Me on the Mount, and I will give you two tables of stone of the Torah and of the commandment, which I have written, that you may teach them.'

2 And Mosheh went up into the mount of YAH, and the splendor of YAH abode on Mount Sinai, and a cloud overshadowed it six days.

3 And He called to Mosheh on the seventh day out of the midst of the cloud, and the appearance of the splendor of YAH was like a flaming fire on the top of the mount.

4 And Mosheh was on the Mount forty days and forty nights, and YAH taught him the earlier and the later history of the division of all the days of the Torah and of the testimony.

5 And He said: 'Incline your heart to every word which I shall speak to you on this mount, and write them in a book in order that their generations may see how I have not forsaken them for all the evil which they have wrought in transgressing the covenant which I establish between Me and you for their generations this day on Mount Sinai.

6 And thus it will come to pass when all these things come upon them, that they will recognize that I am more righteous than they in all their judgments and in all their actions, and they will recognize that I have been truly with them.

7 And do you write for yourself all these words which I declare unto, you this day, for I know their rebellion and their stiff neck, before I bring them into the land of which I swore to their fathers, to Abraham and to Yitschaq and to Yacob, saying: ' Unto your seed will I give a land flowing with milk and honey.

8 And they will eat and be satisfied, and they will turn to strange gods, to (gods) which cannot deliver them from aught of their tribulation: and this witness shall be heard for a witness against them. For they will forget all My commandments, (even) all that I command them, and they will walk after the Gentiles, and after their uncleanness, and after their shame, and will serve their gods, and these will prove unto them an offence and a tribulation and an affliction and a snare. 10 And many will perish and they will be taken captive, and will fall into the hands of the enemy, because they have forsaken My ordinances and My commandments, and the festivals of My covenant, and My Shabbats, and My kodesh place which I have hallowed for Myself in their midst, and My tabernacle, and My sanctuary, which I have hallowed for Myself in the midst of the land, that I should set MY NAME upon it, and that it should dwell (there). **Jubilees 1:1-10**

Speak unto the children of Israel, and say unto them, Concerning the feasts of the Most High God, which ye shall proclaim to be holy convocations, even these are my feasts. Leviticus 23

Three times thou shalt keep a feast unto me in the year. Thou shalt keep the feast of unleavened bread: (thou shalt eat unleavened bread seven days, as I commanded thee, in the time appointed of the month Abib; for in it thou camest out from Egypt: and none shall appear before me empty:)

And the feast of harvest, the first fruits of thy labors, which thou hast sown in the field: and the feast of ingathering, which is in the end of the year, when thou hast gathered in thy labors out of the field.

Three times in the year all thy males shall appear before the Most High God. Exodus 23:14-17

This profound observational study serves as a powerful reminder that keeping the commandments holds a profound promise—a promise to awaken the consciousness of souls on Earth to the prospect of an immortal life. It is through the meticulous observation of calendar systems that we strive to reconstruct what was once lost after the dispersion of the 12 tribes to the four corners of the Earth.

In my journey of constructing a Hebrew calendar, I offer a guide that can elevate our understanding and enhance our studies, particularly in the context of observing the appointed feasts according to the seasons. These feasts are not mere traditions; they are an everlasting covenant, a pathway to an immortal existence, and a commitment to obey the ordinances, laws, and statutes of the Most High God.

This endeavor is not just about dates and calculations; it is a quest for enlightenment in the lunar-solar calendar, a celestial tapestry woven from the movements of the sun, moon, and stars. It is a testament to the glory of YAH's everlasting kingdom of gods, a journey of discovery, and a pursuit of wisdom and understanding.

Hebrew Appointed Times
Holy Days 2022-2023

FEAST OF PURIM

March 1 - 3, 2022 @ 2:00pm
Celebrate 13th - 15th day of 12th Month

BEGINNING OF MONTHS EVEN NEW YEAR

March 18, 2022 @ 7:00 am
Prepare to Clean Leaven Out of House
Celebrate 1st day of 1st Month

PASSOVER

March 31, 2022 @ 8:00 pm
Prepare to Eat Unleavened Bread for 8 days
Celebrate 14th day of 1st Month
April 30, 2022 @ 8:00 pm (2nd Month)

FESTIVAL OF UNLEAVENED BREAD

April 1 - April 7, 2022 @ 2:00 pm
No Servile Work On April 1st & 7th
Eat Unleavened Bread For 7 days
Wave Offering
Men Present First Fruits Offering
April 2, 2022 @ 2:00 pm
Celebrate 15th - 21st day of 1st Month

FESTIVAL OF WEEKS (PENTECOST)

May 31, 2022 @ 2:00 pm
No Servile Work On This Day

Wave Offering
Men Present First Fruits Offering
Celebrate 16th day of 3rd Month

MEMORIAL OF TRUMPETS

September 10, 2022 @ 2:00 pm
No Servile Work On This Day
Celebrate 1st day of 7th Month
Observe at night and day

DAY OF ATONEMENT

Afflict Your Soul on September 18, 2022 @ 8:00 pm
Celebrate Feast on September 19, 2022 @ 8:00 pm
No Work on 10th day even start of fasting
Begin and End Fast
from the going down of sun (9th day)
unto same of the 10th day
Celebrate 10th day of 7th Month at going down of sun

FESTIVAL OF TABERNACLES/SUKKOT/INGATHERING

September 24 - 30, 2022 @ 2:00pm
No Servile Work On October 5th & 11th
Men Present First Fruits Offering
Celebrate 15th - 21st day of 7th Month

LAST GREAT DAY (8TH DAY FEAST)

October 1, 2022 @ 2:00pm
No Servile Work On This Day
Celebrate 22nd day of 7th Month

MEMORIALS OF OBSERVANCE

LED CAPTIVE BY FAMINE AND BABYLON'S ARMY (FAST OF 4TH MONTH)

June 23, 2022 @ 2:00 pm
Free Will Offering - Affliction of Fasting
Day Of Observance (2 Ki 25:4-7)
9th Day of 4th Month

DESTRUCTION OF TEMPLE, ROYAL HOUSES & WALLS OF JERUSALEM (FAST OF 5TH MONTH)

July 20, 2022 @ 2:00 pm
Free Will Offering - Affliction of Fasting
Day Of Observance (2 Ki 25:8-23)
7th Day of 5th Month

CONSECRATION FOR SET-APART SPIRIT (FAST OF 7TH MONTH)

October 3, 2022 @ 2:00 pm
Free Will Offering - Affliction of Fasting
Day Of Observance (Nehemiah 9:1-21)
24th Day of 7th Month

FEAST OF DEDICATION

December 2 - 8, 2022 @ 2:00pm
Celebrate 25th of 9th Month (7 days)

JERUSALEM COMPASSED WITH ARMIES (FAST OF 10TH MONTH)

December 17, 2022 @ 2:00 pm
Free Will Offering - Affliction of Fasting
Day Of Observance (2 Ki 25:1-2, Lk 21:20)
10th Day of 10th Month

PURIM

February 18 - 20, 2023 @ 2:00pm
Celebrate 13th - 15th day of 12th Month

	Spring		Summer		Fall		Winter	
2022	Mar 20	11:30 am EDT	Jun 21	5:13 am EDT	Sep 22	9:03 pm EDT	Dec 21	4:48 pm EST

NEW MOONS OF 2022-2023

Celebrate Every Month @ 7:30 PM

Month	Full Moon Date	Native American Name	Time of Full Moon
1	March 18	Worm Moon	2:17 am
2	April 16	Pink Moon	2:55 PM
3	May 16	Flower Moon	12:14 PM
4	Jun 14	Strawberry Moon	7:51 AM
5	Jul 13	Buck Moon	2:40 PM
6	Aug 11	Sturgeon Moon	10:37 PM
7	Sep 10	Harvest Moon	8:02 AM
8	Oct 9	Full Corn Moon	7:55 PM
9	Nov 8	Hunter's Moon	10:57 AM
10	Dec 7	Beaver Moon	3:57 AM
11	Jan 6	Cold Moon	6:07 PM
12	Feb 5	Wolf Moon	1:28 PM
13	Mar 7	Snow Moon	7:40 AM

2022-2023

ECLIPSES IN 2022

Apr 30, 2022

April 30, 2022 Partial Solar Eclipse

Visible in South/West South America, Pacific, Atlantic, Antarctica.

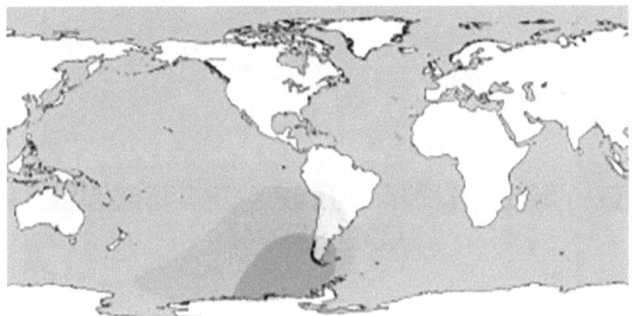

May 15–16, 2022

May 15–16, 2022 Total Lunar Eclipse

Visible in South/West Europe, South/West Asia, Africa, Much of North America, South America, Pacific, Atlantic, Indian Ocean, Antarctica.

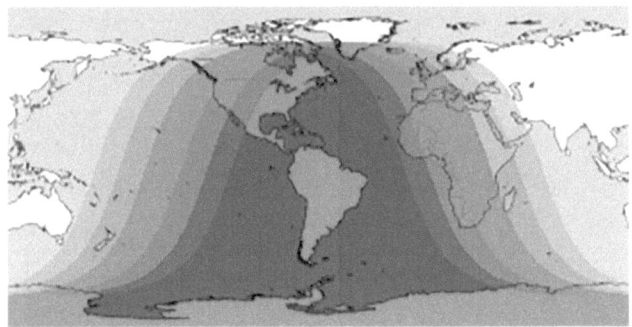

Oct 25, 2022

October 25, 2022 Partial Solar Eclipse

Visible in Europe, South/West Asia, North/East Africa, Atlantic.

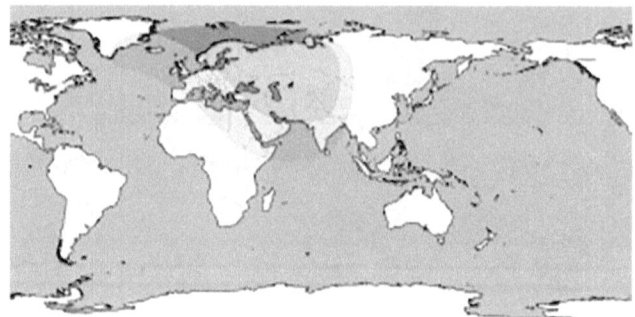

SEVEN YEAR ECLIPSE PATTERN CROSSES OVER USA (2017 - 2024)

Aug 21 of 2017

Solar Eclipse (Total)West in Europe, North/East Asia, North/West Africa, North America, Much of South

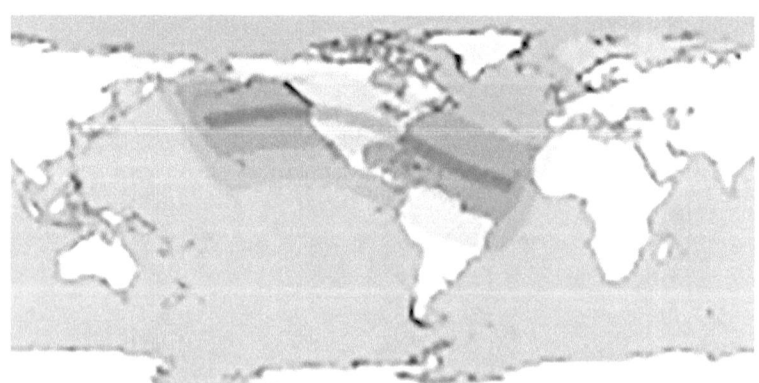

America, Pacific, Atlantic, Arctic

Oct 14 of 2023

Solar Eclipse (Annular)West in Africa, North America,
South America, Pacific, Atlantic, Arctic

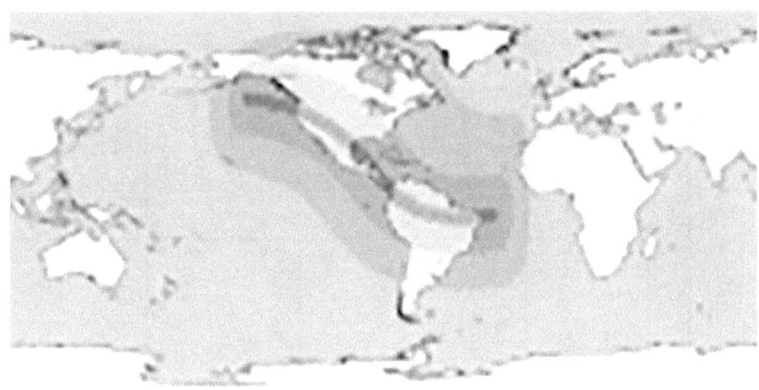

Apr 8 of 2024

Solar Eclipse (Total)West in Europe, North America,
North in South America, Pacific, Atlantic, Arctic

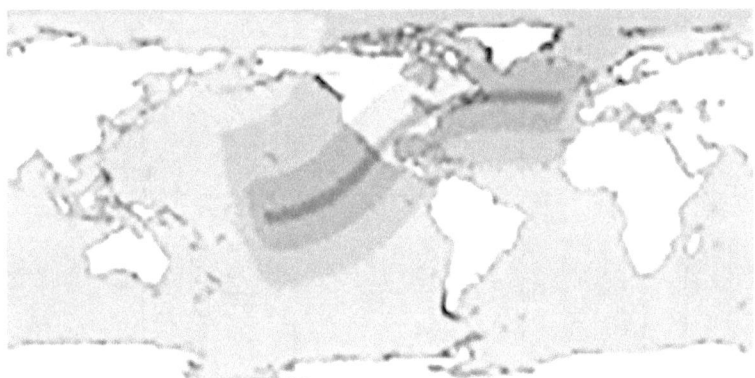

APPOINTED TIMES: ANNUAL FEAST CALENDAR

The Exodus - Red Sea Crossing
Gen. 47:6, Ex. 12:37, 13:20, 14:2

	2	3	4	5	6	7	1 (New Moon)
							1 (New Moon)
	2	3 (A lamb for a house) Exodus 12:3	4	5	6	7	8
	9	10	11	12	13	14 (Passover) Ex. 12:6, Lev. 23:5-8, Num. 33:5-8	15 (1st Day of Unleavened Bread) Ex. 12:18, Num 33:1-3
	16 (Desert of Shur) Ex. 15:22	17 (Desert of Shur)	18 (Desert of Shur)	19	20	21 (7th day of Unleavened Bread)	22
1 week	23 (First Fruits of Harvest) Lev. 23:10-14	24	25	26	27	28	29

Wilderness Crossing

	1 (New Moon)	2	3	4	5	6	7
2nd Week	8 (14 days)	9	10	11	12	13	14 (2nd Passover) Num 9:11
3rd Week	15 (Wilderness of Sin) Ex. 16:1	16 (Quail @ Even & Manna @ Morning) Ex. 16:13-16	17	18	19	20	21
4th Week	22 (28 days)	23	24	25	26	27	28
5th Week	29 (35 days)						

Mount Sinai - Pentecost 50 days

	1 (New Moon)	2	3	4	5	6	7
6th Week	8 (42 days)	9	10	11	12	13	14 (Wilderness of Sinai) Ex. 19:1-16
7th Week	15 (49 days)	16 (Feast of Weeks) Lev. 23:14-17, 21-22	17	18	19	20	21
	22	23	24	25	26	27	28
	29						

Ingathering - End of Harvest

1 (Feast of Trumpets) Lev 23:24	2	3	4	5	6	7
8	9	10 (Day of Atonement) Lev 23:27-32	11	12	13	14
15 (1st Day of Tabernacles) Lev. 23:34-35	16	17	18	19	20	21 (7th day of Tabernacles) Lev 23:36-43
22 (Eighth Day) Lev 23:39	23	24	25	26	27	28
29	30					

4 Blessed winds: 2nd, 5th, 8th, 11th

8 Cursed winds: 1st, 3rd, 4th, 6th, 7th, 9th, 10th, 12th

Portal	Month	Solar Winds	Day	Night	Solar Days	Season	Enoch
4th east	1st	desolation, drought, heat, and destruction	9 parts	9 parts	30	summer (spring)	72:32-35
5th east	2nd	fragrant smells, and dew and rain, prosperity and health	10 parts	8 parts	30	summer (spring)	72:7-11
6th east	3rd	cold and drought	11 parts	7 parts	31	summer (spring)	72:11-14
6th west	4th	hot wind	12 parts	6 parts	30	summer	72:14-16
5th east	5th	fragrant smells, and dew and rain, prosperity and health	11 parts	7 parts	30	summer	72:17-18
4th east	6th	dew, rain, locusts and desolation	10 parts	8 parts	31	summer	72:18-20
3rd east	7th	dew and rain, locusts and desolation	9 parts	9 parts	30	winter (fall)	72:20-23
2nd east	8th	health, rain, dew and prosperity	8 parts	10 parts	30	winter (fall)	72:23-24
1st east	9th	cloud, hoar-frost, snow, rain, dew, and locusts	7 parts	11 parts	31	winter (fall)	72:24-26
2nd east	10th	dew, hoar-frost, cold, snow, and frost	6 parts	12 parts	30	winter	72:26-29
2nd east	11th	dew and rain, and prosperity and blessing	7 parts	11 parts	30	winter	72:29-31
3rd east	12th	drought, desolation, burning, and destruction	8 parts	10 parts	31	winter	72:31-34
After days of following sun for 7 days light, 8th day enter 6th portal for 7 days, enter 5th portal for 7 days to complete							

Beginnings	Constellations	Division of Months	Enoch 82	Enoch 33:1-4
1st Month	Yah'Hudah	I praise Yah	Melkejal	rises first and rules, who is named Tam'aini and sun
2nd Month	Don	Yah hath judged me, and hath also heard my voice	Melkejal	"sweat, and heat, and calms; and all the trees bear fruit, and leaves are produced on all the trees, and the harvest of wheat, and the rose-flowers, and all the flowers which come forth in the field, but the trees of the winter season become withered"
3rd Month	Naph'Ta'Lee	With great wrestlings have I wrestled and I have prevailed	Melkejal	Begining of year = Melkejal rises 1st to rule for 91 days, sweat, heat, calms, trees bear fruit, leaves on trees, harvest of wheat, rose flowers, and all flowers come forth and trees ripen fruits,
4th Month	God	A troop cometh	Hel'emmelek	the shining sun
5th Month	Yah'Seer	Happy am I	Hel'emmelek	"glowing heat and dryness, and the trees ripen their fruits and produce all their fruits ripe and ready, and the sheep pair and become pregnant, and all the fruits of the earth are gathered in, and everything that is 20 in the fields, and the winepress"
6th Month	Yitz'Ah'Kar	Yah hath given me my hire	Hel'emmelek	
7th Month	Zebulun	Yah hath endued me with a good dowry	Mel'ejal	

Beginnings	Constellations	Division of Months	Enoch 82	Enoch 33:1-4
8th Month	Yah'Hasef	Yah hath taken away my reproach; The MOST HIGH GOD shall add to me another son.	Mel'ejal	
9th Month	Ben'Yah'meen	Son of my right hand	Mel'ejal	
10th Month	Re'Ubeen	Yah hath looked upon my affliction; now my husband will love me.	Narel	Adnar'el, and Ijasusa'el, and 'Elome'elech leaders
11th Month	Sim'Ee'on	Be joined unto me	Narel	Milki'el, Hel'emmelek, and Mel'ejal, 14 and Narel.
12th Month	Lee'Vy	Yah hath heard that I was hated, he hath given me this son also	Narel	

PROPHETIC TIMES

					4TH
			Enoch 77	seas of water, the abysses, forests,	
		Dwelling of Men			Zechariah 2:6-13,
					North
			near west (3rd portal)		middle (2nd
			3rd wind	cloud, hoar-frost, snow, rain, dew, and locusts	2nd wind
THE DIMENISHED 3RD QTR		Enoch 76:12	9		8
		West			
		near north (1st portal)			
Revelation 8:6-13	dew, hoar-frost, cold, snow, and frost	1st wind	10		
Ezekiel 5:5-15		middle (2nd portal)	11		
	dew and rain, and prosperity and blessing	2nd wind			
		near south (3rd portal)	12		
	drought, desolation, burning, and destruction	3rd wind			
			6		5
					South
			near west (3rd portal)		middle (2nd
			3rd wind	dew, rain, locusts and desolation	2nd wind
					Deuteronomy 33:2;
					THE MOST HIGH AND
					2ND

QTR				Enoch 77	
rivers, darkness and clouds				7 High Mountains	
6:5-15	Garden of Righteousness			7 Great Rivers	
Enoch 76:10-11				7 Great Islands	
portal)	near east (1st portal)				
health, rain, dew and prosperity	1st wind	dew and rain, locusts and desolation			
	7				
			East	Enoch 76:5-6	1ST QTR
			near north (3rd portal)		
		3	3rd wind	cold and drought	Isaiah 24:1-23
			middle (2nd portal)		Zechariah 14:16-21
		2	2nd wind	rain and fruitfulness and prosperity and dew	
			near south (1st portal)		
		1	1st wind	desolation, drought, heat, and destruction.	
		4			
	Enoch 76:7-8				
portal)		near east (1st portal)			
fragrant smells, and dew and rain, prosperity and health		1 wind	hot wind		
Daniel 12:3					
SAINTS SHALL DESCEND					
QTR					

			Enoch 78:1-3	sun: Orjares	moon: Asonja
Enoch 33:1-4	Uriel gives laws and ordinances				
Enoch 34:1-3	3 north portals blow cold weather hail, frost, snow, dew, and rain.		one portal blows for good (bless wind)	two portals blows violence and affliction on the earth (curse wind)	
Enoch 35:1	"3 west portals as I had seen in the east and the same number of outlets."				
Enoch 36:1	3 south portals blow dew, rain, and wind.				
Enoch 36:1	3 east portals	3 small portals above has stars that run their course to the west portal			
Enoch 60:12-23	breakdown of the portals releasing winds and climate change				
Enoch 72:1,5-11	law of luminaries, 6 portals rise and 6 portal sets		sun leaves the north portal to enter east portal		
Enoch 74:1-4					

Enoch 75:1-4	4 intercalendary days + 360 days = 364 days	
Enoch 77:1-8	4 quarters of the Earth: 1) east, 2) south, 3) west (desolation), 4) north divided into 3 parts	1) dwelling of men, 2) clouds, rivers, forests, abyss, seas 3) garden of righteousness
	Most High will descend on the south	
	7 rivers: 1) flows from west to Great Sea 2) Two rivers flow from east to Erythraean Sea 3) four rivers from north flow to Great Sea & Erythraean Sea	
Enoch 78:1-2	And the names of the sun are the following: the first Orjârês, and the second Tômâs. 2. And the moon has four names: the first name is Asônjâ, the second Eblâ, the third Benâsê, and the fourth Erâe	
Gen 1:14	After completion of light, she enters 4th portal for 7 days, enters 1st portal on 8th day and returns to forth portal for 7 days	

A solar year — the time it takes Earth to orbit the sun — lasts around 365 days, while a lunar year, or 12 full cycles of the Moon, is roughly 354 days.... In these updated calendars, a month is still defined by the moon, but an extra month is added periodically to stay close to the solar year.

"The annual calendar is set by the alignment of both the monthly lunar cycle and the annual solar cycle. The lunar cycle sets the seasons based on the solar equinoctial cycle. The moon and sun together are governing signs. Appointed Year (beginning of months) begins 1st month (Exodus 12:1-2; Deuteronomy 16:1).

This passage clearly sets the full moon apart as the main marker of the seasons, while the sun is to mark the day. The full moon reflects the light of the Sun as a confirmation throughout the month as it waxes full and wanes empty that the created order is not chaotic. Its visible rebirth each month is very orderly and precise, but not absolutely predictable. Therefore, each month has a degree of expectancy about it.

Genesis 8:22 While the earth remaineth, seedtime and harvest, and cold and heat, and summer and winter, and day and night shall not cease. Psalm 74:17

This is determined from the New Moon a.k.a. full moon nearest to the spring equinox in the Northern Hemisphere, which begins the summer season, full moon on or after the vernal equinox at which time the barley crop will be "in the green" ready for harvest at Passover. This month Abib was to be the first of months and, hence, its determination would set the start and finish of the year and, hence, the updated calendar. The autumnal equinox in the Northern Hemisphere begins the winter season. These are the two seasons mentioned by the Bible which are used to determine the beginning of the year to coincide with the appointed feasts of harvest.

The Spring equinox marks when the Northern Hemisphere starts to tilt toward the sun, which means longer, sunnier days. In the Northern Hemisphere, the Spring equinox is called the vernal equinox, because it signals the beginning of spring (vernal means fresh or new like the spring). __The vernal equinox marks the start of spring, and the autumnal equinox marks the start of fall.__ An equinox is one of the two times of the year when the amount of daylight and nighttime hours are just about of equal length. During the equinox, the sun crosses the plane of Earth's equator, making nighttime and daytime (roughly) equal length all over the world.

NEW YEAR

2022	Sunrise/Sunset		Daylength	
Mar	Sunrise	Sunset	Length	Diff.
16	7:46 am (91°)	7:46 pm (269°)	11:59:36	+2:06
17	7:45 am (91°)	7:46 pm (269°)	12:01:42	+2:06

END OF HARVEST YEAR

2022	Sunrise/Sunset		Daylength	
Sept	Sunrise	Sunset	Length	Diff.
26	7:28 am (91°)	7:28 pm (269°)	12:00:08	-2:04
27	7:29 am (91°)	7:27 pm (268°)	11:58:03	-2:04

DIVISION OF DAYS

Portal	Month	Solar Winds	Day	Night	Solar Days	Season	Enoch
4th east	1st	desolation, drought, heat, and destruction	9 parts	9 parts	30	summer (spring)	72:32-35
5th east	2nd	fragrant smells, and dew and rain, prosperity and health	10 parts	8 parts	30	summer (spring)	72:7-11
6th east	3rd	cold and drought	11 parts	7 parts	31	summer (spring)	72:11-14
6th west	4th	hot wind	12 parts	6 parts	30	summer	72:14-16
5th east	5th	fragrant smells, and dew and rain, prosperity and health	11 parts	7 parts	30	summer	72:17-18
4th east	6th	dew, rain, locusts and desolation	10 parts	8 parts	31	summer	72:18-20
3rd east	7th	dew and rain, locusts and desolation	9 parts	9 parts	30	winter (fall)	72:20-23
2nd east	8th	health, rain, dew and prosperity	8 parts	10 parts	30	winter (fall)	72:23-24
1st east	9th	cloud, hoar-frost, snow, rain, dew, and locusts	7 parts	11 parts	31	winter (fall)	72:24-26
2nd east	10th	dew, hoar-frost, cold, snow, and frost	6 parts	12 parts	30	winter	72:26-29
2nd east	11th	dew and rain, and prosperity and blessing	7 parts	11 parts	30	winter	72:29-31
3rd east	12th	drought, desolation, burning, and destruction	8 parts	10 parts	31	winter	72:31-34

YAH said at the dawn of creation, Let there be lights in the firmament of the heaven to divide the day from the night; and let them be for signs, and for seasons, and for days, and years to give light upon the earth. Gen 1:14

		Division of Months	
Beginnings	Constellations	Division of Months	Enoch 82
1st Month	Yah'Hudah	I praise Yah	Melkejal
2nd Month	Don	Yah hath judged me, and hath also heard my voice	Melkejal
3rd Month	Naph'Ta'Lee	With great wrestlings have I wrestled and I have prevailed	Melkejal
4th Month	God	A troop cometh	Hel'emmelek
5th Month	Yah'Seer	Happy am I	Hel'emmelek
6th Month	Yitz'Ah'Kar	Yah hath given me my hire	Hel'emmelek
7th Month	Zebulun	Yah hath endued me with a good dowry	Mel'ejal
8th Month	Yah'Hasef	Yah hath taken away my reproach; The LORD shall add to me another son.	Mel'ejal
9th Month	Ben'Yah'meen	Son of my right hand	Mel'ejal
10th Month	Re'Ubeen	Yah hath looked upon my affliction; now my husband will love me.	Narel
11th Month	Sim'Ee'on	Be joined unto me	Narel
12th Month	Lee'Vy	Yah hath heard that I was hated, he hath given me this son also	Narel

2022 – 2023 New Moons a.k.a. Full Moons

The beginning of months (1st day of 1st Month) occurs on 3/18/2022

1st Month	Mar 18	29 days	spring/fall	7th Month	Sep 10	29 days
2nd Month	Apr 16	29 days	spring/fall	8th Month	Oct 9	30 days
3rd Month	May 15	30 days	spring/fall	9th Month	Nov 8	30 days
4th Month	Jun 14	29 days	summer/winter	10th Month	Dec 7	30 days
5th Month	Jul 13	29 days	summer/winter	11th Month	Jan 6	30 days
6th Month	Aug 11	30 days	summer/winter	12th Month	Feb 5	30 days
			winter	13th Month	Mar 7	29 days

Psalm 74:17 Thou hast set all the borders of the earth: thou hast made summer and winter.

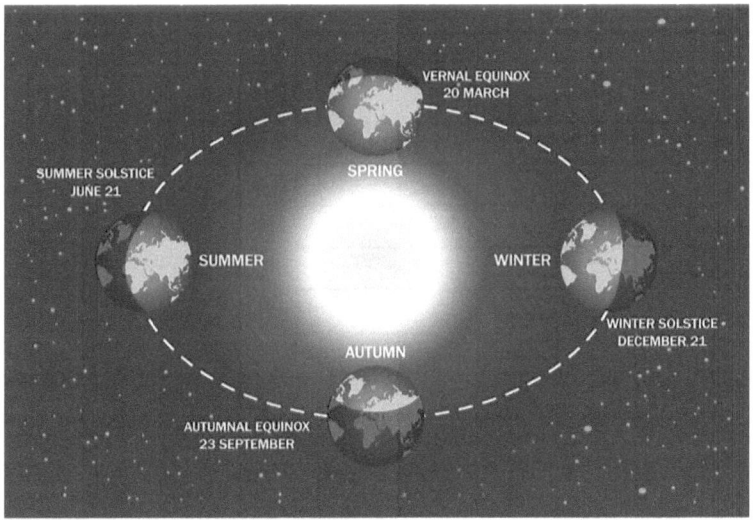

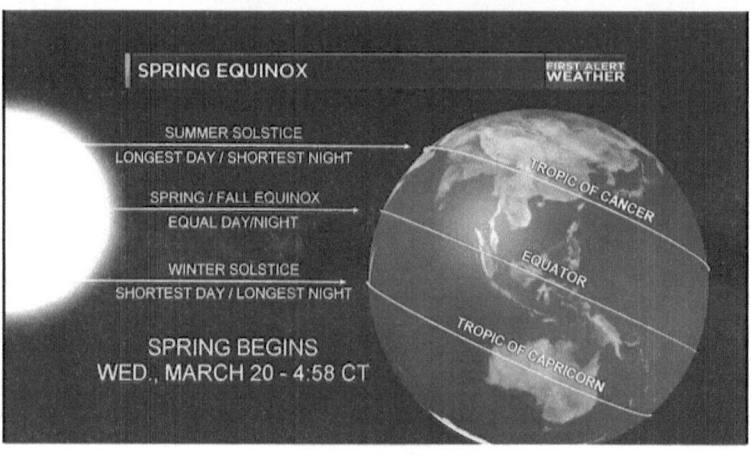

Psalm 104:19 He appointed the moon for seasons: the sun knoweth his going down.

Cycle	Moon	Light
Altering Months	3rd & 4th portal	15 parts
Month 3 & 4	(6) 29/ (6) 30	
Dark		Enoch
		72:6-7; 74:2-3
		74:4
4th portal	7 days	74:5-6
6th portal	8 days	74:6
4th portal	7 days	74:7
5th portal	7 days	74:7-8
	29 days	

Enoch 77:14 And when it is wholly extinguished, its light is consumed in heaven; and on the first day it is called the new moon, for on that day light is received into it.

The first day of the month, that is the New Moon, has special instructions for the New Year of the first day of the First Month. Thus, the Dead Sea Scrolls quite clearly identify the New Moon of the First Month (Abib) as the New Year and as a day of solemn assembly and sacrifice.

These ordinances are followed by the requirements for the seven-day purification of the priesthood, which the Temple Scroll treats as annual, as it is written (Exodus 29:1-35; Leviticus 8-10, 2 Chronicles 29).

"Psalm 81:3-5 Blow up the trumpet in the new moon, in the time appointed, on our solemn feast day. 4 For this was a statute for Israel, and a law of the God of Jacob. 5 This he ordained in Joseph for a testimony, when he went out through the land of Egypt: where I heard a language that I understood not."

Joseph had the power to declare the decree and the people of Egypt, principally the sons of Israel, were delighted to make the recognition of the new moon as a joyful feast. The testimony was to honor Joseph for what he did as a righteous deliverer, who in many ways prefigured the coming Messiah of Israel and the redemption that He would ultimately bring. All Appointed feasts are eternal truths of the Salvation Plan to redeem 12 Tribes of Israel. What Joseph set in place as a testimony, has been established as a "statute for Israel, a law of the Most High God of Jacob"

Numbers 10:10 Also in the day of your gladness, and in your solemn days, and in the beginnings of your months, ye shall blow with the trumpets over your burnt offerings, and over the sacrifices of your peace offerings; that they may be to you for a memorial before Your Almighty Power: I am the Most High God Your Almighty Power.

12 RULERS OF MONTHS				
Chiefs / Captains	Beginnings	KJV	Hebrew Pronunciation	Meaning
Yah'Sho'Bom	1st Month	Jashobeam	(yaw-shob-awm)	People will return
Doda'Ei	2nd Month	Dodai (Dodovah)	(do-dah-ee)	Loving, Amorous (Love of Yah)
Ben'Ah'Yah	3rd Month	Benaiah	(ben-aw-ya)	Yah has built
As'Ah'El	4th Month	Asahel	(as-aw-ale)	Yah has made
Sham'Hooth	5th Month	Shamuth	(sham-hooth)	Desolation
Ei'Rah (Iyra)	6th Month	Ira	(ee-raw)	Wakefulness
Che'Letz	7th Month	Helez	(kheh-lets)	Strength of Yah
Sib'Becha'Ei	8th Month	Sibbechai	(sib-bek-ah-ee)	Weaver
Abi'Ayzer	9th Month	Abiezer	(ab-ee-ay-zer)	My Father of Help
Mahar'Ah'Ei	10th Month	Maharai	(mah-har-ah-ee)	Spontaneous, Hasty, Impulsive
Ben'Ah'Yah	11th Month	Benaiah	(ben-aw-ya)	Yah has built
Chel'Da'Ei	12th Month	Heldai	(kel-da-ee)	Worldly, Experienced, Sophisticated

Numbers 28:11-15 And in the beginnings of your months ye shall offer a burnt offering unto the Most High God; two young bullocks, and one ram, seven lambs of the first year without spot; Moses called the people to assembly on the new moon and spoke to them according to the commandments he had been given by YAH, exhorting them to faith and obedience.

Deuteronomy 1:3 And it came to pass in the fortieth year, in the eleventh month, on the first day of the month, that Moses spake unto the children of Israel, according unto all that the Most High God had given him in commandment unto them;

It is also recorded that YAH chose this sabbatical day to speak to Moses and give him instructions for Israel.

Numbers 1:1-5 And the Most High God spake unto Moses in the wilderness of Sinai, in the tabernacle of the congregation, on the first day of the second month, in the second year after they were come out of the land of Egypt, saying "Jubilees 3:17,32 [17]And after the completion of the seven years, which he had completed there, seven years exactly, [8 A.M.] and in the second month, on the seventeenth day (of the month), the serpent came and approached the woman, and the serpent said to the woman, 'Hath God commanded you, saying, Ye shall not eat of every tree of the garden?' [32] And on the new moon of the fourth month, Adam and his wife went forth from the Garden of Eden, and they dwelt in the land of Elda in the land of their creation." Jasher 9:17; 41:14; 68:4; 88:63; 89:8

"Jubilees 1:13 [13] And they will forget all My law and all My commandments and all My judgments, and will go astray as to new moons, and sabbaths, and festivals, and jubilees, and ordinances." (Enoch 59:5; 64:5; 41:4; 68:28; 71-74, 77-79, 81-82)

"Jubilees 5:17-18, 22 [17] [And of the children of Israel it has been written and ordained: If they turn to him in righteousness, He will forgive all their transgressions and pardon all their sins. [18] It is written and ordained that He will show mercy to all who turn from all their guilt once each year.] [22] And Noah made the ark in all respects as He commanded him, in the twenty-seventh jubilee of years, in the fifth week in the fifth year (on the new moon of the first month). [1307 A.M.]"

The kings of Israel kept the feast of the new moon with its stipulated temple procedure.

- Moses commanded the keeping of the new moons. (2 Chronicles 8:12-13)
- Solomon proclaimed it as an ordinance forever to Israel. (2 Chronicles 2: 3-4)

- Morning and Evening oblations, sabbaths, new moons (1 Chron. 23:31; 2 Chron. 31: 3)
- It was usual during the Temple period to seek guidance from the prophets on the New Moons. (2 Kings 4:23)

"We find a record that Saul held feasts on the new moon, according to the law. When Saul turned against David and he fled and hid in the country, David gave instructions to explain his absence from the feast, indicating that this was a day when David would be missed, if he did not attend the King's table on the New Moon. (1 Samuel 20:4-18, 24)"

"All throughout the scriptures, the New Moon was a day when the prophets heard from YAH, being a day designated for waiting upon YAH, for discerning His purposes and for prophetic revelation. Ezekiel 26:1; 29:17; Haggai 1:1.

There were days of assembly and YAH dealt with Israel at these times, speaking through His servants, the Prophets."

In the New Testament these days are prophetic and foreshadow future events. (Colossians 2:16-17) The celebration of the new moon has great prophetic significance for Israel as the Bride of Yeshua and it was/is an appointed time of His choosing to give prophetic revelation to bring salvation unto His people.

In the restoration of the law under Nehemiah the New Moons were re-instituted and kept from that time through to the destruction of the Temple in 70 CE. Josephus records that they were kept during the entire Temple period and the High Priest attended in the Temple on the New Moons and Sabbaths.

"The word used for New Moon in Hebrew is 'Rosh Chodesh' literally means "beginning, head, or renewal" and thus. the beginning or head of the month. It is a time of spiritual renewal. Deuteronomy 31:9-21, 32:7-43"

The New Moon and the Sabbath were closely linked as both were holy, set-apart days unto Yah and the celebration of the new moon is placed in importance in the scriptures alongside keeping the Sabbath. As written in Numbers 10 as a celebration based upon the testimony of Yah's people being redeemed as His luminaries in the world. Yah called Israel to be a light to the Gentiles, a holy, set-apart nation which reflected His glorious light (Exodus 19:4-6, 10-11; 1 Peter 2: 4-5). At the beginning of each month they were called to come aside from their normal functions for existence in this world, to reflect upon their ordained purpose of reflecting His presence in the world and revitalizing their spiritual lives in Him.

Joseph was given a dream of the sun, moon and stars as it related to their initial household of faith (Gen. 37: 9). This is the fulfillment of Revelation 12 the woman (Zion "Saints of Most High") arrayed with the glory of the sun (representing the glory of the Father), with her feet standing upon the moon (the reflected light of the sun), and the deputation of the twelve stars of His government assigned to her. This portrays that the woman (Yeshua's Bride) in the end days will have come into the glory of the Father in her witness and testimony as the light-bearer of the Son (sun) in her earthly commission (standing upon the moon - i.e., established in her testimony as being THE light to this world).

As His Bride keeps this feast of her appointment with Yeshua and comes into alignment with Him, she will reflect His light even the Morningstar

It is a time of fresh dedication of ourselves to our Heavenly Father and of blessing Him and seeking His direction for the new month ahead. We also take this time to ask His blessings on the planned endeavors for the coming month.

These days are sanctified or set apart as days of sacrifice, for worship, for assembly and for us to make our spiritual offerings to Yahweh. (2 Chronicles 2:4; Nehemiah 10:33; Ezekiel 44:24; 45:17)

It is now a spiritual worship in a spiritual Temple, which makes it more powerful and just as important, as now we see its real significance in preparing us for the kingdom to come. Deuteronomy 30:10-20

Traditionally there is singing and dancing in celebration of the occasion, and the partaking of a festive meal together with suggested scripture reading of Deuteronomy 4: 7-9; Psalm 104; and Psalm 81

The New Moon of Trumpets (Yom Teruah) was also a day of restoration (or reading) of the Law of Yah. (Nehemiah 8: 2, Deuteronomy 29:9-21)

A cleansing process began in the physical temple with the commencement of the new year and this points towards the spiritual cleansing of the spiritual Temple. We are that spiritual Temple and the process of cleansing begins with us on the First New Moon of each year as a preparation for the coming Passover season. It then is repeated throughout the year from New Moon to New Moon as we each come before Yah and renew our life in Him. (Ezekiel 45:18; Numbers 28:11) This will continue in the 1000-year reign of Yeshua. (Isaiah 66:22-23)

The New Moons of the other months of the year are similar to Sabbath days in which no trade or unnecessary work is done. (Amos 8:5; Nehemiah 10:31) [work which has to be done is allowed on the new moon]

The example below shows a 29-day lunar cycle, 1st day of 5th month beginning on June 14, 2022.

Notice how the 14th- 16th are the darkest days of the month. Just as Yeshua was cut off in the midst of the week and confirmed the covenant; causing sacrifice and oblation to cease. (Daniel 9:24-27) He is the head of the church, the firstborn of the dead, proclaimed the "Lamb of God" sent from Heaven to redeem the world from sin and by his blood (Our Passover) a Covenant of an Endless Life sealed unto the day of redemption for them that believe.

CREATION CALENDAR

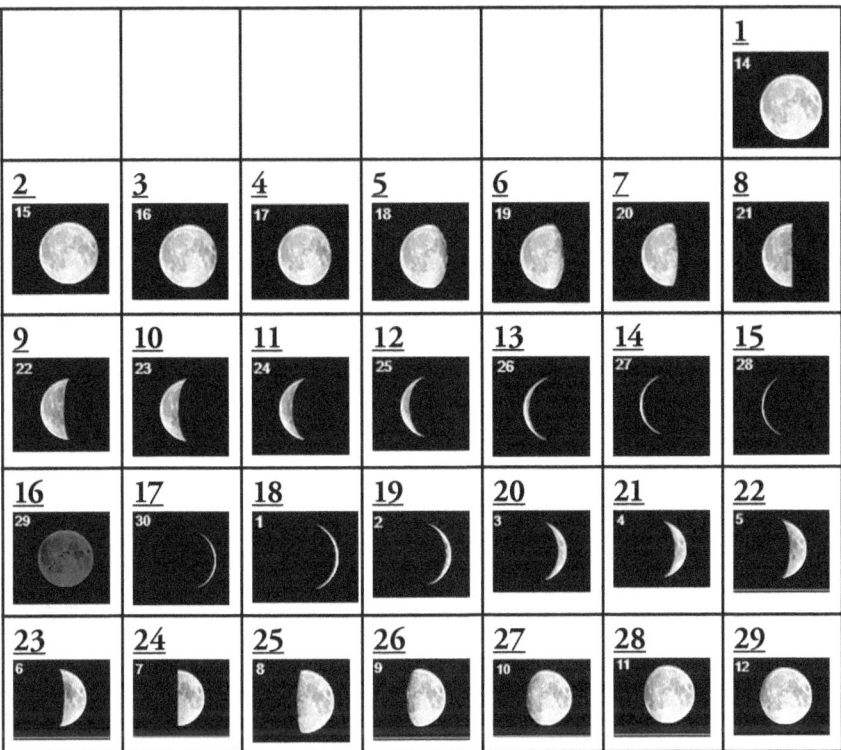

1 Corinthians 5:7-8 Purge out therefore the old leaven, that ye may be a new lump, as ye are unleavened. **For even Christ our Passover is sacrificed for us:** 8 *Therefore let us keep the feast, not with old leaven, neither with the leaven of malice and wickedness*; but with the **unleavened bread of sincerity and truth**.

Hebrews 10:14-25 *For by one offering he hath perfected forever them that are sanctified.* 15 Whereof the Holy Ghost also is a witness to us: for after that he had said before, 16 This is the covenant that I will make with them after those days, saith the Most High God, **I will put my laws into their hearts**, and **in their minds will I write them**; 17 *And their sins and iniquities will I remember no more.* 18 **Now where remission of these is, there is no more offering for sin.**

Appointed Times

Seasons	Lunar Days	Beginnings	Chiefs / Captains	1 Chronicles 27	
summer (spring)	29	1st Month	Yah'Sho'Bom	People will return	
summer (spring)	29	2nd Month	Doda'Ei	Loving, Amorous (Love of Yah)	
summer (spring)	29	3rd Month	Ben'Ah'Yah	Yah has built	
summer	30	4th Month	As'Ah'El	Yah has made	
summer	30	5th Month	Sham'Hooth	Desolation	
summer	30	6th Month	Ei'Rah (Iyra)	Wakefulness	
winter (fall)	30	7th Month	Che'Letz	Strength of Yah	
winter (fall)	30	8th Month	Sib'Becha'Ei	Weaver	
winter (fall)	30	9th Month	Abi'Ayzer	My Father of Help	
winter	29	10th Month	Mahar'Ah'Ei	Spontaneous, Hasty, Impulsive	
winter	29	11th Month	Ben'Ah'Yah	Yah has built	
winter	29	12th Month	Chel'Da'Ei	Worldly, Experienced, Sophisticated	
	177	177		354 lunar	364 solar
				3 years	3 years
				1062 + 30 =	1092
	new moon (full)	14/14	Enoch 78:10-12	addition of 13th month once every 3 years	
	30th day	15 parts of light			
	29th day	14/14			
	takes place for 127 days in the first portal in its season				
	waning occurs in 6 portals		25 weeks & 2 days		
			Enoch 79		

He appointed the moon for seasons: the sun knoweth his going down.
Psalm 104:19

19 Having therefore, brethren, **boldness to enter into the holiest by the blood of Yeshua**, 20 *By a new and living way, which he hath consecrated for us, through the veil, that is to say, his flesh*; 21 And having a **high priest over the house of God**; 22 Let us draw near with a **true heart in full assurance of faith,** having our hearts sprinkled from an evil conscience, and our bodies washed with pure water. 23 Let us hold fast the profession of our faith without wavering; (for he is faithful that promised;) 24 And let us **consider one another to provoke unto love and to good works**: 25 Not forsaking the assembling of ourselves together, as the manner of some is; but exhorting one another: and so much the more, as ye see the day approaching.

The next day John seeth Yeshua coming unto him, and saith, **Behold the Lamb of God, which taketh away the sin of the world. John 1:29, 1:36**

John 6:32-35, 48-58 I am the living bread which came down from heaven: if any man eat of this bread, he shall live forever: and *the bread that I will give is my flesh, which I will give for the life of the world.* **Whoso eateth my flesh, and drinketh my blood, hath eternal life;** and **I will raise him up at the last day.**

Ephesians 1:3-7 Blessed be the Most High God and Father of our Redeemer Yeshua Ha'mashiach, who hath blessed us with all spiritual blessings in heavenly places in Christ: 4 *According as he hath chosen us in him before the foundation of the world, that we should be holy and without blame before him in love*: 5 Having predestinated us unto the adoption of children by Yeshua Ha'mashiach to himself, according to the good pleasure of his will, 6 To the praise of the glory of his grace, wherein he hath made us accepted in the beloved. 7 **In whom we have redemption through his blood, the forgiveness of sins, according to the riches of his grace;**

Matthew 26:26-30 And as they were eating, Yeshua took bread, and blessed it, and brake it, and gave it to the disciples, and said, **Take, eat; this is my body.** 27 And he took the cup, and gave thanks, and gave it to them, saying, Drink ye all of it; 28 **For this is my blood of the new testament, which is shed for many for the remission of sins.** 29 But I say unto you, I will not drink henceforth of this fruit of the vine, until that day when *I drink it new with you in my Father's kingdom.* 30 And when *they had sung an hymn,* they went out into the mount of Olives.

John 6:53 Then Yeshua said unto them, Verily, verily, I say unto you, **Except ye eat the flesh of the Son of man, and drink his blood, ye have no life in you.**

Revelation 5:8-10 And when he had taken the book, the four beasts and four and twenty elders fell down before the Lamb, having every one of them harps, and *golden vials full of odors, which are the prayers of saints.* 9 And *they sung a new song,* saying, Thou art worthy to take the book, and to open the seals thereof: for thou wast slain, and hast <u>redeemed us to God by thy blood out of every kindred, and tongue, and people, and nation</u>; 10 *And hast made us unto Our Almighty Power kings and priests: and we shall reign on the earth.*

Jubilees 2:8 [8] These four great works God created on the third day. And on the fourth day He created the sun and the moon and the stars, and set them in the firmament of the heaven, to give light upon all the earth, and to rule over the day and the night, and divide the light from the darkness.

Jasher 9:17 [17] And Abram saw the stars and moon before him, and he said, Surely this is the Most High God who created the whole earth as well as man, and behold these his servants are gods around him: and Abram served the moon and prayed to it all that night.

Ordinance of Day and Night

Portal	Light	29 Days (3 Months)	Enoch	Light	30 Days (3 Months)	Enoch
4th east	14 parts (east)	1st	78:15-17	14 parts (east)	1st	78:8, 12-13
4th east	13 parts (east)	2nd	74:5-6	13 parts (east)	2nd	78:8
4th east	12 parts (east)	3rd	74:5-6	12 parts (east)	3rd	78:8
4th east	11 parts (east)	4th	74:5-6	11 parts (east)	4th	78:8
4th east	10 parts (east)	5th	74:5-6	10 parts (east)	5th	78:8
4th east	9 parts (east)	6th	74:5-6	9 parts (east)	6th	78:8
4th east	8 parts (east)	7th	74:5-6	8 parts (east)	7th	78:8
6th west	7 parts (west)	8th	74:6	7 parts (west)	8th	78:8
6th west	6 parts (west)	9th	74:6	6 parts west)	9th	78:8
6th west	5 parts (west)	10th	74:6	5 parts (west)	10th	78:8
6th west	4 parts (west)	11th	74:6	4 parts (west)	11th	78:8
6th west	3 parts (west)	12th	74:6	3 parts (west)	12th	78:8
6th west	2 parts (west)	13th	74:6	2 parts (west)	13th	78:8
6th west	1 part (west)	14th	74:6	1 part (west)	14th	78:8
6th west	0 parts	15th	74:6	0 parts	15th	78:8

Covenant of Day and Night: Thus saith the Lord, which giveth the sun for a light by day, and the ordinances of the moon and of the stars for a light by night...
Jer 31:35

Ordinance of Day and Night

Portal	Light	29 Days (3 Months)	Enoch	Light	30 Days (3 Months)	Enoch
4th east	1 part (east)	16th	74:7	1 part (east)	16th	78:10-11
4th east	2 parts (east)	17th	74:7	2 parts (east)	17th	78:14
4th east	3 parts (east)	18th	74:7	3 parts (east)	18th	78:14
4th east	4 parts (east)	19th	74:7	4 parts (east)	19th	78:14
4th east	5 parts (east)	20th	74:7	5 parts (east)	20th	78:14
4th east	6 parts (east)	21th	74:7	6 parts (east)	21th	78:14
4th east	7 parts (east)	22th	74:7	7 parts (east)	22th	78:14
5th west	8 parts (west)	23th	74:7-8	8 parts (west)	23th	78:14
5th west	9 parts (west)	24th	74:7-8	9 parts (west)	24th	78:14
5th west	10 parts (west)	25th	74:7-8	10 parts (west)	25th	78:14
5th west	11 parts (west)	26th	74:7-8	11 parts (west)	26th	78:14
5th west	12 parts (west)	27th	74:7-8	12 parts (west)	27th	78:14
5th west	13 parts (west)	28th	74:7-8	13 parts (west)	28th	78:14
5th west	14 parts (west)	29th	78:15-17	14 parts (west)	29th	78:14
5th west				15 parts (west)	30th	73:4-6, 78:7

20 Thus saith the Lord; If ye can break my covenant of the day, and my covenant of the night, and that there should not be day and night in their season;

21 Then may also my covenant be broken with David my servant, that he should not have a son to reign upon his throne; and with the Levites the priests, my ministers. Jer 33:20-21

Full Moon – a.k.a. biblical new moon (luminous) the brightest phase of the moon in which its whole disk is illuminated. (1st day of month)

New Moon – a.k.a. black moon (dark side of moon) is the darkest phase of the moon when it is in conjunction with the sun and invisible from earth, or shortly thereafter when it appears as a slender crescent. (14th or 15th day of month)

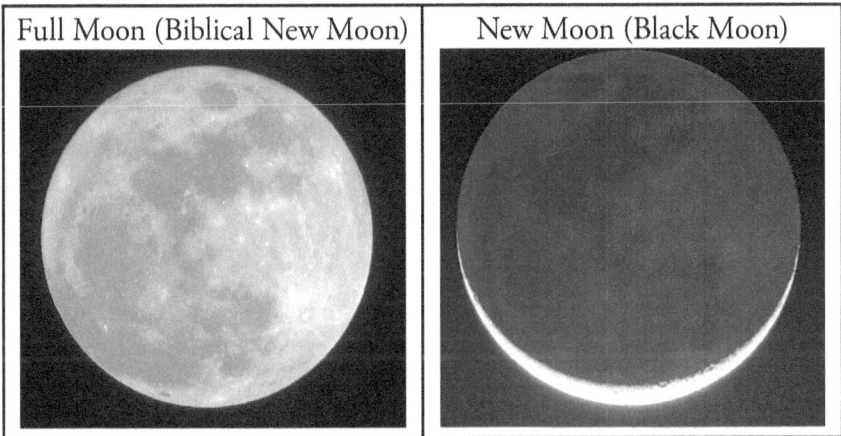

| Full Moon (Biblical New Moon) | New Moon (Black Moon) |

<u>Notice how the earth is between the sun and the moon receiving light for all living beings to grow.</u>

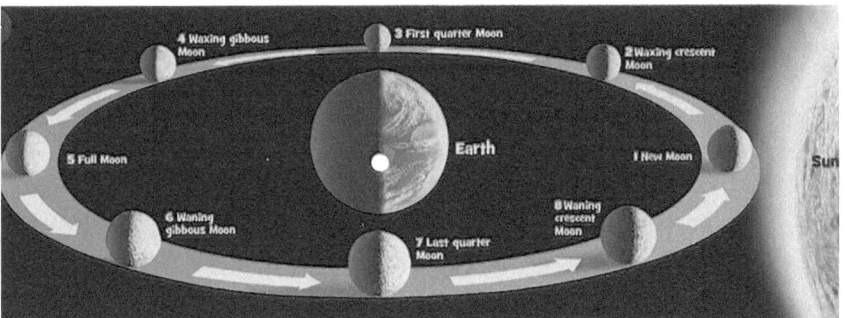

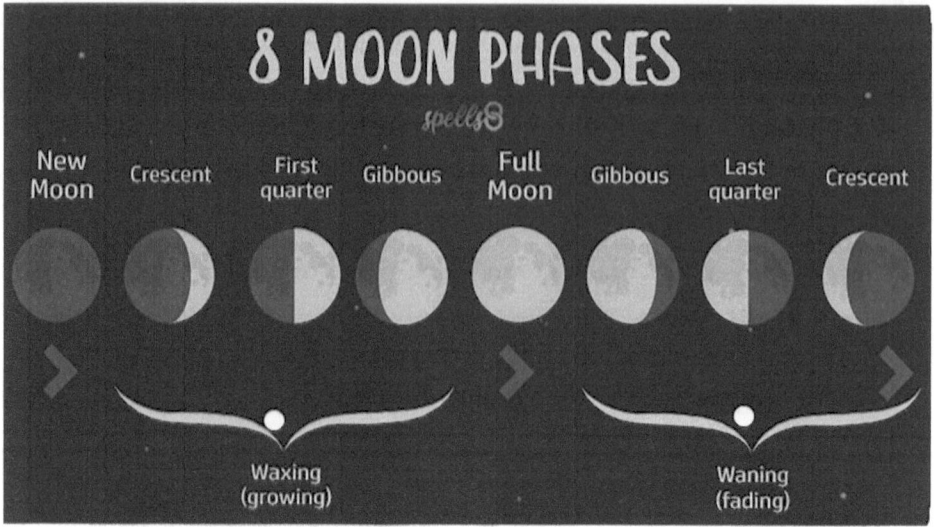

The **waning of the Full Moon** occurs after illumination till the light fades away completely into dark side of the moon. The **waxing of the Dark Moon** occurs after no light is visible save a thin crescent which increases till the light is regenerated in its fullness.

Lunar Eclipse – a celestial event occurs when Earth aligns between the sun and the moon and casts a shadow across the lunar surface. A lunar eclipse only happens during a full moon and can last as long as six hours

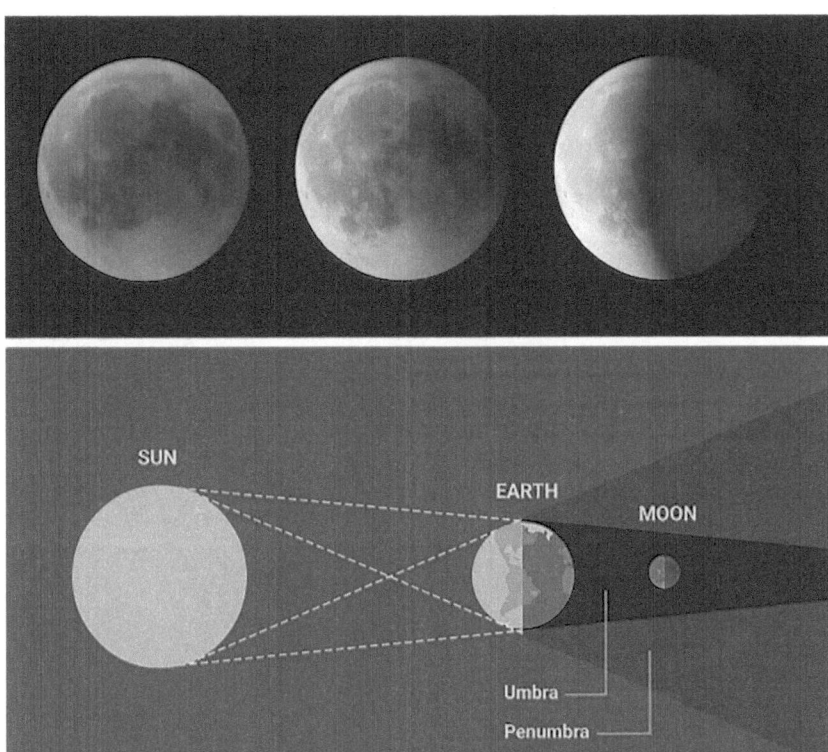

Notice how the lunar eclipse always occur during a full moon.

Solar Eclipse – a celestial event in which the moon passes between the sun and Earth and blocks all or part of the sun for up to about three hours, from beginning to end, as viewed from a given location.

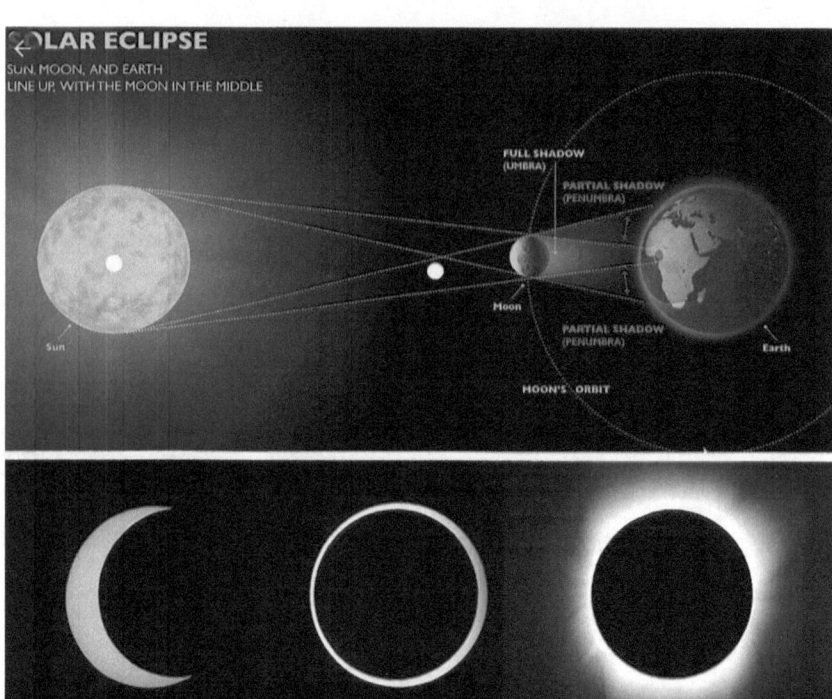

Notice how the solar eclipse takes place during a dark moon.

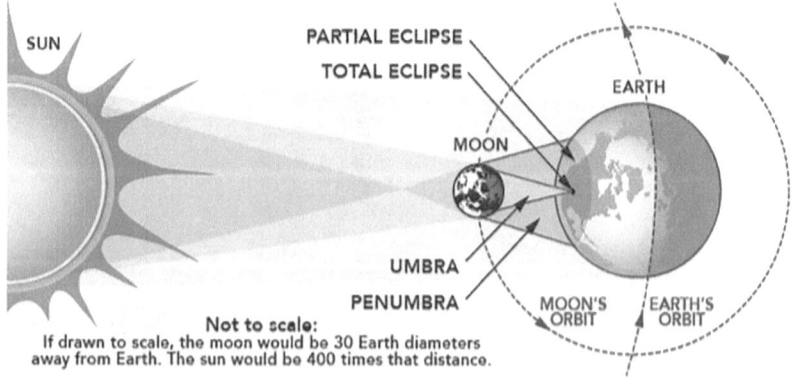

Next occurrence of Total Solar Eclipse happens on **April 8, 2024** and illustrated on the next page.

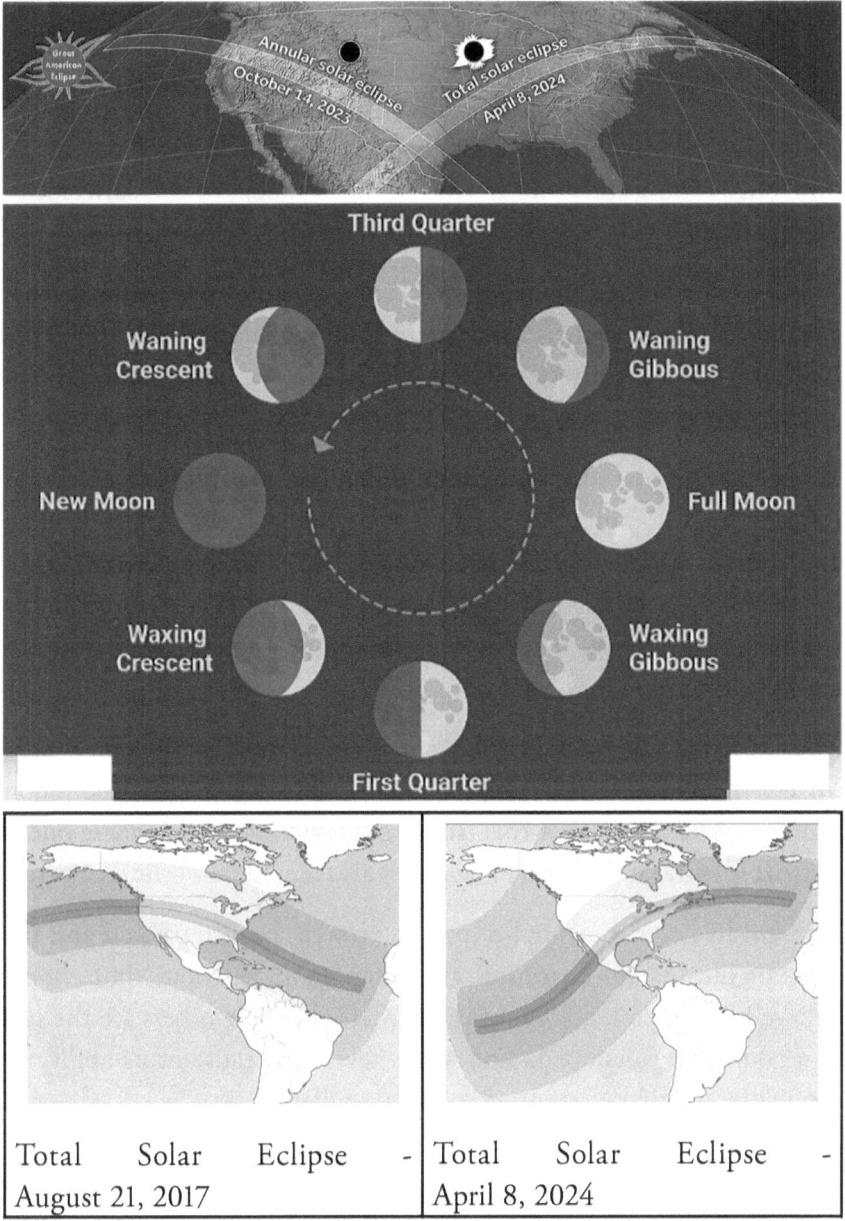

Total Solar Eclipse - August 21, 2017	Total Solar Eclipse - April 8, 2024

Notice the Hebrew Letter Tav 'X' marks this country (2017, 2023, and 2024) *Signs of the Times - Job 22:5*

What is the spiritual significance of the Moon?

The moon is a feminine symbol, universally representing the rhythm of time as it embodies the cycle. The phases of the moon symbolize immortality and eternity, enlightenment or the dark side of Nature herself.

The Sun symbolizes the supreme cosmic power – the life-force that enables all things to thrive and grow. In some cultures, the Sun is the Universal Father. Correspondingly, the Moon symbolizes death, birth and resurrection. Its feminine qualities bind it to Mother Goddess.

When the sun gives its light to the moon and the moon receives and reflects the sun's light, it is man planting life in the womb of woman and woman conceiving and nurturing it; it is the farmer's investment in the soil and the earth's absorption of seed and rain to sprout forth vegetation; it is the rich giving to the poor, the pupil learning from his teachers, the rivers feeding the seas.

The most notable moon symbolism is the symbolism of femininity. Where the sun represents male qualities and male energy, the moon stands for the opposite of that. It's like the yin and yang, where one is not viable without the other. The moon also represents cyclical patterns.

The sun has been a symbol of power, growth, health, passion and the cycle of life in many cultures and religions throughout time. Some believe it is a representation of the higher self, while others see the sun as a god to be worshiped. The sun is revered because of its ability to create life, making crops grow to sustain villages.

I pray this testimony blesses you in knowledge, wisdom, and all understanding of the Immortal Covenant sealed by the Most High God even Yahshua. And the kingdom and dominion, and the greatness of the kingdom under the whole heaven, shall be given to the people of the saints of the Most High, whose kingdom is an everlasting kingdom, and all dominions shall serve and obey him.

Peace be unto you.

Sir Justus Abramelech

Unlocking the Secrets of the Celestial Sphere Protected by Guardians: Navigating Life's Journey with Heavenly Powers

Journey with us as we explore the mystical forces that guard the four corners of the earth – the celestial sentinels of the east, west, north, and south hemispheres. In this captivating exploration, we delve into the observation of stars, our guiding lights across these sacred realms.

Drawing inspiration from sacred scriptures such as Zechariah 2:6, where the Lord urges us to "flee from the land of the north," and references like Dan 7:2, Rev 7:1, Acts 10:11, Isa 11:12, and Matt 24:31, we embark on a profound quest for understanding.

As we gaze upon the living creatures described in Ezekiel 1:4-28 and 10:1-21, and the enchanting visions of Rev 4 & 5, we unveil the profound symbolism of the one wheel upon the earth with its four faces. These revelations offer us insights into the harmonious orchestration of the universe.

Our mission is clear: to enrich our comprehension of the cosmic forces that shape our existence. The knowledge we gain will serve as a compass for navigating the intricate tapestry of life, helping us find direction, purpose, and meaning in our earthly journey.

Join us on this illuminating voyage, where ancient wisdom meets contemporary understanding, all for the purpose of enhancing and enriching our lives.

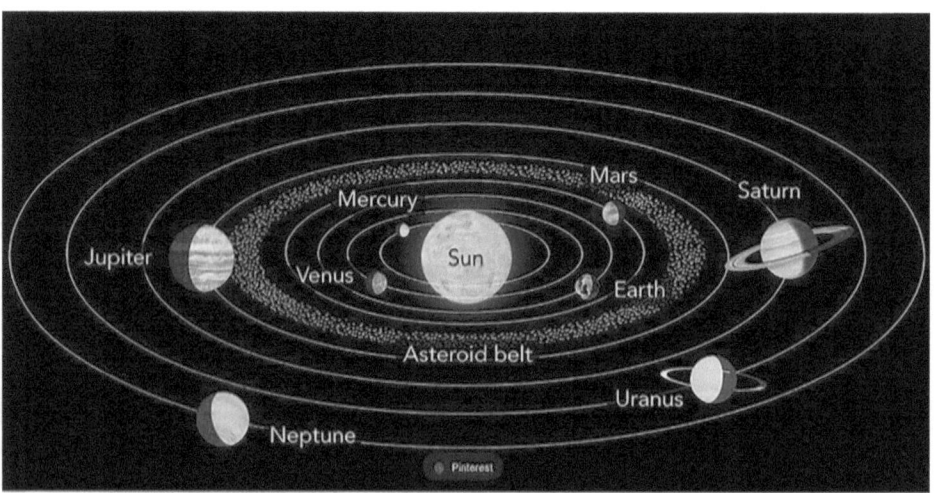

THE NIGHT SKY OF STARS

The sky that surrounds all hemispheres of the Earth, where the stars, planets, moons, and other celestial objects dwell, is commonly referred to as the "celestial sphere" or simply the "sky." This concept is a useful way to visualize the apparent position of celestial objects as if they were all located on the inner surface of a vast, imaginary sphere surrounding our planet.

In this model, celestial objects are projected onto the celestial sphere, allowing astronomers and stargazers to describe their positions relative to one another. While the celestial sphere is a theoretical construct, it simplifies the study and observation of the night sky and provides a practical way to locate and navigate among the stars and planets.

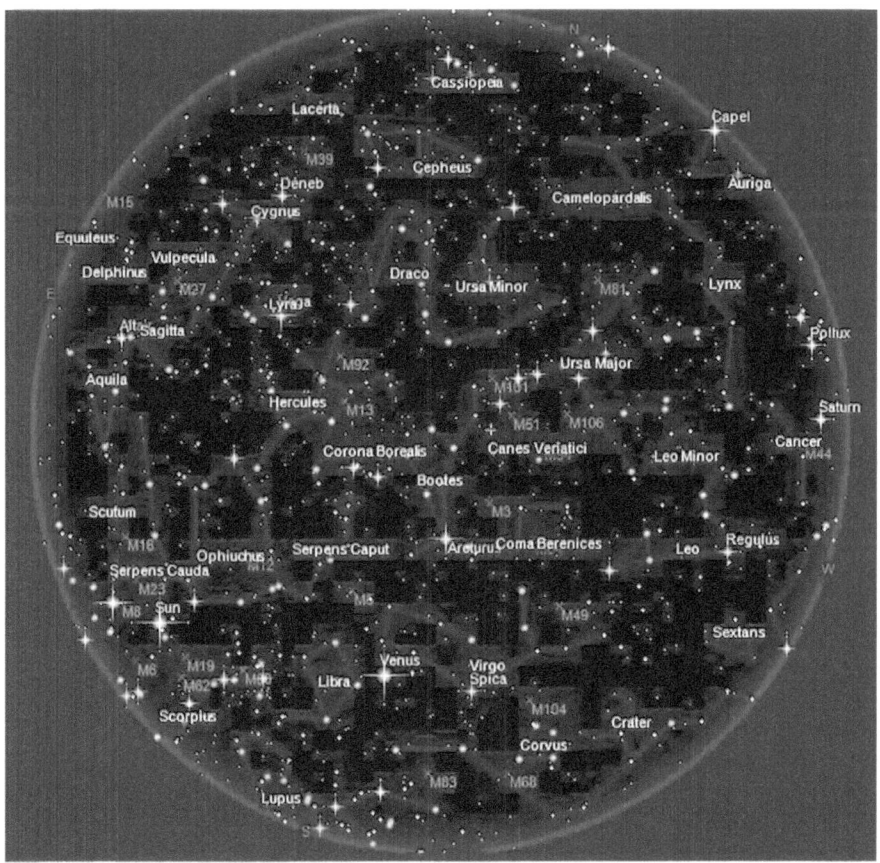

Embark on a captivating journey of celestial discovery, where the allure lies in witnessing the most vibrant and colorful lights that grace the skies of both the northern and southern hemispheres. These mesmerizing displays, such as the Northern Lights and the Southern Lights, paint the heavens with a vivid palette of colors, inspiring wonder and awe.

As you gaze skyward, also find fascination in spotting the brightest stars positioned at the four corners of the Earth, within each hemisphere. These celestial beacons serve as steadfast guides for navigation, offering their brilliance to travelers and explorers, and connecting us to the timeless wonders of the cosmos.

The colorful lights of the Northern Lights, also known as the Aurora Borealis, are primarily visible in the northern hemisphere, particularly in regions close to the Arctic Circle. These regions include places like Norway, Sweden, Iceland, Canada, and Alaska.

In the southern hemisphere, a similar phenomenon known as the Aurora Australis, or the Southern Lights, can be observed. The Southern Lights can display colorful and brilliant lights in the night sky, much like the Northern Lights. The Southern Lights are typically visible in regions near the Antarctic Circle, such as parts of Antarctica, Australia, New Zealand, and southern regions of South America.

So, both the northern and southern hemispheres have their own versions of these dazzling natural light displays, but the specific regions where they are visible differ due to their proximity to the polar circles.

The visibility of the Northern Lights (Aurora Borealis) and the Southern Lights (Aurora Australis) depends on the seasons and the proximity to the polar regions. Here's a general guideline for when these phenomena are most commonly visible:

Northern Lights (Aurora Borealis):

- In the Northern Hemisphere, the best time to see the Northern Lights is during the winter months, from late September to early April. The peak season is typically in the heart of winter, from December to February, when the nights are longest and the skies are darkest.

Southern Lights (Aurora Australis):

- In the Southern Hemisphere, the best time to see the Southern Lights is also during the winter months, which are the opposite of the Northern Hemisphere. So, the prime viewing season for the Southern Lights is from late March to early September. The peak months are generally June, July, and August.

It's important to note that the exact timing and visibility of these phenomena can vary based on factors like solar activity, geomagnetic conditions, and your specific location within the polar regions. To increase your chances of witnessing the Northern or Southern Lights, it's advisable to visit areas near the Arctic or Antarctic Circles during the respective peak seasons and to check local forecasts and aurora tracking tools for the most accurate information on viewing opportunities.

Night Sky of the Northern Hemisphere

In the northern hemisphere, the brightest and one of the most constant stars in the night sky is Polaris, commonly known as the North Star. Polaris is a part of the constellation Ursa Minor (the Little Dipper) and is located very close to the North Celestial Pole.

Due to its proximity to the North Celestial Pole, Polaris appears almost stationary in the northern sky. This makes it an excellent guide for navigation and orientation, especially for those in the northern hemisphere. If you can locate Polaris, you can roughly determine the cardinal directions, with the North Star marking the true north direction.

Throughout the night and across the seasons, Polaris remains a reliable point of reference for anyone navigating by the stars in the northern hemisphere.

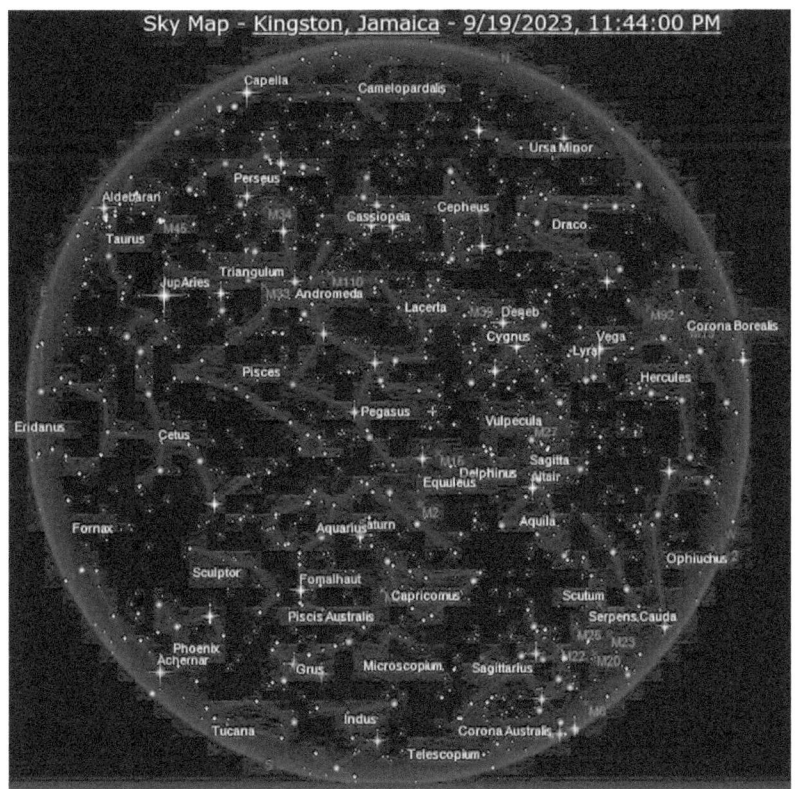

The other brightest stars mentioned in the northern hemisphere's night sky are Vega, Arcturus, and Capella. These stars are among the brightest in the entire night sky and are easily recognizable:

1. Vega: Vega, part of the constellation Lyra, is one of the brightest stars in the northern hemisphere and the entire night sky. It has a bluish-white hue and is especially prominent during the summer months.

2. Arcturus: Arcturus, part of the constellation Boötes, is another exceptionally bright star in the northern hemisphere's night sky. It is prominent during late spring, summer, and early autumn.

3. Capella: Capella, located in the constellation Auriga, is one of the brightest stars and is visible throughout much of the year in the northern hemisphere.

These stars are notable for their brightness and prominence, and they play a significant role in celestial navigation and stargazing in the northern hemisphere.

Arcturus is a prominent star in the northern hemisphere's night sky and can be visible during different months depending on the time of year. Here's a general guideline for when Arcturus is visible in the north, east, and west night sky:

1. North Sky Visibility (Generally Visible Year-Round): Arcturus is located in the northern celestial hemisphere, relatively close to the north celestial pole, which means it's circumpolar for many northern hemisphere locations. This means it can be visible year-round in the northern sky, including the north-northeast and north-northwest directions.

2. East Sky Visibility (Spring to Autumn): Arcturus is often visible in the eastern sky during the late winter months but becomes particularly prominent in the eastern sky from late spring through summer and into early autumn. It's one of the first stars to appear in the evening, and it's high in the eastern sky during these months.

3. West Sky Visibility (Late Summer to Early Winter): After its prominence in the eastern sky, Arcturus gradually moves toward the western sky as the night progresses. So, you can observe Arcturus in the west during the late summer, fall, and early winter months.

Keep in mind that the exact months of visibility can vary depending on your specific location and local time. Arcturus is part of the constellation Boötes and is known for its bright and distinctive appearance, making it a notable feature of the night sky throughout much of the year in the northern hemisphere.

Night Sky of the Western Hemisphere

The prominence of stars in the western hemisphere's night sky varies with the seasons. Here's a general guideline for when each of the prominent stars mentioned earlier is most prominent in the western night sky:

1. Vega: Vega is most prominent in the western evening sky during the summer months in the western hemisphere. This visibility typically starts in late spring and extends through the summer and into early autumn. It is part of the "Summer Triangle" a prominent asterism formed by Vega, Altair, and Deneb which shines brightly during this period.

2. Arcturus: Arcturus is often visible in the western evening sky during the late spring, summer, and early autumn months. It becomes particularly prominent in the western sky as the evening progresses during these seasons.

3. Sirius: Sirius is more prominent in the southern hemisphere but can be visible in the southwestern evening sky during the winter months in the western hemisphere. It is often referred to as a "winter star" and shines brightly during the late autumn and winter months.

Keep in mind that the exact months of visibility can vary slightly depending on your specific location within the western hemisphere and the progression of the seasons. These stars are still visible outside of the mentioned months but are at their most prominent during the specified periods.

In the western hemisphere, the brightest and most constant light of the night sky is the star Sirius. Sirius is part of the constellation Canis Major and is often referred to as the "Dog Star." It is the brightest star visible from Earth and has a luminosity that makes it stand out prominently in the night sky.

Today, Sirius continues to be a prominent and easily recognizable star in the western night sky, making it a useful guide for stargazers and navigators.

The visibility of Vega in the night sky varies with the seasons and your specific location within each hemisphere. Here's a general guideline for when Vega is visible in both the eastern and western hemispheres:

In the Northern Hemisphere:

- Vega is most prominently visible during the summer months, starting in late spring, peaking in summer, and extending into early autumn.
- It is often one of the first stars to become visible in the evening and remains visible for a significant portion of the night during this period.
- So, you can generally see Vega from late spring through summer and into early autumn in the northern hemisphere.

In the Southern Hemisphere:

- While Vega is a star of the northern hemisphere, it can also be seen in parts of the southern hemisphere during the summer months when it's higher in the northern sky.
- The visibility of Vega in the southern hemisphere is limited to certain latitudes and specific times of the year, primarily during the southern summer months (corresponding to the northern winter).

Keep in mind that the exact timing and visibility of Vega can vary depending on your specific location within each hemisphere, but it is generally most prominent during the summer in the northern hemisphere and may be visible in limited regions of the southern hemisphere during its summer.

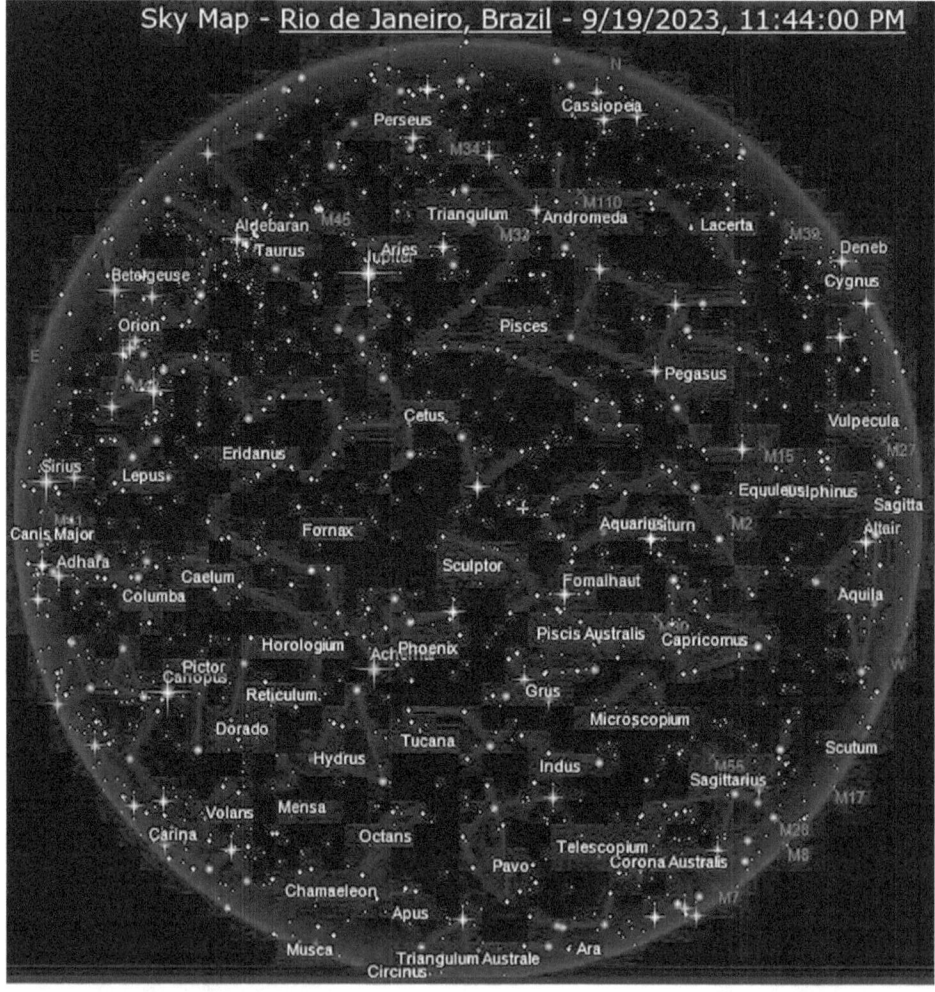

Sky Map - Rio de Janeiro, Brazil - 9/19/2023, 11:44:00 PM

Night Sky of the Southern Hemisphere

In the southern hemisphere, the brightest and most constant light of the night sky is the star Canopus. Canopus is the second brightest star in the entire sky, after Sirius, which is in the northern hemisphere. It belongs to the constellation Carina and is sometimes referred to as the "Southern Star."

Canopus is known for its striking brightness and its steady presence in the southern night sky, making it an excellent guide for navigation and stargazing in the southern hemisphere. It is especially prominent for observers in the southern parts of Africa, South America, Australia, and other regions of the southern hemisphere. Canopus's position near the celestial south pole also makes it useful for navigation, as it can serve as a reference point for determining direction.

Given its brilliance and prominence, Canopus has been a significant star in the mythology and navigation of various cultures in the southern hemisphere.

The Southern Cross, or Crux, is indeed another prominent and recognizable constellation in the southern hemisphere. While it is not a single bright star like Sirius or Canopus, Crux is a distinctive group of stars that forms a cross-like pattern and is one of the most well-known constellations in the southern sky.

Crux is often used as a guide for navigation and orientation in the southern hemisphere. It is positioned close to the south celestial pole, making it a valuable reference point for determining direction, especially for those in the southern parts of the world. Sailors, explorers, and indigenous cultures in the southern hemisphere have long used Crux as a navigational aid.

While Crux is not as bright as Canopus or Sirius, its distinctive shape and its role as a celestial marker have made it an important guidepost for those who navigate and observe the night sky in the southern hemisphere.

The visibility of Vega in the night sky varies with the seasons and your specific location within each hemisphere. Here's a general guideline for when Vega is visible in both the eastern and western hemispheres:

In the Northern Hemisphere:

- Vega is most prominently visible during the summer months, starting in late spring, peaking in summer, and extending into early autumn.
- It is often one of the first stars to become visible in the evening and remains visible for a significant portion of the night during this period.
- So, you can generally see Vega from late spring through summer and into early autumn in the northern hemisphere.

In the Southern Hemisphere:

- While Vega is a star of the northern hemisphere, it can also be seen in parts of the southern hemisphere during the summer months when it's higher in the northern sky.
- The visibility of Vega in the southern hemisphere is limited to certain latitudes and specific times of the year, primarily during the southern summer months (corresponding to the northern winter).

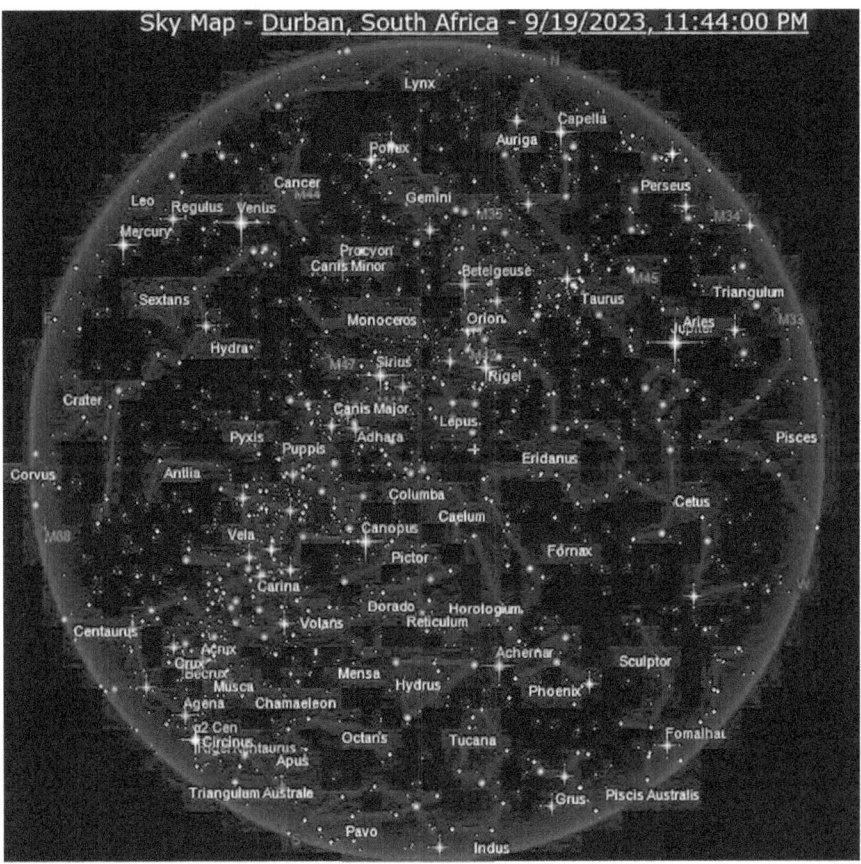

Keep in mind that the exact timing and visibility of Vega can vary depending on your specific location within each hemisphere, but it is generally most prominent during the summer in the northern hemisphere and may be visible in limited regions of the southern hemisphere during its summer.

Night Sky of the Eastern Hemisphere

Vega, Sirius, and Arcturus are indeed among the most prominent and brightest stars in the eastern hemisphere's night sky, but their prominence can vary with the seasons. Here's a brief overview of each:

1. Vega: Vega is a bright bluish-white star located in the constellation Lyra. It is most prominent during the summer months in the eastern hemisphere. It's often one of the first stars to become visible in the evening, particularly in late spring, summer, and early autumn.

2. Sirius: Sirius, also known as the Dog Star, is the brightest star in the entire night sky. It is part of the constellation Canis Major and is most prominent during the winter months in the eastern hemisphere. It shines brilliantly and is easily visible during the winter evenings.

3. Arcturus: Arcturus is a reddish-orange star located in the constellation Boötes. It is prominent in the eastern hemisphere's night sky during late spring, summer, and early autumn. It becomes one of the first stars to appear in the evening sky, especially during the late spring and summer months.

These stars are valuable reference points for stargazers and navigators in the eastern hemisphere and are notable for their brightness and distinctive appearances. However, their visibility and prominence change with the seasons, so the most prominent star can vary depending on the time of year.

Sirius is the brightest star in the night sky and is visible from most parts of the world. Its brilliance makes it stand out prominently, and it can be seen in the eastern hemisphere's night sky throughout the year. Sirius is especially conspicuous when it rises in the east just before sunrise, and it remains visible during the night. It rises in the east-southeastern part of the sky and is highly recognizable due to its intense white-blue color and its status as the brightest star in the night sky.

However, please note that the night sky's appearance and which stars are most prominent can vary with your specific location and the time of year. Other bright stars and constellations, such as Orion and its stars like Betelgeuse and Rigel, are also notable features of the eastern hemisphere's night sky during the winter months.

Due to its constant visibility and striking brightness, Sirius has been a notable celestial reference point for various cultures and has often been associated with myths and legends.

The Orion constellation is visible in both the Northern Hemisphere and the Southern Hemisphere. It's one of the few constellations that can be seen from almost anywhere on Earth, making it a prominent and recognizable feature of the night sky.

The Pleiades, also known as the Seven Sisters, is another constellation that can be seen from both hemispheres. It's located in the Taurus constellation and is easily visible to the naked eye.

These constellations are visible in different parts of the sky depending on the time of year and your specific location, but they are not limited to one hemisphere or the other.

Certainly because of its brightness and the fact that it is visible for much of the year in the western hemisphere, Sirius has been used as a guide and reference point for navigation and timekeeping for millennia. In ancient Egypt, for example, the heliacal rising of Sirius (its first appearance in the dawn sky just before sunrise) marked the beginning of the annual flooding of the Nile River, which was a vital event for agriculture.

Arcturus is often used as a guide in the eastern hemisphere due to its prominent position in the sky during certain times of the year. It's one of the first bright stars to appear in the evening and remains visible for a significant portion of the night. This makes it a valuable reference point for stargazers and navigators in the eastern part of the world.

Keep in mind that the appearance and visibility of stars can vary depending on your location and the time of year, so Arcturus may not always be visible, but when it is, it serves as a reliable and recognizable guide in the night sky.

When Arcturus is not visible due to its position below the horizon or other factors, another bright and reliable star that is often visible in the night sky is Vega. Vega is part of the constellation Lyra and is one of the brightest stars in the northern hemisphere's summer sky.

Vega is known for its bluish-white brilliance and its prominent location in the summer months. It's frequently used as a reference point for celestial navigation and stargazing. During the summer, Vega is one of the first stars to become visible in the evening and remains prominent throughout the night.

So, when Arcturus is not visible, especially during the summer in the northern hemisphere, Vega is a trustworthy and easily recognizable star in the night sky.

Vega is indeed visible as a guide in the night sky in both the eastern and western hemispheres. Its location in the sky makes it an excellent reference point for stargazers and navigators in many parts of the world.

Western Hemisphere: In the western hemisphere, Vega is especially prominent during the summer months, where it is often one of the first stars to appear in the evening. It remains visible throughout the night.

Eastern Hemisphere: In the eastern hemisphere, Vega is also visible, although its position and visibility may vary slightly depending on your specific location and the time of year. It is generally considered one of the bright stars that can be used as a guide in the night sky.

Vega's prominence and visibility make it a valuable reference point for celestial navigation and stargazing in various parts of the world, making it a useful guide in both hemispheres.

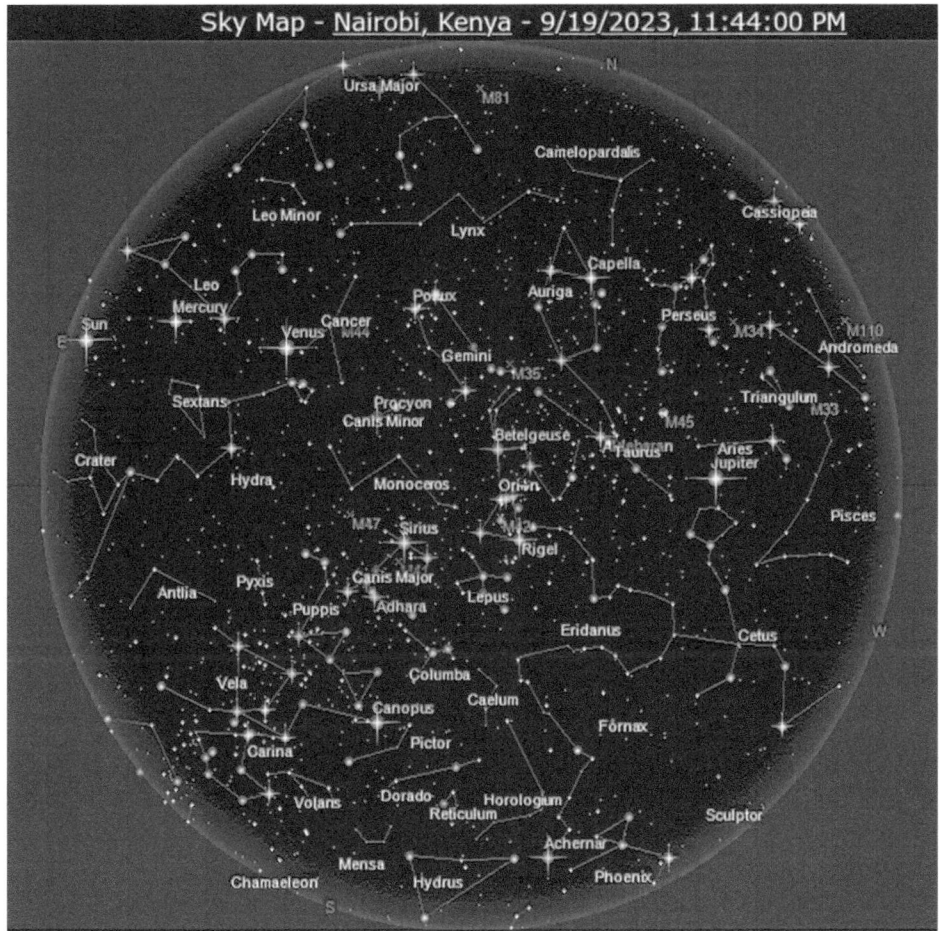

Evening Star or West/Morning Star of East

Venus orbits the Sun at a closer distance than Earth, and its orbit is inside Earth's orbit. This means that from the perspective of an observer on Earth, Venus can be seen both in the western sky after sunset (as the "Evening Star") and in the eastern sky before sunrise (as the "Morning Star").

Here's how this works:

1. Evening Star (Western Sky): When Venus is on the same side of the Sun as Earth but trailing behind it in its orbit, or slightly to the east of the Sun it appears in the western sky after sunset. This is why it's called the "Evening Star" during this phase. Venus is visible shortly after sunset (dusk) for a period of time, and it sets in the west and is often one of the brightest objects in the evening sky.

2. Morning Star (Eastern Sky): When Venus is visible in the eastern sky just before sunrise, it is known as the "Morning Star." As Venus continues its orbit, it eventually moves to the opposite side of the Sun from Earth or slightly to the west of the Sun. At this point, it appears in the eastern sky just before sunrise. This is why it's known as the "Morning Star" during this phase. Venus is visible for a while before sunrise (dawn) and then disappears into the sunrise.

The visibility of Venus in the west and east sky is related to its position as either an "Evening Star" or a "Morning Star." This relationship is due to Venus's orbit around the Sun and its relative position to Earth. The transition from being an Evening Star to a Morning Star (or vice versa) is known as "inferior conjunction." During this time, Venus passes between Earth and the Sun, changing its position in the sky. The exact timing of these transitions can vary, but they occur roughly every 19 months.

The period just before sunrise is commonly referred to as the "dawn" or "pre-dawn" hours. This is the time when the sky begins to brighten as the Sun approaches the horizon, but before it actually rises above it. The pre-dawn period is characterized by low light levels, often with beautiful colors in the sky, such as shades of blue, pink, and orange, depending on atmospheric conditions and location. It's a tranquil and visually appealing time of day, favored by photographers and early risers.

The period just after sunset is commonly referred to as "dusk." Dusk is the transitional time between day and night when the sky gradually darkens as the sun disappears below the horizon. It's a beautiful and often serene time of day when the colors in the sky can range from bright oranges and reds to softer pinks and purples before eventually transitioning into nighttime.

Venus's appearance as either the Evening Star or the Morning Star is a fascinating phenomenon and one of the most prominent planets visible in the night sky.

A CONNECTION AMONG HUMANS CELESTIAL BOND

In various cultures and belief systems, there is a long history of associating celestial bodies such as the Sun, Moon, stars, and planets with human characteristics, personalities, and destinies based on a person's birth date and time. This practice is known as astrology. Astrology is a belief system that suggests a connection between celestial phenomena and events on Earth, including individual personalities and life paths.

Here's a brief overview of how astrology connects humans with celestial bodies in the Milky Way galaxy:

1. The Sun: In astrology, the Sun sign (e.g., Aries, Taurus, Gemini) is determined by the position of the Sun at the time of a person's birth. The Sun sign is often associated with a person's core identity, ego, and general characteristics.

2. The Moon: The Moon sign is determined by the position of the Moon at the time of birth. It is associated with a person's emotions, instincts, and subconscious. The Moon's phases are also considered in some astrological interpretations.

3. Planets: Astrology assigns meaning to the positions of various planets in the zodiac at the time of birth. For example, Mercury is linked to communication and intellect, Venus to love and relationships, Mars to energy and drive, and so on. The positions of these planets in a person's birth chart are believed to influence their personality and life path.

4. Stars: Certain fixed stars and star clusters, like the Pleiades, have been associated with astrological meanings and used in chart interpretations. However, their influence is generally less emphasized than that of planets.

5. Constellations: The zodiac consists of 12 constellations along the ecliptic, and each zodiac sign is associated with a specific constellation. Astrology uses the positions of these constellations as a backdrop for interpreting planetary influences.

The relationship between humans and celestial bodies like the Sun, Moon, stars, and planets has long been a subject of interest, folklore, and cultural significance, especially in the context of astrology and beliefs about how celestial bodies may influence human life. Here are some perspectives on this relationship:

1. Astrology: Astrology is the belief that the positions and movements of celestial bodies at the time of a person's birth can influence their personality, behavior, and life events. Astrologers study the positions of the Sun, Moon, planets, and stars in the zodiac at the moment of a person's birth to create a natal or birth chart. This chart is used to make predictions and interpretations about an individual's life and characteristics.

2. Cultural Significance: Throughout history, various cultures have attached cultural and religious significance to celestial bodies. For example, the Sun has often been associated with life, light, and energy, while the Moon has been linked to cycles, emotions, and femininity. Stars and planets have also been named and incorporated into myths, stories, and religious beliefs.

3. Navigation: Celestial bodies have played a crucial role in navigation for centuries. Sailors, for example, used the positions of stars to determine their location and direction at sea. The North Star (Polaris) has been especially important for navigation in the Northern Hemisphere.

4. Timekeeping: The movements of celestial bodies have been used to measure time. The day is based on the rotation of the Earth relative to the Sun, and the year is based on Earth's orbit around the Sun. Lunar calendars, which are based on the phases of the Moon, have also been used in various cultures.

5. Inspiration: The beauty and mystery of the night sky have inspired humans for millennia. Many people find wonder, awe, and inspiration in observing celestial bodies. Astronomy, the scientific study of celestial objects and phenomena, seeks to understand the universe and our place in it.

6. Scientific Exploration: Humans have explored and continue to explore the Moon, Mars, and other celestial bodies in our solar system through robotic and human missions. This scientific exploration enhances our understanding of these bodies and our potential for future space exploration.

7. Astronomy: Astronomy is the scientific study of celestial objects and phenomena, including the Sun, Moon, stars, planets, and galaxies, without the metaphysical or predictive aspects associated with astrology. Astronomical observations and research contribute to our understanding of the cosmos and the physical properties of celestial bodies.

It's important to note that while celestial bodies have cultural, symbolic, and historical significance, there is no scientific evidence to support the notion that they directly influence individual human lives or personalities, as suggested by astrology. Astronomy and astrology are distinct fields, with astronomy being a science focused on understanding the universe, while astrology is a belief system based on celestial interpretations.

I will live forever by the things I do and say
The spirit of life even truth is with me
I am immortal and will not fall into the hands of man.
The ways of man leads to death
Even my breath shall never sting with sin.
Many men have learned the ways of the world
Bringing baby girls and boys, toys, no knowledge of the Almighty.
How shall we have leaders, the very few awaken not shaken from
The truth are heard in words received and believed.
Can it be reality to find true love without praising
Live forever, his majesty on high, Oh King of the Saints! The
Most High!

The Celestial Symphony and Divine Guidance

The celestial night sky, as described in various sacred scriptures, serves as a profound testament to the glory and wisdom of the divine. In the Bible, Psalms 19:1-2 declares that the heavens themselves declare the glory of God, and the skies proclaim His handiwork. The purpose of the celestial bodies, including the North Star (Polaris) and the stars of Gemini (Castor and Pollux), is not merely to adorn the night sky but to guide and inspire.

In the Quran (Surah Al-Baqarah 2:164), the alternation of night and day, the ships sailing through the sea, and the rains that bring life to the earth are identified as signs for those who reflect and use reason. The celestial bodies are intricately woven into the fabric of creation, serving as symbols of divine knowledge and order.

The Bhagavad Gita (Chapter 15, Verse 6) beautifully captures the idea that the sun, a prominent celestial body, is not only a radiant source of heat but also a reflection of a cosmic reality within the self.

Genesis 1:14 from the Torah reinforces the intentional design of the celestial bodies, indicating that they are not haphazard occurrences but deliberate markers for sacred times and seasons.

These verses from various books of the Bible convey a powerful message about the divine authority and omnipotence of the Almighty, referred to as YAH or the Most High God. Collectively, they underscore the universal recognition and worship of YAH, extending from the rising to the setting of the sun.

Psalm 50:1: The Mighty One, YAH, the Most High God, is portrayed as an active speaker, summoning the entire earth. The span from the rising to the setting of the sun signifies the comprehensive reach of YAH's authority and influence over the entire creation.

Malachi 1:11: This verse emphasizes the global greatness of YAH's name among the Gentiles. It envisions a time when incense will be offered to YAH's name in every place, emphasizing the universality of worship and the purity of offerings. It speaks to a future where YAH's name transcends cultural and geographical boundaries.

Jeremiah 31:35: Here, YAH is portrayed as the cosmic orchestrator, appointing the sun to shine by day and decreeing the moon and stars to illuminate the night. The mention of stirring up the sea symbolizes YAH's control over the forces of nature. The Almighty YAH is presented as the supreme architect of the universe, whose name is to be revered.

Isaiah 45:6: This verse declares that from the rising to the setting of the sun, people will come to the realization that there is none besides YAH. The affirmation of being the Almighty underscores YAH's unmatched power and uniqueness. The verse stresses monotheism, proclaiming that there is no other deity besides YAH.

Collectively, these verses instill a sense of awe and reverence for YAH as the all-encompassing, universal Creator. The rising and setting of the sun symbolize the entirety of existence, from east to west, and serve as a metaphor for the omnipresence of YAH. The verses evoke a profound connection between the divine, nature, and humanity, emphasizing that the recognition of YAH's supreme authority should extend across all borders and be acknowledged by people from every corner of the earth. In essence, they invite the audience to contemplate the grandeur of creation and to recognize YAH as the singular, almighty force governing the entire cosmos.

Rigveda's verse (Mandala 10, Sukta 85, Verse 1) complements the chorus, acknowledging the enduring brilliance of the celestial lights even after the sun's departure.

The Celestial Elegance: Names of the Stars that Grace Our Night Sky

1. Polaris - The Guiding Star:

   Ever pondered about the North Star? Look no further – it's Polaris. Nestled within Ursa Minor, Polaris has earned its celestial fame as the Guiding Star. Throughout history, its radiant glow has played a pivotal role in crafting navigation charts.

2. Castor - Gemini's Luminary Twin:

   Castor, an integral part of the Gemini constellation, is the celestial sibling of Pollux. In ancient Greece, it wore the moniker Apollo, while in China, it embodied Yin, a fundamental force symbolizing life's balance.

3. Pollux - The Benevolent Greek Star:

   Of Greek origin, Pollux means kindness. This orange-red gem is the brightest in Gemini, standing as the seventeenth familiar beacon in our night sky.

4. Orion - Celestial Splendor at Plain Sight:

   Orion, a constellation renowned for its visibility, boasts the famed Orion's Belt, comprised of Mintaka, Alnitak, and Alnilam. Their alignment weaves through nebulas and stellar dust clouds, creating a captivating celestial tapestry.

5. Sirius - The Luminous Canis Major Gem:

   Sirius, the brightest star in Canis Major, graces the night sky with its brilliance. Visible from every corner of our planet, this radiant beauty captivates observers with the naked eye.

6. Altair - Soaring Arabic Brilliance:

   With an Arabic origin meaning "flying," Altair belongs to the Eagle constellation. As the twelfth brightest star, it adds a touch of celestial majesty to the night sky.

7. Sun - Our Radiant Celestial Center:

Yes, the Sun is also a star! This colossal powerhouse of energy serves as the heart of our solar system. Its radiant light and energy sustain life on Earth, and it's poised to remain stable for another 5 billion years, eventually transforming into a resplendent red giant.

8. Antares - The Fiery Alpha Scorpii:

Often known as Alpha Scorpii, Antares is a red giant approaching the twilight of its existence. Blazing 10,000 times brighter than the sun, Antares is on an extraordinary journey, destined to culminate in a breathtaking supernova display.

The purpose of the celestial stars and the rhythmic cycle of day and night, as depicted in these verses, extends beyond their aesthetic beauty. They are celestial signposts, guiding humanity in its journey of self-discovery, spiritual reflection, and alignment with divine principles. The alternation of light and darkness is a metaphor for life's journey, urging individuals to navigate through challenges, appreciate moments of clarity and introspection (Full Moon), express gratitude (Waning Gibbous Moon), evaluate and release burdens (Last Quarter Moon), and prepare for new beginnings (Dark Moon).

The Celestial Elegance: Divine Order that Grace Our Night Sky

In essence, the celestial symphony serves as a constant reminder of the divine order, providing guidance, inspiration, and opportunities for spiritual growth throughout the seasons of life. Before we embark on the journey through the seasons of life, let us recognize the divine order of the Night Sky.

Psalm 104:19 This verse acknowledges the purposeful creation of the moon by the Almighty. The moon is described as a celestial timekeeper, marking the seasons. In this context, the moon becomes a celestial signpost, guiding the cyclical changes in nature. Its presence and phases contribute to the order and rhythm of the created world.

Psalm 136:9 Here, the moon and stars are recognized as cosmic authorities that govern the night. The enduring love of the Almighty is linked with the constancy and reliability of these celestial bodies. Their role as governors of the night implies a divine order and purpose, providing both light and a sense of continuity during the darkness.

Isaiah 66:23 This verse presents a future vision where the worship of the Almighty transcends temporal boundaries. The mention of "New Moon to another" signifies a continual, unbroken cycle of worship. The celestial markers, including the New Moon, are highlighted as occasions when all of humanity will gather to bow down before the Almighty. This reinforces the idea that the celestial bodies play a role in the divine order and worship.

2 Chronicles 8:13 This verse references the celestial cycles in the context of religious observances. The daily requirements for offerings, as commanded by Moses, include specific observances related to the New Moons. The alignment of religious practices with celestial events suggests a divine connection between the earthly rituals and the celestial order, reinforcing the idea that the moon has a role in the structure of religious life.

In the context of Hebrew customs performed by the Children of Israel, the New Moon holds significance for several reasons:

1. Sacred Observances: The New Moon is often associated with sacred observances and festivals held at appointed times. The beginning of each month, marked by the New Moon, is crucial for determining the timing of various festivals and sacred feasts. Keeping track of the lunar-solar calendar, including

the New Moon, ensures the proper observance of holy events and ceremonies.

2. Calendar and Festivals: The Hebrew calendar is a lunisolar calendar, meaning it is based on both the solar and lunar cycles. The New Moon marks the start of each lunar month, and its observation is integral to the accurate reckoning of time for appointed festivals. This includes the celebration of Passover, Feast of Weeks (Shavuot), Feast of Ingathering (Sukkot), and other significant events that are determined by the lunar calendar.

3. Cultural and Historical Significance: The New Moon has cultural and historical significance in the traditions of the Children of Israel. It is a symbol of renewal and the beginning of a new month even the sign of the covenant to be sealed at the last day. The concept of marking time through the lunar cycle is deeply ingrained in the cultural and appointed times on the Hebrew calendar for all 12 tribes of Israel. Remembering the 7th day is set apart to be holy and the sign of the covenant.

4. Preventing Astray Behavior: The emphasis on observing the New Moon and adhering to the lunar-solar calendar can be seen as a way to maintain set apart discipline and prevent the Children of Israel from going astray. Following the prescribed calendar and appointed times is a way to ensure the continuity of cultural and holy days, reinforcing a sense of identity and connection to YAH.

5. Scriptural Guidance: The importance of the New Moon is reflected in various biblical verses that reference its observation. For example, in Psalms 81:3 (NIV), it is written: "Sound the ram's horn at the New Moon, and when the moon is full, on the day of our festival."

In summary, the New Moon is crucial for the Children of Israel to maintain the proper timing of holy observances, festivals, and cultural practices. It serves as a symbol of renewal, adherence to scriptural guidance, and the preservation of their unique identity and virtuous heritage.

These verses collectively underscore the celestial bodies, particularly the moon, as significant components of divine creation and order. The moon is portrayed as more than a mere astronomical object; it is a purposeful creation that marks time, governs the night, and plays a role in the worship and religious observances of humanity. The constancy and order represented by the moon and stars reflect the enduring love and authority of the Almighty, creating a seamless connection between the celestial and the divine in the grand tapestry of creation.

The Seasons of Life unfold in a rhythmic dance, mirroring the phases of the moon, with each quarter bringing its unique theme and purpose.

Spring Theme (March, April, May):

In this season, the Waxing Crescent Moon ushers in the first signs of life. Decisions made in the shadows manifest, and it's time to fulfill the work of taking action on intentions. The Waxing Crescent Moon offers a boost of hope and positivity, providing the momentum needed to accomplish goals. Embrace the dreams envisioned, meditate on desires, and manifest intentions with unwavering hope.

Summer Theme (June, July, August):

With the warmth of summer comes the Waxing Gibbous Moon, a phase for redefining goals and prioritizing what aligns with innermost feelings. Evaluate for personal growth, recite affirmations to boost confidence, and release under the illuminating Full Moon. It's a period for introspection, evolving relationships, breaking habits, and focusing on healing.

Fall Theme (September, October, November):

As the Fall Theme approaches, the Waning Gibbous Moon prompts expressions of gratitude for goals achieved and obstacles conquered. Take inventory of accomplishments, revisit intentions, and express gratitude. The Last Quarter Moon urges self-evaluation, prompting the removal of burdens and non-serving elements. Clear the clutter to evolve positively.

Winter Theme (December, January, February):

The Winter Theme brings the Waning Crescent Moon, a time of peaceful reflection. Rest in harmony, focusing on value-based opportunities. Reflect on past lessons, preparing for a new journey ahead. The Dark Moon ushers in new beginnings and fresh starts. Visualize goals, declare intentions in a journal, and embrace the potential for personal growth.

As the months unfold, embrace the elegance of self-discovery, growth, and renewal in harmony with the changing seasons and the cosmic dance of the moon.

Spring Theme:

1st - Waxing Crescent Moon: In the embrace of the burgeoning Spring, decisions from the dark moon manifest under the Waxing Crescent. Fulfill the work of translating intentions into actions. This phase offers a hopeful boost, encouraging positivity to accomplish goals. It's a time to embrace imagined dreams, meditate on desires, and sow the seeds of growth.

2nd - Manifest Intentions, Hope & Momentum: As Spring unfolds, the second phase is dedicated to manifesting intentions, fostering hope, and building momentum. It's a period of nurturing the seeds of aspiration, allowing them to sprout with unwavering optimism.

3rd - First Quarter Moon: With the First Quarter Moon, adjustments to lifestyle and situations can be made to refine goals. Momentum is offered to overcome obstacles, emphasizing that intentions are respected by the universe. This is the time for revisions and decisions, welcoming success as the universe applauds authenticity.

Summer Theme:

4th - Waxing Gibbous Moon: Summer brings the Waxing Gibbous Moon, urging a redefinition of goals. It's a phase of evaluating priorities aligned with inner feelings. Confidence is bolstered through affirmations, fostering the necessary changes for personal growth.

5th - Recite Affirmations & Release: Amidst the warm nights, reciting affirmations becomes a ritual, affirming confidence and releasing what hinders growth. The Full Moon illuminates clarity, offering introspection and the potential for relationships to evolve. It's a time to release what doesn't belong, break habits, and focus on healing.

6th - Full Moon: The Full Moon, a pinnacle of the Summer Theme, marks a time of clarity, introspection, and intuition. Relationships can grow if past issues are left behind. It's a moment to release what no longer serves, take control, and start anew. Relax, unwind, and honor the Moon's glory, preparing for the next lunar journey.

Fall Theme:

7th - Waning Gibbous Moon: In the autumnal breeze, the Waning Gibbous Moon prompts expressions of gratitude for goals achieved. Journaling events to the universe enhances the acknowledgment of personal power. This phase is about taking inventory, revisiting intentions, and expressing gratitude.

8th - Gratitude & Self Evaluation: As leaves fall, expressing gratitude and self-evaluating become paramount. The Last Quarter Moon signals a time of clearing burdens, releasing what hinders growth, and making room for effective self-evolution.

9th - Last Quarter Moon: The Last Quarter Moon becomes the catalyst for effective results, urging action to free oneself from burdens. It's the season's end, calling for a thorough evaluation and decluttering of the house of habits.

Winter Theme:

10th - Waning Crescent Moon: Winter's chill brings the Waning Crescent Moon, a time for reflection and stillness. Resting in harmony, focus shifts to value-based opportunities. Reflect on the journey, understanding the life lessons brought to attention. It's a peaceful preparation for the upcoming new journey.

11th - Reflection & New Beginnings: Amidst the winter quiet, reflection paves the way for new beginnings. It's a time to understand where you are and prepare for the next chapter. Recall the lessons, find peace, and embrace the potential for new growth.

12th - Dark Moon: The Dark Moon, a veil over the winter night, marks a time of new beginnings. Visualize goals, declare intentions, and create a fresh start in your journal. Whether it's a new relationship, improved personality, or increased abundance, declare it as your new beginning as the Seasons of Life continue their eternal dance.

People's beliefs and attitudes toward these relationships can vary widely, and they may find personal meaning and significance in different ways.

The Zodiac constellations are a group of 12 constellations that lie along the ecliptic, the apparent path that the Sun, Moon, and planets follow through the sky. Here are the Zodiac constellations, along with the months during which they are most prominent:

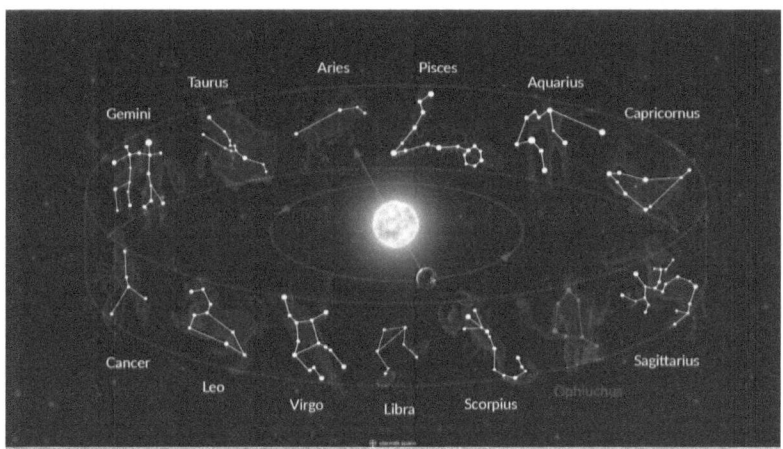

1. Aries (The Ram): Aries is typically visible from late November through early June. The Sun passes through Aries from late March to mid-April.

2. Taurus (The Bull): Taurus is visible from late September through early March. The Sun passes through Taurus from late April to mid-May.

3. Gemini (The Twins): Gemini is visible from late December through early July. The Sun passes through Gemini from late May to mid-June.

4. Cancer (The Crab): Cancer is visible from late January through early August. The Sun passes through Cancer from late June to mid-July.

5. Leo (The Lion): Leo is visible from late February through early September. The Sun passes through Leo from late July to mid-August.

6. Virgo (The Virgin): Virgo is visible from late March through early October. The Sun passes through Virgo from late August to mid-September.

7. Libra (The Scales): Libra is visible from late April through early November. The Sun passes through Libra from late September to mid-October.

8. Scorpius (The Scorpion): Scorpius is visible from late May through early December. The Sun passes through Scorpius from late October to mid-November.

9. Sagittarius (The Archer): Sagittarius is visible from late June through early January. The Sun passes through Sagittarius from late November to mid-December.

10. Capricornus (The Sea Goat): Capricornus is visible from late July through early February. The Sun passes through Capricornus from late December to mid-January.

11. Aquarius (The Water Bearer): Aquarius is visible from late August through early March. The Sun passes through Aquarius from late January to mid-February.

12. Pisces (The Fishes): Pisces is visible from late September through early April. The Sun passes through Pisces from late February to mid-March.

Please note that these are general time frames for when each Zodiac constellation is visible in the night sky. The exact visibility may vary depending on your location and local light pollution conditions. Additionally, the Sun's passage through each Zodiac constellation corresponds to the astrological signs used in Western astrology.

VISIBLE CELESTIAL PHENOMENA IN THE NIGHT SKY

Here's a list of observable celestial phenomena in the night sky:

1. Stars: The twinkling points of light created by distant suns. Stars are the most abundant and constant objects in the night sky. They emit their own light and appear as tiny points of light. Some stars are bright and easily recognizable, while others are faint.

2. Planets: Bright, non-twinkling objects that move against the backdrop of stars. Certain planets in our solar system are often visible to the naked eye. The five visible planets (Mercury, Venus, Mars, Jupiter, and Saturn) are known as "wandering stars" because they appear to move against the background of fixed stars.

3. The Moon: Earth's natural satellite, which goes through phases from crescent to full. Earth's natural satellite, the Moon, is one of the most prominent objects in the night sky. Its phases change as it orbits Earth, from the New Moon to the Full Moon and back again.

4. Constellations: Recognizable patterns of stars, often named after mythological figures or animals. Constellations are patterns of stars that form recognizable shapes or figures in the night sky. They have been used for navigation and storytelling for thousands of years. Examples include Orion, the Big Dipper, and the Southern Cross.

5. Meteor Showers: Meteor showers occur when the Earth passes through the debris left behind by comets. During these events, numerous meteors (shooting stars) can be seen streaking across the sky.

6. Auroras: Dazzling displays of light in polar regions, caused by solar wind interacting with Earth's magnetic field. The Northern Lights (Aurora Borealis) and Southern Lights (Aurora Australis) are colorful displays of light caused by interactions between charged particles from the Sun and Earth's magnetic field. They are typically visible at high latitudes.

7. Eclipses: When the Moon passes between Earth and the Sun (solar eclipse) or when Earth passes between the Sun and the Moon (lunar eclipse). Solar and lunar eclipses are rare but dramatic events. A solar eclipse occurs when the Moon passes between the Earth and the Sun, blocking out the Sun's light. A lunar eclipse happens when the Earth casts its shadow on the Moon, causing it to darken and change color.

8. Satellites: Artificial satellites, such as the International Space Station (ISS), can be seen moving across the night sky. They appear as bright points of light moving steadily across the heavens.

9. ISS Passes: The ISS is often visible from Earth as a bright, moving point of light.

10. Double Stars: Pairs of stars that appear close together in the sky.

11. Nebulas: Clouds of gas and dust, often seen through telescopes.

12. Galaxies: Vast collections of stars, like the Milky Way, which are visible in dark sky areas.

13. Zodiacal Light: Zodiacal light is a faint, pyramid-shaped glow that can be seen in the west after sunset or in the east before sunrise. It is caused by sunlight reflecting off dust particles in the solar system.

14. Comets: Occasionally, comets become visible in the night sky when they approach the Sun. They often exhibit a bright nucleus and a tail, which can be quite striking.

These celestial phenomena provide a captivating and ever-changing view of the night sky for those who take the time to observe and appreciate them.

The visibility of constellations and planets in the night sky changes throughout the year due to Earth's orbit around the Sun. Here's a general overview of which constellations and planets are visible during each month of the year. Keep in mind that the visibility can vary based on your location and time of night.

January	February	March
Constellations: Orion, Taurus, Gemini, Canis Major	Constellations: Orion, Taurus, Gemini, Canis Major	Constellations: Leo, Cancer, Gemini, Taurus, Orion
Planets: Venus is often visible in the evening sky, and you may see Jupiter and Saturn as well.	Planets: Venus, Jupiter, and Saturn can still be seen in the evening sky.	Planets: Venus may still be visible, and Mars becomes more prominent in the evening sky.

April	May	June
Constellations: Leo, Cancer, Gemini, Taurus, Orion	Constellations: Ursa Major (part of it), Leo, Cancer, Gemini	Constellations: Ursa Major (part of it), Leo, Virgo
Planets: Mars, Jupiter, and Saturn continue to be visible, with Venus appearing in the morning sky.	Planets: Mars, Jupiter, and Saturn are still visible, and Venus shines brightly in the morning.	Planets: Venus dominates the morning sky, and you may see Jupiter and Saturn as well.

July	August	September
Constellations: Ursa Major (part of it), Virgo, Libra	Constellations: Cygnus, Lyra, Aquila, Hercules	Constellations: Pegasus, Andromeda, Cassiopeia
Planets: Venus remains prominent in the morning sky, and Jupiter and Saturn are visible.	Planets: Venus continues to shine in the morning, and Jupiter and Saturn are still visible.	Planets: Venus is still a morning "star," and Jupiter and Saturn remain in the evening sky.

October	November	December
Constellations: Pegasus, Andromeda, Cassiopeia	Constellations: Orion, Taurus, Auriga	Constellations: Orion, Taurus, Auriga
Planets: Venus transitions from the morning to the evening sky, and Jupiter and Saturn are visible.	Planets: Venus becomes more prominent in the evening sky, while Jupiter and Saturn remain visible.	Planets: Venus shines brightly in the evening, and you can still see Jupiter and Saturn.

Here's a simplified overview of some key constellations you can look for in different seasons: The visibility of constellations in relation to the Northern Lights (Aurora Borealis) changes throughout the year due to the Earth's axial tilt and the changing seasons. Here's a rough guide to some prominent constellations that can be visible in the Northern Hemisphere during the you seasons when the Northern Lights are more likely to occur:

Spring (March - May)	Summer (June - August)	Autumn (September - November)	Winter (December - February)
- Leo: Becomes visible in the *eastern sky. - Virgo: Still visible, now in the *northern sky. - Boötes: Rises in the *east, near the Big Dipper. - Ursa Major (part of it): Visible throughout the night. - Ursa Minor (Little Dipper): Visible throughout the night. - Draco: Visible throughout the night. - Hercules: Best seen in the evening.	- Cygnus: Appears in the *northeast. - Lyra: Rises in the *east. - Aquila: Best seen in the evening. - Scorpius: Best seen in the evening. - Sagittarius: Best seen in the evening. - Cassiopeia: Visible throughout the night. - Ursa Major (part of it): Visible throughout the night. - Hercules: Visible in the eastern sky. - Draco: Can be seen in the north, near the Little Dipper.	- Pegasus: Best seen in the evening. - Andromeda: Best seen in the evening in the east. - Perseus: Best seen in the evening. - Auriga: Best seen in the evening. - Cassiopeia: Visible throughout the night in the northern sky, often near the Northern Lights. - Ursa Major (Big Dipper): Visible partly throughout the night. - Ursa Minor (Little Dipper): Visible throughout the night.	- Orion: Prominent in the southern sky during winter evenings. - Taurus: Also visible in the *winter sky, near Orion. - Gemini: Seen in the *east. - Canis Major: Best seen in the evening. - Ursa Major (part of it): Visible throughout the night. - Ursa Minor (Little Dipper): Visible throughout the night with Polaris (North Star) in the north. - Cassiopeia: Visible throughout the night. - Auriga: Found in the northwestern sky.

Note* Best seen in the evening.

Remember that the Northern Lights are most commonly visible during the fall and winter months when the nights are longest and darkest. Keep in mind that this is a simplified list, and the visibility of constellations can vary depending on your location within the Northern Hemisphere and the specific time of night. Additionally, some constellations, like the ones in the Ursa Major and Ursa Minor groups, are visible year-round in this hemisphere.

The Southern Lights, also known as the Aurora Australis, are most commonly visible in the southern hemisphere during the winter months. Here's a general guideline for when the Southern Lights are most frequently observed:

- Peak Season: The peak season for viewing the Aurora Australis is generally from late March to early September in the southern hemisphere. This corresponds to the southern hemisphere's winter and early spring.
- Strongest Months: The strongest and most reliable displays of the Southern Lights often occur during the winter months of June, July, and August.

During this time, the nights are longer, and the skies are darker, providing better conditions for observing the colorful displays of the Aurora Australis. However, it's important to note that the exact timing and visibility of the Southern Lights can vary based on your specific location within the southern hemisphere and other factors like solar activity and geomagnetic conditions.

To increase your chances of witnessing the Southern Lights, it's advisable to visit regions closer to the Antarctic Circle during the peak season and to check local forecasts and aurora tracking tools for the most accurate information on viewing opportunities.

A HEBREW CALENDAR OBSERVATION

This profound observational study serves as a powerful reminder that keeping the commandments holds a profound promise—a promise to awaken the consciousness of souls on Earth to the prospect of an immortal life. It is through the meticulous observation of calendar systems that we strive to reconstruct what was once lost after the dispersion of the 12 tribes to the four corners of the Earth.

In my journey of constructing a Hebrew calendar, I offer a guide that can elevate our understanding and enhance our studies, particularly in the context of observing the appointed feasts according to the seasons. These feasts are not mere traditions; they are an everlasting covenant, a pathway to an immortal existence, and a commitment to obey the ordinances, laws, and statutes of the Most High God.

This endeavor is not just about dates and calculations; it is a quest for enlightenment in the lunar-solar calendar, a celestial tapestry woven from the movements of the sun, moon, and stars. It is a testament to the glory of YAH's everlasting kingdom of gods, a journey of discovery, and a pursuit of wisdom and understanding.

Prepare to embark on a journey of understanding, where we delve into the intricate construction of the Hebrew calendar. Preferably the agricultural calendar which is based on the appointed times of the feasts held three times a year. At its heart lies the harmonious dance between solar years and lunar months, a delicate balance that shapes the rhythm of time. Uncover the profound significance of jubilee years, the sacred pause of sabbatical years, and the graceful leap years that keep this ancient calendar in sync with the cosmos. Join us as we explore the timeless wisdom behind the Hebrew calendar, a masterpiece of celestial and earthly alignment.

In accordance with Hebrew chronology, we currently reside within the sixth millennium. The Hebrew calendar commences its year count from the year 3761 BCE, a dating convention famously affirmed by the 12th-century Jewish philosopher Maimonides as the biblical Date of Creation.

In the Jewish calendar, years are denoted as AM (Anno Mundi), signifying their inclusion in the Anno Mundi epoch, which represents the age of the world as indicated in the Bible. To illustrate, the onset of the year 2023 in the Gregorian calendar corresponds to the year AM 5783 in the Jewish calendar.

The Jewish calendar consists of several different calendar systems, each serving different purposes. Two of the primary calendar systems used by Jewish communities are the civil calendar and the agricultural calendar:

Civil Calendar (Jewish Civil Year)	Agricultural Calendar (Jewish Agricultural Year)
- The Jewish civil calendar, also known as the "Hebrew calendar" or "lunar-solar calendar," is primarily used for determining the dates of holidays, festivals, and religious observances. - It is a lunisolar calendar, which means it is based on the cycles of the moon and adjusted to keep it synchronized with the solar year. - The civil year begins with the month of Tishrei and is used to calculate the dates for the High Holy Days, such as Rosh Hashanah (Jewish New Year) and Yom Kippur, as well as other major festivals like Sukkot, Passover, and Shavuot. - This calendar is crucial for religious and cultural events, and it follows a 19-year cycle, including leap months to align with the solar year.	- The Jewish agricultural calendar, often referred to as the "agricultural cycle" or "festivals related to agriculture," is focused on the agricultural cycles and the biblical festivals associated with the harvest seasons. - It is closely tied to the agricultural practices of ancient Israel and includes festivals like Pesach (Passover), Shavuot (Pentecost), and Sukkot (Feast of Tabernacles), which coincide with planting, harvest, and other agricultural activities. - While the civil calendar is primarily used for religious observances, the agricultural calendar is more aligned with the seasons and the land of Israel's agricultural rhythms.

In summary, the main difference between the civil and agricultural calendars used by Jewish communities lies in their purposes. The civil calendar is primarily for religious and cultural observances, while the agricultural calendar is rooted in the agricultural cycles of ancient Israel and includes festivals related to the land and its produce. Both calendars are important for understanding the rich tapestry of Hebrew tradition and history. Now lets take a look at how this hebrew calendar is constructed.

Hebrew Calendar Design

The Jewish year 5783 in the Hebrew calendar corresponds to the Gregorian calendar year of 2023. To find the Gregorian equivalent of a Jewish year, you generally need to subtract 3760 from the Jewish year. This method helps you convert Hebrew calendar years to Gregorian calendar years.

Metonic Cycle	Metonic Period	Hebrew Year Range	Gregorian Year Range
1	1-19 (1-7)	1 AM to 20 AM	3760 BCE to 3741 BCE
2	20-38 (8-14)	21 AM to 40 AM	3740 BCE to 3721 BCE
3	39-57 (15-21)	41 AM to 60 AM	3720 BCE to 3701 BCE
4	58-76 (22-28)	61 AM to 80 AM	3700 BCE to 3681 BCE
5	77-95 (29-35)	81 AM to 100 AM	3680 BCE to 3661 BCE
6	96-114 (36-42)	101 AM to 120 AM	3660 BCE to 3641 BCE
7	115-133 (43-49)	121 AM to 140 AM	3640 BCE to 3621 BCE

The Metonic cycle is a 19-year cycle used in the Hebrew calendar to reconcile lunar months with solar years. It helps determine the timing of leap years and other adjustments in the Hebrew calendar. To find the Metonic cycle for the Hebrew year 5783, you can use the following steps:

1. Start with the Hebrew year: 5783.

2. Add 1 (since the Metonic cycle starts with year 1): 5783 + 1 = 5784.

3. Divide by 19 (the length of the Metonic cycle): 5784 ÷ 19 = 304 remainder 8.

So, the Hebrew year 5783 is in the 8th year of the 304th Metonic cycle.

Metonic Cycle	Metonic Period	Hebrew Year Range	Gregorian Year Range
304	1-19 (1-7)	5777-5796	2017-2036
2	20-38 (8-14)	5797-5816	2037-2056
3	39-57 (15-21)	5817-5836	2057-2076
4	58-76 (22-28)	5837-5856	2077-2096
5	77-95 (29-35)	5857-5876	2097-2116
6	96-114 (36-42)	5877-5896	2117-2136
7	115-133 (43-49)	5897-5916	2137-2156

Civil & Agricultural Calendar

The Hebrew calendar has multiple New Year's days, but the most widely recognized and celebrated is Rosh Hashanah, which marks the beginning of the Jewish civil year. Rosh Hashanah typically falls in the Gregorian calendar during September or October. It's observed on the first and second days of the Hebrew month of Tishrei, which is the seventh month in the Hebrew calendar.

However, there is another important New Year's day on the Hebrew Agricultural calendar known as Rosh Hashanah La'ilanot, which marks the beginning of the tree-planting season. This New Year's day falls on the 15th day of the Hebrew month of Shevat and is observed as Tu B'Shevat, a holiday celebrating trees and nature.

The sign for the beginning of the Jewish civil year is the holiday of Rosh Hashanah. Rosh Hashanah is observed on the first and second days of the Hebrew month of Tishrei, which typically falls in September or October on the Gregorian calendar. It is known as the Jewish New Year and is marked by special prayers, the blowing of the shofar (a ram's horn), and the consumption of symbolic foods like apples dipped in honey to signify a sweet year ahead.

Rosh Hashanah is the moment when the Jewish civil calendar advances to the next year. For example, the arrival of Rosh Hashanah in the year 5783 in the Hebrew calendar would signify the beginning of that Jewish civil year. The Hebrew year advances by one year on Rosh Hashanah.

The Hebrew civil calendar months do not have alternating days like the days of the week. Instead, they are based on a lunar calendar, which means that the length of each month alternates between 29 and 30 days. Here is a list of the Hebrew calendar months, along with their typical lengths:

Civil Calendar (1st half)	(2nd half)
1. Tishrei תִּשְׁרֵי (30 days)	7. Nisan נִיסָן (30 days)
2. Cheshvan חֶשְׁוָן (29 or 30 days) (varies in leap years)	8. Iyar אִיָּ ר (29 days)
3. Kislev כִּסְלֵו (29 or 30 days) (varies in leap years)	9. Sivan סִיוָן (30 days)
4. Tevet טֵבֵת (29 days)	10. Tammuz תַּמּוּז (29 days)
5. Shevat שְׁבָט (30 days)	11. Av אָב (30 days)
6. Adar אֲדָ ר (29 days) (30 days in leap years, with an additional month of Adar II)	12. Elul אֱלוּ ל (29 days)

Please note that the lengths of Cheshvan and Kislev vary in leap years to ensure that certain Jewish holidays, like Passover (Pesach), continue to fall in the spring season. In leap years, they each have 30 days. In non-leap years, they each have 29 days. Additionally, there is a second month of Adar (Adar II) added in leap years to maintain the synchronization of the lunar and solar calendars.

So, while Rosh Hashanah in Tishrei is the more widely known New Year's day in the Hebrew calendar, Tu B'Shevat in Shevat marks another New Year related to trees and agriculture.

The Hebrew calendar consists of 12 or 13 months in a year, alternating between 29 and 30 days each. The Hebrew agriculture calendar aligns with the seasons and agricultural activities in ancient Israel and here are the corresponding Gregorian calendar approximate equivalents:

Agricultural Calendar (1st half)	(2nd half)
1. Nisan (נִיסָן) -Typically March to April	7. Tishrei (תִּשְׁרֵי)- Typically September to October
2. Iyar (אִייָר) -Typically April to May	8. Marcheshvan (מַרְחֶשְׁוָן)- Typically October to November
3. Sivan (סִיוָן) -Typically May to June	9. Kislev (כִּסְלֵו) - Typically November to December
4. Tammuz (תַּמּוּז) - Typically June to July	10. Tevet (טֵבֵת) - Typically December to January
5. Av (אָב) - Typically July to August	11. Shevat (שְׁבָט) -Typically January to February
6. Elul (אֱלוּל) - Typically August to September	12. Adar (אֲדָר) - Typically February to March (Adar I in leap years)
	13. Adar II (אֲדָר ב) - Typically February to March (Adar II in leap years)

The Hebrew calendar is a lunisolar calendar, so it incorporates an extra month (Adar II) in leap years to ensure that the Jewish holidays, particularly Passover (Pesach), which must occur in the spring, remain aligned with the seasons. In non-leap years, Adar II is not present, and Adar is the only Adar in the calendar.

Discover a fascinating tool that unveils the secrets of accounting for the 13th month, the start of the year, prophetic cycles, and even the extraordinary years of jubilee. Dive into the ancient wisdom of timekeeping, where time itself is measured in the pages of history. The Book of Jubilees reveals a world where weeks of years are the measure of life's grand tapestry. Unlock the mysteries of time in a journey that transcends the ordinary and explores the extraordinary.

Hebrew Calendar Overview

The Hebrew calendar, also known as the Jewish calendar, is a lunar-solar calendar system that has been in use for centuries to determine the dates of Jewish holidays and events. It is based on both lunar and solar cycles and is designed to keep the Jewish holidays, particularly Passover (Pesach), in alignment with the seasons. Here's how the Hebrew year corresponds to the Gregorian year:

1. Lunar Months: The Hebrew calendar is primarily lunar, with months based on the moon's phases. A lunar month is approximately 29.5 days long. To keep the calendar roughly in sync with the solar year, the Hebrew calendar uses a 19-year cycle known as the Metonic cycle. In this cycle, seven of the 19 years are leap years, each with an extra month (Adar II), making those years 13 months long. This adjustment helps to account for the approximately 365.25 days in a solar year.

2. Start of the Hebrew Year: In the Hebrew calendar, the year begins with the month of Tishrei, which usually falls in September or October of the Gregorian calendar. The exact date varies from year to year because the Hebrew calendar is based on lunar months.

3. Alignment with Gregorian Year: The Hebrew year corresponds to the Gregorian year from one Rosh Hashanah (the Jewish New Year, which occurs on the 1st day of Tishrei) to the next. For example, if Rosh Hashanah falls in September 2022, it marks the beginning of the Hebrew year 5783, which runs from September 2022 to September 2023.

4. Adjustments: Due to the differences in the lengths of lunar and solar months, the Hebrew year can vary in length from 353 to 385 days. The leap years help maintain alignment with the seasons over time.

5. Astronomical Accuracy: The Hebrew calendar's design aims to ensure that certain holidays, like Passover, always occur in the spring. This is achieved through careful calculations involving the moon's phases and the solar year.

In summary, the Hebrew year corresponds to the Gregorian year from one Rosh Hashanah to the next, with the exact date of Rosh Hashanah varying within the Gregorian calendar due to the lunar nature of the Hebrew calendar. The use of leap years and the Metonic cycle helps maintain alignment with the seasons and ensures that holidays are celebrated at their appropriate times in the Jewish calendar.

Now constructing the Hebrew calendar is a complex process that involves intercalating (inserting) months to keep it synchronized with the solar year. The Hebrew calendar is a lunisolar calendar, which means it combines lunar months with a solar year. Here is a simplified overview of how the Hebrew calendar is constructed:

1. Start with the Lunar Months: The Hebrew calendar is based on lunar months, with a typical lunar month lasting either 29 or 30 days. The months alternate in length, creating a basic lunar year of 354 days.

2. Incorporate Leap Years: To adjust for the discrepancy between the lunar year and the solar year (which is approximately 365.24 days), the Hebrew calendar includes leap years. Leap years have an extra month, known as Adar II or Adar Sheni, inserted. In a leap year, there are 13 months instead of the usual 12. This extra month helps bring the Hebrew calendar closer to the solar year.

3. Determine Leap Years: To decide which years are leap years, the Hebrew calendar follows a 19-year cycle called the Metonic cycle. In this cycle, seven out of every 19 years are leap years. The leap years occur in years 3, 6, 8, 11, 14, 17, and 19 of the cycle.

4. Calculating the Months: The length of the months in the Hebrew calendar depends on several rules and traditions, including the observation of the new moon and the avoidance of certain months for religious holidays. The months are adjusted to ensure that Passover (Pesach) falls in the spring.

5. Use of Moladot: The Hebrew calendar uses a system called "Moladot" to calculate the new moons and determine the beginnings of months. This involves mathematical calculations based on the lunar and solar cycles.

6. Insert Leap Month: If the Molad (calculated new moon) of Tishrei (the seventh month) occurs later than a specific time on the 30th day of Elul (the sixth month) in a leap year, then a leap month (Adar II) or 13th month is inserted before Nisan (the first month) to ensure that Passover occurs in the spring.

Again the practice of adding an extra month, known as Adar II (Adar Bet), occurs in a leap year. A leap year is inserted according to the Metonic cycle, which is a 19-year cycle that incorporates seven leap years. Remember each of these years inserts a leap month in the Hebrew calendar.

The purpose of adding an extra month is to ensure that the lunar-solar calendar stays synchronized with the solar year. The Hebrew calendar is based on lunar months, which are approximately 29.5 days long, resulting in a lunar year of about 354 days. To align with the solar year, which is approximately 365.25 days long, an extra month is added seven times during each 19-year cycle.

This additional month, Adar II, is inserted before the standard month of Adar, extending the year to 13 months. This adjustment helps to ensure that the Jewish holidays, especially Passover (Pesach), remain in their appropriate seasons.

This is a highly simplified overview of the Hebrew calendar construction. The actual calculations and rules are more intricate, and they require expertise in Jewish calendar calculations. It's a calendar that has been refined over centuries to ensure the proper timing of religious observances and festivals.

Hebrew Calendar Background

According to historical tradition, the Jewish calendar, designed to align religious holidays accurately, is attributed to the renowned sage Hillel, who served as the head of the Sanhedrin from 320 to 385 C.E. This calendar is a product of intricate mathematical and astronomical calculations. It operates on a 19-year cyclical system, punctuated by seven leap years strategically positioned to maintain the precise timing of significant holidays.

In antiquity, before these mathematical methods were established, the determination of leap years relied heavily on natural phenomena. Specifically, the Sanhedrin relied on observations of the environment: the behavior of weather, animals, and crops, as well as the arrival of the spring equinox. If these elements did not manifest a distinctly "spring-like" quality, and if the spring equinox did not occur prior to the midpoint of the month of Nissan, it was a clear signal to the judges that a leap year, characterized by an additional month known as Adar I, was required to preserve the accurate timing of Passover. This extra month was systematically inserted into the third, sixth, eighth, 11th, 14th, 17th, and 19th years of the 19-year cycle.

The calendrical precision achieved by Hillel and his collaborators derives from the harmonious synchronization of three key celestial factors: the Earth's rotation (approximately 24 hours per day), the moon's orbit around the Earth (approximately 29½ days per lunar month), and the Earth's orbit around the sun (approximately 365¼ days per solar year). Through comprehensive incorporation of these factors, Hillel devised a 19-year cycle, which featured seven leap years, each encompassing an additional month of 13 lunar months.

To ascertain whether a given year qualifies as a leap year, one must determine its position within the current 19-year Metonic cycle. This is accomplished by dividing the Jewish year's numerical value by 19 and examining the remainder. Specifically, years associated with a remainder of 3, 6, 8, 11, 14, 17, or 0 (representing the 19th year) are indicative of leap years within this cyclical framework.

In the Hebrew calendar, a standard year consists of precisely 12 months, yet a misalignment of approximately 11 days exists between 12 lunar cycles and a single solar cycle. The duration of

Earth's orbital journey around the Sun encompasses 365.25 days. Over the course of one year, 12 lunar cycles transpire, summing to a total of $12 \times 29.53059 = 354.36708$ days. Thus, the deviation between these lunar cycles and a solar cycle precisely amounts to $365.25 - 354.36708 = 10.88292$ days.

To harmonize the lunar reckoning of days with the solar cycle, a leap year is introduced every 19 years. During a leap year, the month of Adar is substituted with two months, Adar Alef and Adar Beit (אדר א' ואדר ב). Consequently, a Hebrew leap year comprises 13 months.

The scheduling of leap years adheres to a 19-year cyclic pattern. Within 19 years, the cumulative difference between lunar and solar cycles amounts to $19 \times 10.88292 = 206.77548$ days. This disparity corresponds to roughly seven 30-day intervals ($206.77548 / 7 = 6.892516$). However, the number 19 does not evenly divide by 7. Consequently, the Hebrew sages established that leap years occur in the following years within a 19-year cycle: 3, 6, 8, 11, 14, 17, and 19. The inclusion of seven 30-day months introduces an additional discrepancy of 3 days ($210 - 207 = 3$) over each 19-year period. To rectify this variation, 3 days are appended to the months of Cheshvan and Kislev at the culmination of each 19-year cycle.

Lunisolar Metonic Cycle

Every 19 years, a reconciliation between the solar and lunar cycles takes place within the Hebrew calendar. During this period, seven leap years are strategically added to the calendar to ensure that the measurement of time on Earth remains accurate and harmonized. Let's begin with how the synodic month relates to the phases of the moon and year for the calculation of the Metonic cycle.

A synodic month, also known as a lunar month, is the period of time it takes for the Moon to return to the same phase, such as from one full moon to the next full moon. On average, a synodic month lasts approximately 29.53 days.

A synodic year, on the other hand, refers to the time it takes for a planet, such as Earth, to return to the same position in its orbit with respect to the Sun, while considering the phases of a specific celestial body, like the Moon. For Earth, a synodic year is approximately 365.24 days, which is why we use leap years to adjust our calendar.

In summary, a synodic month relates to the Moon's phases, and a synodic year takes into account the relative positions of celestial bodies in their orbits, usually concerning a specific phase or position of one of those bodies, such as the Moon.

The Metonic cycle is primarily related to the synchronization of lunar and solar calendars. It's a period of 19 solar years (or 235 lunar months) that closely approximates the number of days in both calendar systems. The primary celestial sign related to the Metonic cycle is the alignment of the lunar and solar calendars.

Again the Metonic cycle is a 19-year cycle used in the Hebrew calendar to reconcile lunar months with solar years helps to determine the timing of leap years and other adjustments in the Hebrew calendar. To find the Metonic cycle for the Hebrew year 5783, you can use the following steps:

1. Start with the Hebrew year: 5783.
2. Add 1 (since the Metonic cycle starts with year 1): 5783 + 1 = 5784.
3. Divide by 19 (the length of the Metonic cycle): 5784 ÷ 19 = 304 remainder 8.

So, the Hebrew year 5783 is in the 8th year of the 304th Metonic cycle.

However, the Metonic cycle is a mathematical and astronomical concept used to reconcile lunar months and solar years within various calendar systems. It helps ensure that important religious or agricultural events in societies with lunar-based calendars, such as the Hebrew calendar, stay relatively synchronized with the seasons and solar year.

The Metonic year, named after the ancient Greek astronomer Meton, is a period of 19 solar years that closely approximates 235 lunar months. To determine a Metonic year, follow these steps:

1. Understand the Relationship: A Metonic year consists of 19 solar years, which means it's the time it takes for the Sun to return to the same position in the sky on the same date (for example, from one vernal equinox to the next). This period of 19 years closely matches 235 lunar months (synodic months), which is the time it takes for the Moon to return to the same phase (e.g., from one new moon to the next new moon).

2. Calculate Days: In one solar year, there are approximately 365.24 days. In one lunar month, there are about 29.53 days on average.

3. Multiply Lunar Months: Multiply the number of lunar months (235) by the average number of days in a lunar month (approximately 29.53). This gives you the total number of days in 235 lunar months.

   235 lunar months * 29.53 days/month ≈ 6,939.7 days

4. Divide by Solar Days: Divide the total number of lunar days (6,939.7) by the number of days in a solar year (365.24) to find the number of solar years in a Metonic cycle.

6,939.7 days ÷ 365.24 days/year ≈ 19 solar years

So, a Metonic year consists of 19 solar years. This cycle is used in various calendar systems, including the Hebrew calendar, to reconcile the differences between the lunar and solar calendars by adding leap months or years at specific intervals.

To determine which Metonic year corresponds to the current year, you would need to find the start of the Metonic cycle and count forward. The Metonic cycle consists of 19 solar years. Since it is based on the synchronization of lunar and solar cycles, it doesn't align precisely with the Gregorian calendar year. Keep in mind the leap month is added every 2 to 3 years according to the Metonic cycle.

The Metonic cycle starts with year 1, and the next Metonic year begins after 19 solar years. The current year within the Metonic cycle depends on when you start counting.

For example, if you start counting from the Gregorian year 2017, the Metonic years would be as follows:

- - 2017 (Year 1 in the Metonic cycle)
- - 2036 (Year 19 in the Metonic cycle)
- - 2037 (Year 1 in the next Metonic cycle)
- - 2056 (Year 19 in the next Metonic cycle)

So, if you're referring to the current Gregorian year, you would need to specify when you want to start counting within the Metonic cycle to determine the corresponding Metonic year.

Metonic Cycle	Leap Year Number	Hebrew Year	Gregorian Year
1st year excluded	1	5777	2017
(1 - 3)	3	5780	2020
(4 - 6)	6	5783	2023
(7 - 8)	8	5785	2025
(9 - 11)	11	5788	2028
(12 -14)	14	5791	2031
(15 - 17)	17	5794	2034
(18 - 19)	19	5796	2036

In order to mitigate the occurrence of certain Jewish holidays, such as Rosh Hashana, aligning with specific days of the week, adjustments are made by either adding an extra day to the 8th month (Marcheshvan) or subtracting a day from the 9th month (Kislev) within the Jewish calendar. Consequently, a year in the Jewish calendar can manifest in six distinct durations:

1. Cheserah or Deficient Year: These years consist of 353 days in common years and 383 days in leap years.

2. Kesidrah or Regular Year: Regular years encompass 354 days in common years and 384 days in leap years.

3. Shlemah or Complete Year: Complete years encompass 355 days in common years and 385 days in leap years.

These designations delineate the various year lengths within the Jewish calendar, which serve to harmonize the alignment of holidays with specific days of the week. Appointed Times for Passover (Pesach), Feast of Unleavened Bread, and the counting of the Omer are transposed on the Gregorian calendar according to the ordinance.

April 2023

Sunday	Monday	Tuesday	Wednesday	Thursday	Friday	Saturday
						1 10th of Nisan Shabbat HaGadol Yom HaAliyah **19:40** Havdalah (42 min)
2 11th of Nisan	**3** 12th of Nisan	**4** 13th of Nisan	**5** 14th of Nisan **05:10** Fast begins Ta'anit Bechorot Erev Pesach **18:21** Candle lighting	**6** 15th of Nisan **Pesach I**	**7** 16th of Nisan Pesach II (CH"M) **19:44** Havdalah (42 min) 1st day of the Omer **18:22** Candle lighting	**8** 17th of Nisan Pesach III (CH"M) 2nd day of the Omer **19:45** Havdalah (42 min)
9 18th of Nisan Pesach IV (CH"M) 3rd day of the Omer	**10** 19th of Nisan Pesach V (CH"M) 4th day of the Omer	**11** 20th of Nisan Pesach VI (CH"M) 5th day of the Omer **18:25** Candle lighting	**12** 21st of Nisan **Pesach VII** 6th day of the Omer **19:48** Havdalah (42 min)	**13** 22nd of Nisan 7th day of the Omer	**14** 23rd of Nisan 8th day of the Omer **18:27** Candle lighting	**15** 24th of Nisan Mevarchim Chodesh Iyyar 9th day of the Omer **19:50** Havdalah (42 min)
16 25th of Nisan 10th day of the Omer	**17** 26th of Nisan 11th day of the Omer	**18** 27th of Nisan Yom HaShoah 12th day of the Omer	**19** 28th of Nisan 13th day of the Omer	**20** 29th of Nisan 14th day of the Omer	**21** 30th of Nisan Rosh Chodesh Iyyar 15th day of the Omer **18:31** Candle lighting	**22** 1st of Iyyar, 5783 Rosh Chodesh Iyyar 16th day of the Omer **19:55** Havdalah (42 min)
23 2nd of Iyyar 17th day of the Omer	**24** 3rd of Iyyar 18th day of the Omer	**25** 4th of Iyyar Yom HaZikaron 19th day of the Omer	**26** 5th of Iyyar Yom HaAtzma'ut 20th day of the Omer	**27** 6th of Iyyar 21st day of the Omer	**28** 7th of Iyyar 22nd day of the Omer **18:36** Candle lighting	**29** 8th of Iyyar 23rd day of the Omer **20:00** Havdalah (42 min)
30 9th of Iyyar 24th day of the Omer						

*Candle lighting occurs 40 min. prior to sunset.

ANNUAL FESTIVALS APPOINTED TIMES ON AGRICULTURAL/ CIVIL CALENDAR

The Hebrew calendar, an officially recognized calendar in Israel, operates as a lunisolar system, wherein months are governed by lunar cycles, while years are synchronized with solar periods. Within this calendar, the chronological sequence of years is computed from the estimation of Earth's creation. This calendar comprises 12 months, with an additional month, Adar II, intercalated during leap years. Notably, the year 2022 (or 5782 in the Hebrew calendar) marked the most recent occurrence of a leap year.

The Hebrew calendar is deeply rooted in religious and agricultural traditions, and its festivals are organized around various cycles, including seven-week cycles, lunar months, and years.

The Passover, Offers Eternal Life (An Atonement for Sin)

Purge out therefore the old leaven, that ye may be a new lump, as ye are unleavened. For even Christ our passover is sacrificed for us: 1 Corinthians 5:7 And the priest shall make an atonement for all the congregation of the children of Israel, and it shall be forgiven them; for it is ignorance: and they shall bring their offering, a sacrifice made by fire unto the Lord, and their sin offering before the Lord, for their ignorance: Numbers 15:25-28 But that ye may know that the Son of man hath power on earth to forgive sins, (he saith to the sick of the palsy,) Mark 2:10
Whither the forerunner is for us entered, even Yeshua, made a high priest forever after the order of Melchisedec. Hebrews 6:20 Seeing then that we have a great high priest, that is passed into the heavens, Yeshua the Son of YAH, let us hold fast our profession.
Having therefore, brethren, boldness to enter into the holiest by the blood of Yeshua,
20 By a new and living way, which he hath consecrated for us, through the veil, that is to say, his flesh; And having a high priest over the house of YAH. Hebrews 10:19-21

Having abolished in his flesh the enmity, even the law of commandments contained in ordinances; for to make in himself of twain one new man, so making peace; And that he might reconcile both unto YAH in one body by the cross, having slain the enmity thereby: And came and preached peace to you which were afar off, and to them that were nigh. Ephesians 2:15-18 For through him we both have access by one Spirit unto the Father. Luke 22:18 For I say unto you, I will not drink of the fruit of the vine, until the kingdom of YAH shall come. 19 And he took bread, and gave thanks, and brake it, and gave unto them, saying, This is my body which is given for you: this do in remembrance of me. 20 Likewise also the cup after supper, saying, This cup is the new testament in my blood, which is shed for you. 1 Corinthians 11:24-25 Whoso **eateth my flesh**, and **drinketh my blood**, hath **eternal life**; and I will raise him up at the last day. John 6:54

Spring is constant in all four seasons.
Knowing everything in the world.

1. Spring Indian Azaleas (Rhododendron indicum):

- Blooming Season: Indian Azaleas typically bloom in spring, typically from late March to early May, depending on the climate and location.
- Characteristics: Indian Azaleas produce vibrant clusters of trumpet-shaped flowers in various colors, including shades of pink, red, white, and purple. They are known for their lush and showy blooms.

2. Summer Royal Poignant Blossoms (Lilies, such as Oriental Lilies):

- Blooming Season: Lilies, including Oriental Lilies, are known for their summer blooms, which generally occur from late spring to midsummer, usually from June to August.
- Characteristics: Oriental Lilies are renowned for their large, fragrant, and trumpet-shaped flowers that come in various colors, including white, pink, and deep crimson. They make striking additions to summer gardens.

Gregorian Date ▸ 0	1	2	3	4	5	6	7
Day of Hebrew Month — **Day 0** Example Day Note regarding Hebrew Day	**Day 1** New Month	**Day 2**	**Day 3**	**Day 4**	**Day 5**	**Day 6** Preparation Day	**Shabbat**
New months in new seasons always fall on the Gregorian Sunday, starting with the first Sunday in April. 8	**Day 8**	9 **Day 9**	10 **Day 10**	11 **Day 11**	12 **Day 12**	13 **Day 13** Preparation Day	14 **Shabbat** Passover at Sunset
To see why Passover is at the end of a 7th Day Shabbat, read our article: *The Death and Resurrection of the Messiah*. 15	**Day 15** Unleavened Bread (Day 1)	16 **Day 16** Unleavened Bread (Day 2)	17 **Day 17** Unleavened Bread (Day 3)	18 **Day 18** Unleavened Bread (Day 4)	19 **Day 19** Unleavened Bread (Day 5)	20 **Day 20** Unleavened Bread (Day 6)	21 **Shabbat** Unleavened Bread (Day 7)
Passover is observed from evening to morning, followed by Unleavened Bread Day 1, making it a high Sabbath. 22	**Day 22** Wave Sheaf	23 **Day 23**	24 **Day 24**	25 **Day 25**	26 **Day 26**	27 **Day 27** Preparation Day	28 **Shabbat**
	29 **Day 29**	30 **Day 30**					
			They finished investigating all the men who had marr... ...rst day of the first month. 🌐 kingdompreppers.org **Ezra 10:17**				

Prepare Yourself for the Passover to Eternal Life.

The Son of man came **eating** and **drinking**, and they say, Behold a man gluttonous, and a winebibber, a friend of publicans and sinners. But **wisdom** is justified of her **children**.

Here's an overview of some of the key festivals and cycles in the Hebrew calendar:

1. **Weekly Cycle:** Shabbat (Sabbath)

- Frequency: Every week, from Friday evening (sunset) to Saturday evening (sunset).

- Observance: A day of rest, prayer, and family activities.

2. **Monthly Cycle:** Rosh Chodesh (New Moon)

- Frequency: Occurs at the beginning of each Hebrew month.

- Observance: A special time for prayer and reflection, often marked by additional synagogue services and festive meals.

3. **Seven-Week Cycle:** Counting the Omer (Sefirat HaOmer)

- Frequency: Occurs during the 49 days (7 weeks) between Passover (Pesach) and Shavuot.

- Observance: Each day, a blessing is recited, and the count is made in anticipation of Shavuot.

4. **Festivals by Month:**

- Nisan (1st Month of Passover):

- Passover (Pesach): Celebrates the 14th day Exodus from Egypt, typically in March or April. Lasts for 7 or 8 days (15th - 21st day).

- Iyar (2nd Month of Shavuot):

- Lag BaOmer: Occurs on the 33rd day of the Omer count, often marked by bonfires and outdoor celebrations.

- Sivan (3rd Month of Shavuot):

- Shavuot: Celebrates the 16th day giving of the Torah at Mount Sinai, typically in May or June. Often associated with dairy foods and all-night Torah study.

- Tammuz (4th Month):

- 17th of Tammuz: A fast day commemorating the breach of the walls of Jerusalem before the destruction of the First and Second Temples.

2023

Jewish Festivals:	
Feb 05	Tu Bishvat
Mar 06	Purim
Mar 08	Shushan Purim
Apr 05	Passover-First Day
Apr 13	Passover-Final Day
Apr 18	Yom Hoshoah
Apr 25	Yom HaZikaron
Apr 26	Yom HaAtzma'ut
May 05	Second Passover
May 09	Lag BaOmer
May 19	Yom Yershalayim
May 25	Shavuot (Ist Day)
May 26	Shavuot
Jul 26	Tish'a B'Av
Sep 15	Rosh HaShana
Sep 17	Rosh HaShana Ends
Sep 18	Fast of Gedaliah
Sep 25	Yom Kippur
Sep 29	Sukoot Starts
Oct 06	Sukoot Ends
Oct 06	Shimini Atzeret
Oct 07	Simchat Torah
Dec 07	Hanukkah Starts
Dec 15	Hanukkah Ends

- Av (5th Month):

- Tisha B'Av: Tisha B'Av is a day of fasting and mourning for the destruction of both the First Temple by the Babylonians in 586 BCE and the Second Temple by the Romans in 70 CE. Tisha B'Av falls on the 9th day of 5th month. Therefore, it is referred to as "Tisha" (9) "B'Av" (Av), and it is observed on the 9th of Av every year typically in July or August.

- Elul (6th Month)::

- Selichot: Special penitential prayers and preparatory rituals leading up to the High Holy Days.

5. High Holy Days:

- Rosh Hashanah: The Jewish New Year, observed in Tishrei, 1st day of 7th month usually in September or October. A memorial of blowing the Shofars (Trumpets).

- Yom Kippur: The Day of Atonement, observed in Tishrei, takes place on the 9th day at evening until the evening of the 10th day of the 7th month.

- Sukkot: The Festival of Booths (Tabernacles), observed in Tishrei on the 15th - 21st day of the 7th month, featuring the construction of temporary booths (sukkot) and the Four Species (Lulav and Etrog).

- Simchat Torah: Celebrates the completion of the annual Torah reading cycle, observed in Tishrei, immediately following Sukkot on the 22nd day of the 7th month.

These festivals and cycles are integral to Jewish life and tradition, and they serve as a means of commemorating historical events, renewing spiritual commitments, and fostering community bonds throughout the Hebrew calendar year.

Here's the meaning of each festival held throughout the year.

Holidays begin the evening before because a Jewish "day" begins and ends at sunset, rather than at midnight.

Rosh Hashanah* (Jewish New Year)	Traditions include eating apples dipped in honey and blowing the *shofar* (ram's horn). Most Jews attend synagogue on these two days and the preceding evening.
Yom Kippur* (Day of Atonement)	Considered by Jews to be the holiest and most solemn day of the year. Fasting begins at sundown and ends after nightfall the following day. Most Jews attend synagogue on this day and the preceding evening.
Sukkot* (Feast of Tabernacles or Booths)	A seven-day festival. One of the three pilgrimage festivals mentioned in the Bible. Celebrated by the building of a *sukkah*, or temporary dwelling, outdoors. Work is traditionally prohibited on the 1 st and 2nd days.
Shemini Atzeret* (Eighth day of Sukkot)	Immediately follows the conclusion of Sukkot. Work is traditionally prohibited.
Simchat Torah* (Rejoicing of the Law)	Concludes and begins anew the annual reading cycle of the *Torah*, the Five Books of Moses that make up the Jewish Bible. Immediately follows Sukkot and Shemini Atzeret. Work is traditionally prohibited.
Hannukkah* (Festival of Lights)	An eight-day festival marked by the lighting of candles—one the 1st night, two the 2nd, etc.—using a special candle holder called a *menorah* or *chanukiah*. Traditions include spinning *dreidels* (tops), eating potato *latkes* (pancakes), and giving gifts.
Tu B'Shevat (New Year of the Trees)	Originally celebrated as an agricultural festival marking the emergence of spring, today celebrations focus on environmental awareness. Trees are often planted in honor or memory of loved ones.
Purim	Commemorates the events in the Book of Esther. One of the most joyous holidays. Traditions include wearing costumes and giving care packages to those in need.
Passover* (Pesach)	Commemorates the liberation of the Hebrew slaves from Egypt. A feast called a *seder* is held on the 1st two nights of the eight-day holiday. Leavened food (e.g., bread, cake) and most grain products are not eaten. *Matzah* (unleavened bread) is often eaten instead. Work is traditionally prohibited on the 1st, 2nd, 7th, and 8th days.

Yom Ha'Shoah* (Holocaust Remembrance Day)	Yom Ha'Shoah is a Jewish observance commemorating the lives and heroism of the six million Jewish people and five million others who perished in the Holocaust between 1933 and 1945.
Yom Hazikaron* (Israeli Memorial Day)	Yom Hazikaron is Israel's Official Memorial Day for her fallen soldiers and victims of terrorism. Falling either in late April or early May every year, Yom Hazikaron is an especially solemn time and marked by ceremonies and silences across the country.
Yom HaAtzmaut* (Israeli Independence Day)	Yom HaAtzmaut marks the anniversary of the establishment of the modern state of Israel in 1948. It is observed on or near the 5th of the Hebrew month of Iyar on the Jewish calendar, which usually falls in April.
Shavuot* (Feast of Weeks, Pentecost)	According to Rabbinic tradition, the Ten Commandments were given to the Jewish people at Mt. Sinai on this day. It is traditional to eat meals containing dairy.
Tisha B'Av	Annual fast day commemorating the destruction of the First and Second Temples in Jerusalem and the subsequent exile of the Jews from the land of Israel. Today in many modern Jewish communities, Tisha B'Av stands as a day to reflect on the suffering that still occurs in our world.

'Commonly observed by synagogue attendance or family gatherings. On these days and on the Sabbath (Friday evening through Saturday evening), work is traditionally prohibited; individuals may be absent from school or work.

6. Jubilee Cycle: Yovel (Jubilee Year)

- Occurs every 50 years observed in Tishrei on Yom Kippur (Day of Atonement), marked by the release of slaves, return of ancestral land, and a year of rest and renewal.

These festivals and cycles are integral to Jewish life and tradition, and they serve as a means of commemorating historical events, renewing spiritual commitments, and fostering community bonds throughout the Hebrew calendar year.

Jubilee of 7 Year Cycles

The Jubilee year in the Hebrew calendar is a special year that occurs every 50 years. It is known as the "Yovel" in Hebrew and has several unique features, including the release of slaves, the return of ancestral land, and a year of rest and renewal. Determining the Jubilee year involves a combination of counting cycles and observing specific commandments from the Hebrew Bible (Old Testament). Here are the key steps:

1. Start with the Counting: The Jubilee year follows a 49-year cycle, which means it's the 50th year after seven cycles of seven years each (7 x 7 = 49). This cycle is known as the "Shemitah" cycle.

2. Identify the Shemitah Year: The seventh year in each seven-year cycle is called the Shemitah year. It is a year of rest for the land, and debts are generally forgiven during this year. Count seven Shemitah cycles (7 x 7 = 49 years) to reach the year right before the Jubilee.

3. Declare the Jubilee: The Jubilee year begins on the Day of Atonement (Yom Kippur) following the 49th year. On Yom Kippur of the 49th year, the Jubilee year is declared.

4. Observe Jubilee Commandments: During the Jubilee year, several commandments are observed, including:

   - The release of Hebrew slaves.
   - The return of ancestral land to its original owner or their descendants.
   - The land lies fallow, just as in the Shemitah year.
   - A time of renewal and celebration.

It's important to note that there is limited historical evidence of the observance of the Jubilee year in ancient Israel, and there are differing interpretations and practices among Jewish communities today. Determining the specific year of the Jubilee in the Hebrew calendar may vary among different Jewish traditions and authorities. Therefore, consulting with religious authorities or scholars within a specific Jewish community is often necessary to ascertain the timing of the Jubilee year.

Jubilee Year Calculation

To determine if 5783 is a Jubilee year, you should use the following steps:

1. Identify the current year in the Hebrew calendar. In your question, you mentioned the year 5783.

2. Check the last Jubilee year before the current year. The Jubilee year occurs every 50 years. 5783 divided by 50 equals approximately 115.66.

3. If the result is a whole number, then the current year is a Jubilee year. If the result has a decimal part, then it is not a Jubilee year.

In this case, 5783 divided by 50 equals approximately 115.66, so it is not a Jubilee year.

Therefore we can conclude that year 5750 is the most recent Jubilee year in the Hebrew calendar since its is fully divisible as a whole number:

1. Identify the year 5750 in the Hebrew calendar.

2. Check the last Jubilee year before the year 5750. The Jubilee year occurs every 50 years. 5750 divided by 50 equals 115.

3. Since the result is a whole number (115), the year 5750 is indeed a Jubilee year in the Hebrew calendar.

4. Now to determine which year according to the 49 year cycle we are subtract 5783 from 5750 equals 33.

So, the Hebrew year 5783 is in the 33rd year of the 49th Jubilee cycle.

In the Hebrew calendar, a Jubilee cycle consists of seven sets of seven-year cycles culminating in the Jubilee year, seven Shemitah (Sabbatical) cycles lead up to and conclude with the arrival of the Jubilee year. In the Hebrew calendar, a Jubilee year is a significant and special year that follows the completion of seven cycles of seven years each, totaling 49 years.

Here's how it works:

1. Seven-Year Cycles: There are seven Shemitah (Sabbatical) cycles of seven years each, totaling 49 years.

2. Jubilee Year: The 50th year is the Jubilee year, which follows the completion of the seven cycles. It is a special year of celebration and observance, including the release of slaves, the return of ancestral land, and other significant events.

So, while there are seven sets of seven-year cycles (49 years) within a Jubilee cycle, the Jubilee year itself is distinct and separate from these regular cycles, occurring every 50 years.

The significance of the Jubilee year includes:

1. Release of Slaves: During the Jubilee year, Hebrew slaves were to be set free, and they could return to their families and ancestral land.

2. Return of Ancestral Land: Land that had been sold or leased was to be returned to its original owner or their descendants.

3. Rest for the Land: The land was left fallow, given a year of rest, similar to the Shemitah (Sabbatical) year.

4. Reaffirmation of Social and Economic Equality: The Jubilee year was a time to reset social and economic imbalances and provide a fresh start for individuals and families.

5. Religious Observance: The Jubilee year carried spiritual and religious significance, with special rituals and observances.

The term "culminating" here means that after the completion of seven cycles of seven years (49 years), the Jubilee year arrives, marking a special time of renewal, freedom, and restoration in various aspects of society, including personal and economic life. It is a unique and important concept in the Hebrew calendar and holds cultural, religious, and historical significance.

Once the Jubilee year concludes, the next year marks the beginning of a new seven-year cycle. The first year of this cycle is counted as the first year (Year 1), and the seventh year within that cycle is the Shemitah year (Year 7), which is a year of rest for the land and the remission of certain debts.

So, to clarify, the sequence is as follows:

- Jubilee Year (Year 1 of the Jubilee cycle)
- Year following the Jubilee (Start of the new seven-year cycle, Year 1)
- Years 2 through 6 within the seven-year cycle
- Shemitah (Sabbatical) Year (Year 7 within the seven-year cycle)
- Years 8 through 13 within the next seven-year cycle
- And so on, with each Shemitah year occurring every seventh year within the seven-year cycle.

This pattern continues, with the Shemitah year occurring at the end of each seven-year cycle, after the Jubilee year.

The seven-year cycle in the Hebrew calendar, including the Shemitah (Sabbatical) year, is based on a combination of solar years and lunar months. The Hebrew calendar is a lunisolar calendar, which means it uses both lunar months and adjustments for the solar year to keep its months and holidays synchronized with the seasons.

Here's how the seven-year cycle works:

1. Solar Year: A solar year is approximately 365.24 days, which is the time it takes for the Earth to orbit the Sun. The Hebrew calendar accounts for this by having a 7-year cycle that includes 2 or 3 leap years.

2. Lunar Months: A lunar month, or synodic month, is approximately 29.53 days, which is the time it takes for the Moon to go through its phases (e.g., from one new moon to the next new moon). The Hebrew calendar months are based on lunar months.

3. Shemitah (Sabbatical) Year: Every seventh year in the Hebrew calendar is a Shemitah year, which corresponds to the Sabbatical year. During this year, the land lies fallow, and debts are forgiven. This cycle of seven years is based on the interaction between the lunar and solar calendars.

4. Leap Years: To reconcile the lunar and solar years, the Hebrew calendar adds an extra month (Adar II) to the calendar in leap years. This ensures that the Jewish holidays, particularly Passover (Pesach), which must occur in the spring, remain aligned with the seasons.

In summary, the seven-year cycle in the Hebrew calendar is primarily based on the lunar months, but it incorporates adjustments for the solar year through the addition of leap months. This lunisolar calendar system is designed to maintain the timing of religious observances and holidays in alignment with both lunar and solar events.

After the Jubilee year in the Hebrew calendar, the new year begins with the month of Tishrei. Specifically, the Jewish New Year, known as Rosh Hashanah, falls on the first and second days of Tishrei. This marks the beginning of the Jewish civil year.

Tishrei is also the seventh month in the Hebrew calendar, but it is the month associated with many important holidays, including Rosh Hashanah (the Jewish New Year), Yom Kippur (the Day of Atonement), and Sukkot (the Feast of Tabernacles).

So, after the Jubilee year, the cycle of months begins anew with Tishrei as the starting point for the Jewish civil year. Pesach (Passover), Shavuot (Pentecost), and Sukkot (Feast of Tabernacles) are all significant Jewish holidays with specific dates in the Hebrew calendar. Here are the months in which these holidays begin: Ex 23:17 & Deu 16:16

1. Pesach (Passover): Pesach begins on the 15th day of the Hebrew month of Nisan. It typically falls in March or April of the Gregorian calendar.

2. Shavuot (Pentecost): Shavuot begins on the 16th day of the Hebrew month of Sivan. It usually falls in May or June of the Gregorian calendar.

3. Sukkot (Feast of Tabernacles): Sukkot begins on the 15th day of the Hebrew month of Tishrei. It generally falls in September or October of the Gregorian calendar.

   These holidays are observed based on the lunar-solar Hebrew calendar, and their dates may vary slightly from year to year in the Gregorian calendar.

This verse is part of the instructions given to the Israelites regarding the three annual pilgrimage festivals:

"Three times a year all the men are to appear before the Most High God…"

Spring is constant in all four seasons.
Knowing everything in the world.

1. Spring Indian Azaleas (Rhododendron indicum):

   - Blooming Season: Indian Azaleas typically bloom in spring, typically from late March to early May, depending on the climate and location.
   - Characteristics: Indian Azaleas produce vibrant clusters of trumpet-shaped flowers in various colors, including shades of pink, red, white, and purple. They are known for their lush and showy blooms.

2. Summer Royal Poignant Blossoms (Lilies, such as Oriental Lilies):

   - Blooming Season: Lilies, including Oriental Lilies, are known for their summer blooms, which generally occur from late spring to midsummer, usually from June to August.
   - Characteristics: Oriental Lilies are renowned for their large, fragrant, and trumpet-shaped flowers that come in various colors, including white, pink, and deep crimson. They make striking additions to summer gardens.

3. Autumn Sweet Osmanthus (Osmanthus fragrans):

   - Blooming Season: Sweet Osmanthus, also known as Fragrant Olive or Tea Olive, typically blooms in the autumn months, often from late September to November.
   - Characteristics: Sweet Osmanthus produces small, highly fragrant, and tiny white or orange-yellow flowers that release a delightful, sweet scent. The flowers are often used to make perfumes and teas.

Spring is constant in all four seasons.
Knowing everything in the world.

4. Winter Plum Blossoms (Prunus mume):

- Blooming Season: Plum blossoms are famous for their winter blooms, usually occurring from late winter to early spring, typically from January to March, depending on the climate.
- Characteristics: Plum blossoms are known for their delicate, five-petaled flowers in shades of white, pink, or red. They are associated with the arrival of spring in East Asian cultures and are highly symbolic.

Africa is home to a diverse range of beautiful flowers, and choosing the "most beautiful" can be subjective as it depends on personal preferences. However, one of the stunning flowers that bloom in the springtime in various parts of **Africa is the African Lily (Agapanthus africanus)**.

Here are some details about the African Lily:

• **Blooming Season:** African Lilies typically bloom in late spring to early summer, which in the southern hemisphere, including parts of Africa, corresponds to the months of October to December.

Africa is a continent with an incredibly diverse range of climates and ecosystems, and it's home to many beautiful flowers that bloom during the summer months. One of the striking and iconic flowers of Africa that blooms in summer is the **Bird of Paradise flower (Strelitzia reginae)**.

Bird of Paradise Flower (Strelitzia reginae):

• Blooming Season: Bird of Paradise flowers typically bloom during the summer months, which vary depending on the specific region within Africa but often occur from late spring to early autumn.

One of the most striking and beautiful flowers that blooms in autumn in various parts of the African continent is the **African Lily** or **Agapanthus** (Agapanthus spp.).

Characteristics:

- **Blooming Season:** Agapanthus typically blooms in late summer and early autumn, often from late August to October, depending on the specific region and climate in Africa.

One of the most beautiful winter-blooming flowers in Africa is the African Violet (Saintpaulia ionantha). Although African Violets are native to East Africa, they are widely cultivated and cherished as ornamental houseplants around the world, including Africa.

African Violet (Saintpaulia ionantha):

- **Blooming Season:** African Violets are known for their ability to bloom throughout the year, including during the winter months.

Each of these flowers has its unique blooming season, which contributes to the diversity and beauty of gardens and landscapes throughout the year. Gardeners and nature enthusiasts can plan their gardens to enjoy a continuous display of blooms across the seasons by choosing a variety of plants that flower during different times of the year.

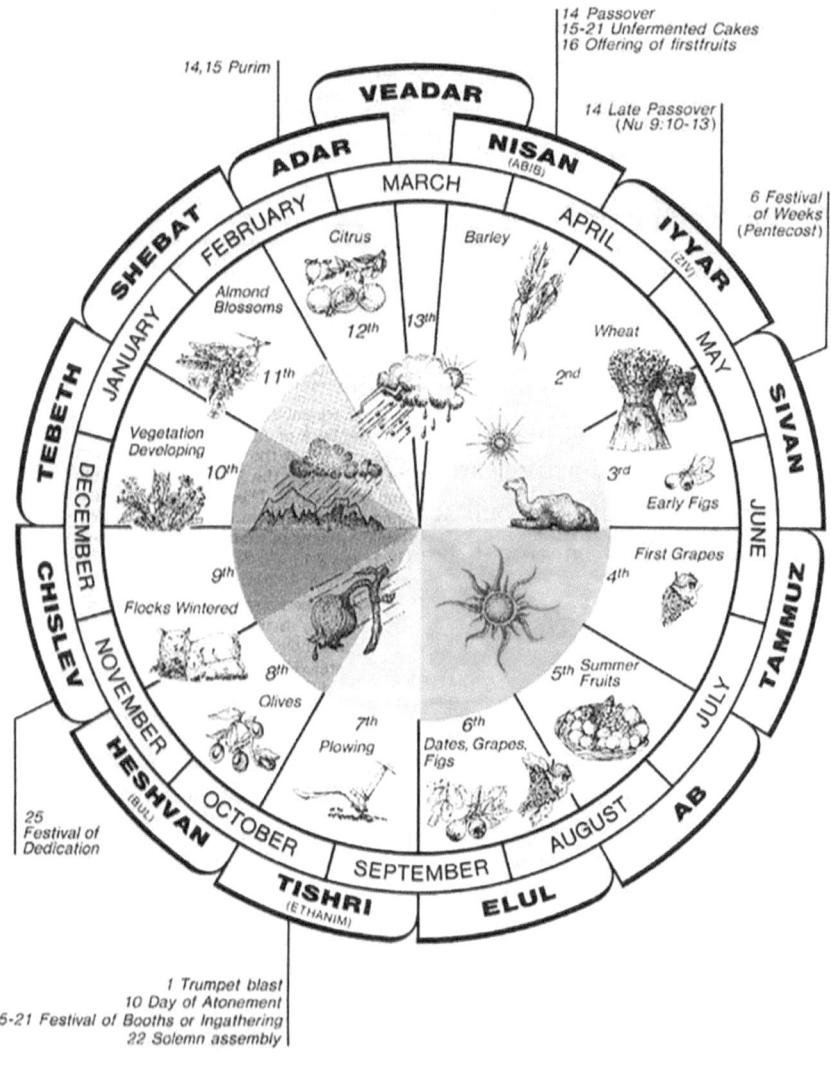

14 Passover
15-21 Unfermented Cakes
16 Offering of firstfruits

14,15 Purim

14 Late Passover
(Nu 9:10-13)

6 Festival
of Weeks
(Pentecost)

VEADAR

ADAR

NISAN
(ABIB)

SHEBAT

FEBRUARY

MARCH

APRIL

IYYAR
(ZIV)

TEBETH

JANUARY

Almond
Blossoms

Citrus

Barley

Wheat

MAY

SIVAN

12th

13th

2nd

11th

3rd

Early Figs

JUNE

Vegetation
Developing

10th

First Grapes

TAMMUZ

CHISLEV

DECEMBER

9th

4th

Flocks Wintered

5th Summer
Fruits

JULY

NOVEMBER

8th

Olives

6th

7th

Dates, Grapes,
Figs

AB

HESHVAN
(BUL)

OCTOBER

Plowing

AUGUST

25
Festival of
Dedication

TISHRI
(ETHANIM)

SEPTEMBER

ELUL

1 Trumpet blast
10 Day of Atonement
15-21 Festival of Booths or Ingathering
22 Solemn assembly

Shavuot of 7 Week Cycles

During the period of the Temple in Jerusalem, an Omer of barley was brought as an offering on the second day of Passover (Pesach). This offering marked the beginning of the barley harvest and was presented in conjunction with the festival. After this offering was made, the Counting of the Omer would commence, a practice that continued for a total of 49 days, leading up to the holiday of Shavuot.

Omer: an ancient Hebrew unit of dry capacity equal to $^1/_{10}$ ephah. 2. a. often capitalized: the sheaf of barley traditionally offered in Jewish Temple worship on the second day of the Passover.

The last verse of Exodus 16 clarifies that an omer consisted of a tenth of an ephah. An "ephah" was equal to about twenty quarts in today's measurements, so an "omer" was about two quarts.

An "Omer" is an ancient Hebrew unit of measurement for grain or produce. In the context of Jewish tradition, particularly during the Counting of the Omer, it refers to a specific offering of barley made in the Temple during biblical times.

Today, during the Counting of the Omer, Jewish people engage in a daily count of these 49 days as a spiritual practice, connecting the themes of physical liberation (Passover) with spiritual revelation (Shavuot). While the original agricultural significance remains, it has taken on a more symbolic and spiritual meaning in contemporary Jewish practice.

Counting the weeks from the end of Pesach to celebrate Shavuot is a tradition known as "Counting the Omer" (Sefirat HaOmer). It involves counting the days and weeks between these two Jewish holidays. Here's how you can do it:

1. Start on the Second Night of Pesach: Counting the Omer begins on the second night of Pesach (Passover), which is the first night of the festival where the Israelites were freed from Egypt.

2. Count Each Day: Starting from that night, count each day, both in Hebrew and in your native language. For example, you would say, "Today is the first day of the Omer" and "Today is 1 day of the Omer."

3. Count Each Night: The counting is traditionally done in the evening after sunset but before nightfall. It is customary to count the Omer in a synagogue or at home with a blessing, followed by the count.

4. Count for 49 Days: Continue counting each day for a total of 49 days, which is seven weeks. The 49th day is the day before Shavuot.

5. Celebrate Shavuot: Shavuot begins on the 50th day, which is the day after the completion of the counting of the Omer. It is the festival that commemorates the giving of the Torah at Mount Sinai.

During this period, some people also reflect on personal growth and self-improvement, as it is seen as a time of spiritual preparation leading up to the receiving of the Torah on Shavuot.

It's important to note that there are specific blessings that are traditionally recited when counting the Omer, so you may want to consult with a rabbi or refer to a Jewish calendar or guide for the correct blessings and instructions for the year you are observing.

Shabbat of 7 Day Cycles

The seven-day cycle in which the seventh day, the Shabbat (Sabbath), is observed as a day of rest is a fundamental part of various religious and cultural traditions of the Hebrews, Judaism, and Christianity. To determine the seven-day cycle and identify the Sabbath as a day of rest, follow these steps:

1. Start with a Calendar: Begin with a calendar that indicates the days of the week. In many cultures, including the Gregorian calendar used in much of the world today, the week starts with Sunday and ends with Saturday.

2. Count Seven Days: Count seven days from any starting point on the calendar. For example, if you start with a Sunday, the next day is Monday, then Tuesday, and so on, until you reach the seventh day, which is Saturday.

3. Identify the Sabbath: In the seven-day cycle, the seventh day is recognized as the Sabbath. In Judaism, the Sabbath begins at sunset on Friday evening and continues until sunset on Saturday evening. In Christianity, many denominations observe the Sabbath on Sunday, while others follow the Hebrew tradition and observe it on Saturday.

4. Rest and Religious Observance: On the Sabbath, individuals and communities typically engage in ritual worship, rest from work or certain activities, and spend time with family and community. The specific rules and traditions related to Sabbath observance can vary among different religious groups and cultures.

5. Repeat Weekly: The seven-day cycle, with the Sabbath as a day of rest, repeats weekly, and it forms an essential part of religious and cultural observance in various traditions.

It's important to note that while the seven-day cycle is widely recognized, the specific day chosen for the Sabbath and the customs associated with it can vary among different religious and cultural groups. For example, in Islam, Friday is considered a holy day and a day of congregational prayer, while in Hinduism, there is no fixed day of rest, but certain lunar phases are considered auspicious for religious activities.

To determine the Sabbath and the seven-day cycle in a specific religious or cultural context, it's best to refer to the practices and traditions of that particular group.

The observation of the Shabbat, particularly in Judaism, is generally from Friday evening at sunset to Saturday evening at sunset. This period covers a 24-hour day, but the Shabbat is defined as the period from Friday evening (the start of the Jewish day) to Saturday evening (the end of the Jewish day).

The reasoning behind observing the Shabbat from sunset to sunset is rooted in the biblical account of creation in the Book of Genesis. In Genesis 1, it is said, "And there was evening and there was morning, the first day," which sets the pattern for each subsequent day of creation. In Jewish tradition, the day begins with the onset of darkness (sunset) and continues until the following sunset, aligning with the biblical narrative.

During the Shabbat, Jewish individuals and communities engage in worship, rest from work and certain activities, and spend time with family and community. The specific customs and practices associated with the Sabbath may vary among Jewish denominations and communities.

It's important to note that while the Hebrew Shabbat follows this pattern of sunset to sunset, other religious traditions may have different definitions of their holy days and may observe them from sunrise to sunrise or according to other criteria.

Remember these three annual festivals are Pesach (Passover), Shavuot (Pentecost), and Sukkot (Feast of Tabernacles), during which Israelite men were instructed to present themselves before the Most High God at the central sanctuary in ancient Israel. These festivals are important ritual observances in ancient Israel and continue to be celebrated throughout the generations as an everlasting ordinance. (Exodus 23:14, Deuteronomy 16:16)

YAH's name shall endure for ever: his name shall be continued as long as the sun: and men shall be blessed in him: all nations shall call him blessed. Blessed be YAH ALMIGHTY ELOHIM, the Most Holy of Israel, who only doeth wondrous things. And blessed be his glorious name for ever: and let the whole earth be filled with his glory; Shelah, and Shelah. Psalm 72:17-19

Wherefore YAH also hath highly exalted him, and given him a name which is above every name: That at the name of Yeshua every knee should bow, of things in heaven, and things in earth, and things under the earth; And that every tongue should confess that Yeshua HaMashiach is Almighty God, to the glory of YAH the Father. Philippians 2:9-11 And out of his mouth goeth a sharp sword, that with it he should strike down the nations: and he shall rule them with a rod of iron: and he treadeth the winepress of the fierceness and wrath of Almighty YAH. Revelation 19:15 And I heard as if it were the voice of a great multitude, and as the voice of many waters, and as the voice of mighty thunderings, saying, Alleluia: for the Almighty YAH omnipotent reigneth. Revelation 19:6 And after these things I heard a great voice of much people in heaven, saying, Alleluia; Salvation, and glory, and honor, and power, unto the Almighty Power our God: Bless the eyes and ears of the soul who takes heed to walk in spirit of truth to love your neighbor as yourself and the Most High God with all your heart.

www.ingramcontent.com/pod-product-compliance
Lightning Source LLC
Chambersburg PA
CBHW021609120626
46545CB00001B/143